NOT BY THE COLOR

OF THEIR SKIN

The Impact of Racial Differences on the
Child's Development

NOT BY THE COLOR
OF THEIR SKIN

The Impact of Racial Differences on the
Child's Development

MARJORIE McDONALD, M.D.

INTERNATIONAL UNIVERSITIES PRESS, INC.

Library of Congress Catalog Card Number: 73-134334

Manufactured in the United States of America

I HAVE A DREAM THAT MY FOUR LITTLE CHILDREN WILL ONE DAY LIVE IN A NATION WHERE THEY WILL NOT BE JUDGED BY THE COLOR OF THEIR SKIN, BUT BY THE CONTENT OF THEIR CHARACTER.

MARTIN LUTHER KING, JR.
The Lincoln Memorial
Washington, D.C.
August, 1963

FOREWORD

This is a psychoanalytic book about skin color and personality development, and about object relationships and racial integration. It is based upon experiences with racial integration in a therapeutic nursery school and kindergarten. It is not a study about Negroes or any other segregated group. It is about all skin colors and their effects upon personality. It is also a study of integration in action, and of everyone—white or nonwhite, child or parent or staff—who participated in it.

Part I is the work of countless contributors, the most important of whom must remain nameless. They are the nursery and kindergarten children and their parents, of all races, but especially those of minority races, who have attended the Hanna Perkins School. Those Negroes, Orientals, and Indians who came to us with their children proved to be leaders in the movement toward integration and improvement of living conditions for their own races. We discovered that our school, with its therapeutic orientation, imposed a special selectiveness upon minority groups. Mostly it fell to the leaders in these groups to take initial steps to enable them to admit and accept help for problems in their children. Hence it was the leaders who came to us. Their character strengths were reflected in their work with us and in their devoted upbringing of their children. Whatever the emotional conflicts of child and parents, we found time and again a soundness of ego development, a strength of character, being passed on from one generation to the next. It was our privilege to become a part of the development of these children and to work with their parents, and we hope that their gain was as great as our own. Should any of these people read this work we hope they will do so as participants, not as unsuspecting subjects of a research study. Every effort has been made to protect privacy and preserve anonymity of all concerned individuals—children, parents, and staff—without compromising the honesty of the reporting and the benefits that our experiences may have for others.

Some contributors must be named. Miss Lois Archer, Educational Director, started us off because of her deep concern that the school, with its major focus on treatment, was in danger of ignoring a civic responsibility to become better integrated. She also saw that the school's psychoanalytic perspective could contribute to improved understanding of racial reactions in young children and their parents. Further, her consistent concern and interest and her regular attendance at our staff meetings set for all of us an example of integration at work. Miss Eleanor Hosley, Executive Director of the Day Nursery Association of Cleveland, brought us the financial support and good wishes of that organization. The Cleveland Center for Research in Child Development, under the directorship of Dr. Robert A. Furman, gave both financial support and professional consultation and encouragement. Miss Sandra Redmond and Miss Marilyn Hamre, head teachers in the nursery and kindergarten, respectively, were leaders in the work. Other teachers whose participation was invaluable were Mrs. Christine Beeke, Mrs. Nicki Cordes, Miss Linda Fetter, Miss Sally Jenkins, Mrs. Julie Limbert, and Mrs. Isabella McMillin.

Dr. Anny Katan, Clinical Director, often discussed racial problems in her regular seminars at the school and gave us many valuable suggestions which we followed up at our special staff meetings. Many of the school's child therapists were also helpful contributors. Those active in the school program during the years of this work include Marion Barnes, Elizabeth Daunton, David Fairman, Eleanor Fiedler, Erna Furman, Robert Furman, Eleanor Hosley, Carla Polak, Edward Schiff, and Yolande Tanguay.

The responsibility for Parts II and III is my own. The theoretical aspects of Part II represent a recent outgrowth of the several years of clinical experience reported in Part I. Although I have not quoted her work extensively, I believe that my indebtedness to Edith Jacobson's *The Self and the Object World* is obvious. In my discussions I have used her terminology. I hope that I have applied it, as well as her theoretical conceptions, correctly.

I also feel indebted to Phyllis Greenacre's work on identity, and to Anna Freud's work on the concept of developmental lines, especially as it applies to the development of object relationships.

Part III is a broad, though incomplete, survey of professional literature on racial problems. My review of the psychoanalytic and psychiatric literature is more detailed than it is of the sociological, social work, psychological, and educational literature. My inexperience in these latter specialties has been a constant frustration to me in attempting to do them justice in my review, and I assume that this limitation will be apparent to any reader knowledgeable in these areas. The question may rightly be asked why I have tried to include a broad literature survey ranging far beyond the psychoanalytic facet that is our own work. I was, of course, searching for reflections of our clinical and theoretical findings, especially with regard to skin color anxiety. But my intent has also been to try to place this psychoanalytic facet in its proper setting within a multifaceted historical perspective. In this setting, with its opportunities for comparisons and contrasts, the contributions—in fact the distinct identities—of each separate profession gain in clarity and value. Respected professional identities and a professional integration are necessary in the work of establishing respected racial identities and racial integration.

During the years of this work I was fortunate in having at first a full-time, and later a part-time office in Hanna Perkins School. It made possible a frequent and informal association with the teaching staff and repeated school visits which enabled me to know the children well. As for my personal qualifications I recognize, but perhaps take for granted, the significance of my psychiatric and psychoanalytic education. At times I find myself reflecting gratefully upon my medical internship in the South, at Grady Memorial Hospital in Atlanta, Georgia. "The Gradies," as the old white and colored hospitals were then known, before the new integrated hospital was built, opened my closed Northern eyes to our complex racial problems. It was an invaluable, if often overwhelming, experience. It had lasting effects on my life, some of which have found their way into this book.

I want to thank Mrs. Lottie M. Newman for her invaluable editorial help with both style and content. Her thorough knowledge of the analytic literature led her to make many stimulating suggestions which I have incorporated in the book.

Lastly, I want to thank especially Miss Elizabeth Daunton, a child analyst on the Hanna Perkins staff and the school's Kindergarten Consultant, for her careful reading and discussion of the entire manuscript with me.

ACKNOWLEDGMENT OF PERMISSIONS

Acknowledgment is gratefully given for permission to quote from the following publications: *Monet*, by William C. Seitz, published by Harry N. Abrams, Inc.; *The Nature of Prejudice*, by Gordon W. Allport, and *Race Awareness in Young Children*, by Mary Ellen Goodman, both published by Addison-Wesley Publishing Company; *Prejudice and Your Child*, by Kenneth B. Clark, published by Beacon Press; *Race Attitudes in Children*, by Bruno Lasker, published by Holt, Rinehart & Winston, Inc.; *Children of Crisis*, by Robert Coles, published by Little, Brown & Company; *The History of Impressionism*, by John Rewald, published by the Museum of Modern Art; *Why We Should Suspend the Studies of Negroes*, by Whitney M. Young, Jr., published by The National Observer; *Killers of the Dream*, by Lillian Smith, published by W. W. Norton & Co.; *Now Is the Time*, by Lillian Smith, published by The Viking Press and permission for quotation granted by Miss Paula Snelling, co-executor of the estate of Lillian Smith.

CONTENTS

PART I

THE NURSERY SCHOOL AND ITS RACIAL INTEGRATION

Integration is a creative job—a process
that will take effort, imagination, and faith.

—LILLIAN SMITH
(*Now Is the Time*)

1

INTRODUCTION

A few years ago our school decided to "do something" to improve its racial integration. Like so many others, we were responding to that combination of public, nationwide pressure toward integration, generated especially in the wake of our Supreme Court's momentous *Brown* decision in 1954, and the private, highly personal pressure generated by shifting forces within our own individual personalities. Although we had never been a segregated school, we began to face the fact that neither were we a truly integrated school. In retrospect, perhaps we did not fully understand at that time just what is a truly integrated school. We just sensed that something was not right with us.

What to do was not difficult to decide. Up until then we had been suffering from *de facto* segregation, with only an occasional Negro or Oriental child finding his way to our school for children with emotional problems. So first we would make a more active effort to search out community referrals of Negro and other minority group children. In Cleveland, with its large Negro population, we expected mostly referrals of Negro children. Second, we would pay more conscious, organized attention to happenings within what we pictured as our newly integrated school community. We would notice more about the children and somehow we would use our observations to help them grow into unprejudiced people. To this end the teachers and I met regularly. In the course of our efforts we hoped to learn something about the interweaving of perception of racial difference, personality development, and prejudice.

We found out immediately that putting our two sound and simple objectives into practice was not easy. When we tried to fulfill our first goal, we could not get the influx of referrals we

3

sought. When we tried to fulfill our second goal—the setting up of some plan of operation for ourselves—we did not know just what to do and consequently were more vulnerable than we realized to doing the wrong thing. We could have acted in a number of ways which might have forestalled or even foreclosed our efforts toward integration.

ESTABLISHING PHYSICAL INTEGRATION

We discovered that, for many reasons, it was not easy for victims of prejudice to avail themselves of a therapeutic nursery school. The most deprived had urgent material needs which we could not meet. Their inability to sustain relationships with people who could not provide their basic needs meant that they in turn could not meet the basic requirements of our school. The mothers could not meet consistently enough with a therapist or bring their children regularly enough to the school to use our program. Day care programs elsewhere in the city were geared much more to their needs. For these deprived people a psychological disturbance which not only could take precedence over a physical need but also demand time and effort in its behalf was an unknown luxury of life.

Negro families who had risen above the level of unmet material needs often could not come to us for another reason. Through a combination of more favorable early life experiences and their own strivings as adults these people had broken through many segregation barriers—in their jobs, in the location of their homes, and even in their marriages. They were leaders with high ideals and strong ambitions, and their personalities were responding in the healthiest way to our cultural crisis. But as at least two mothers from this group told us, it is not easy for these Negro families to admit having any difficulties in raising children. An application to our school required just such an admission. The children of these people naturally were the carriers of their parents' conscious ideals for the future. But in the timeless and contradictory state of the unconscious mind these children represented for the parents a current idealized (often white) version of life in the integrated hereafter, in the unbearable conditions of the segregated here and now. Their children had to be perfect children. They were not allowed the ordinary developmental conflicts and anxieties of childhood, or any internalized neurotic reactions with symptom formations. Conflicts, anxieties, and symptoms meant weakness, and weakness to someone just barely liberated meant threat of a return to a state of dependency and servitude. Under such conditions a therapist threatened to be an oppressor, not a helper. Once again, experiencing an internalized psychological need had become an unattainable luxury in life.

Some referrals from minority groups proved unsuitable for reasons not primarily relating to racial problems. However, much as these referral failures might resemble ordinary failures in referrals of white children, racial conflicts usually glimmered below the surface.

Charles, a three-year-old Negro boy, is a good example of the fallacy of a too-active recruitment for a school whose primary reason for existence is its therapeutic program. Charles's mother brought him to our school with rather ill-defined developmental problems, the most specific being that he dawdled over his meals. She came more through our recruiting efforts than because of her own concerns about her child. She was extremely indecisive about enrolling him, revealing in the course of her deliberation unmistakable signs of her obsessional neurosis. She was tempted by our excellent educational facilities, from which Charles, a boy with a very superior intelligence, could have benefited greatly. Her decision, after Charles's school visit, not to enroll him seemed independent of racial conflicts. Her bright adolescent twins were experiencing serious emotional conflicts which roused strong guilt in this obsessional mother. Working with a therapist about Charles seemed to threaten her with unbearable insight into her own neurosis and her guilt concerning the rearing of her older children. We have had similar early withdrawals of white children. But even though race apparently was not the issue in the case of Charles, we felt that indirectly it must have entered into the unique picture which this child displayed on his visit. His mother, his family, his neighborhood had come to regard this verbal, bright, friendly little boy as a child leader of men, a Christ. In fact Charles bore the full name of a famous historical personage noted for his messianic character. Little three-year-old Charles was consulted about all sorts of things, and his sayings were taken as gospel. In his visit with us Charles captivated children and adults alike and was soon leading the school's activities. At three years he seemed already to have internalized the charisma surrounding him and to have made it a part of his own self representation.

Warren illustrates the unusual case where an economically deprived child proved to be a successful referral. Warren was the youngest child in a very large Negro family. Both parents were chronically and seriously ill and could work only irregularly. For a while Warren's place to sleep was across the foot of the bed of his newlywed brother and his wife. Warren's mother managed to bring him regularly to the nursery and to meet fairly regularly with the child therapist only because this skilled therapist was also a social worker whose community connections enabled her to help meet Warren's family's basic material as well as psychological needs. The therapist was secure in adjusting and limiting the usual psychological goals of our work to the realistic conditions of Warren's family life.

Pamela was brought by her college graduate Negro parents for help with her toilet training. She withheld her bowel movements and was beginning to bite her siblings. These developmental problems improved rapidly after the mother began to work regularly with the therapist. Pamela was a charming child who made an excellent school adjustment. But when she confronted her parents with her disappointment at being Negro instead of white, her parents found their child's distress unbearable. They defended against recognition of it largely through denials and projections. Since Pamela expressed her feelings to the teachers, but not at home, the parents concluded from the teachers' reports that we were instilling prejudicial ideas into Pamela's mind through *our* talk about Pamela's color. When the therapist further threatened the parents' defenses by introducing more examples from the child's school experience, the parental projection only increased. They repressed the developmental difficulties for which they had sought our help and expressed the belief that we had accepted Pamela only in order to have a Negro child to study. Throughout Pamela's stay at school she made many gains, especially in ego activities, where her parents gave her much devoted help. But her feelings about her color remained largely segregated from her otherwise well-integrated personality development. She continued to give evidence of feeling inferior and rejected as a Negro. Her parents could not permit any awareness of her feeling because they unconsciously regarded her as a white child in a white school, who had no reason to feel sad or angry about her color. When another Negro girl entered her class both Pamela and her mother seemed irritated, and for a long time succeeded in ignoring the newcomer and her mother.

We found that so long as the school remained predominantly white it remained a confirmation in reality of any denial a Negro might have about being Negro. Unconsciously Negro parents could regard themselves as white in a white private school. Minority group families most able to accept enrollment in a therapeutic setting on a realistic basis were those who were themselves engaged in helping professions such as teaching, medicine, social work. The spirit of liberation, integration, and helping others in these professions in turn helped these families to accept identification with the goals of our work.

We are still unsatisfied with the limitations of our physical integration, which has not gone higher than 25 percent. Efforts to obtain Negro teachers for our staff have not yet met with any success.

Our efforts toward integration introduced us not only to the problems of segregated people but also to the problems of the segregators. Inevitably they bared to each of us the guilty feelings of every normal white person living in our segregated society. This white guilt is an ever-present problem and repeated reference was made to it in our work. Its fate is as important a part of the problem of integration as is the fate of the feelings of the Negro. In our recruiting efforts we found that our guilt, so long as it remained mostly unconscious, was most apt to be defended from consciousness through unrealistic rescue activities. (Later, other defenses prevailed. These will be discussed in Chapter 2.) We were in danger of allowing too many exceptions to our usual working methods in order to make it possible for a minority group child to attend the school. Exceptional arrangements were permissible only when they did not compromise the general aims of the school.

A Negro mother was permitted some realistic special privileges to make it possible for her child to attend the school. One privilege was an unusual appointment time with the therapist, when the school classrooms and therapy offices ordinarily were closed. The mother often came a little late for her weekly appointment and maintained an aloof reserved manner toward the therapist. When she was able to express her feeling of guilt about intruding upon the therapist's free time, the hindrance to the working relationship decreased considerably. However, it was the therapist's feeling that the undeniable fact of the special arrangement supported a residual guilt in the mother—very likely a guilt that she had used her color to gain special privileges through an appeal to a white person's guilt. The realistic fact, shared with the mother, that the therapist's schedule included appointments in a nearby clinic following the mother's own appointment did not change the effect of being seen specially in an empty school building.

ESTABLISHING PSYCHOLOGICAL INTEGRATION

In planning the meetings which the teachers and I would have we were uncertain of what procedure to follow. We could not yet appreciate what only forthcoming experience could teach us—that these meetings ought to be an active part of our putting integration into practice. To be effective they could not be just a static study of a physically integrated school setting. They had to be working-through sessions for the conflicts which children, parents, teachers, and therapists experienced in relation to each other about racial differences. They had to be a means of extending a physical integration to a true psychological integration.

It would have been easy to divert the purpose of these meetings to some other goal which would have subtly interfered with our manifest wish to promote integration. In the university environment in which the school existed, reading and study seminars would have been acclaimed as proper purposes for holding meetings. A "research"-centered series of meetings might also have been conducted, with the emphasis upon collecting data and using them for the primary purpose of making new and reportable discoveries. Indeed, no sooner had we announced our intentions to promote integration in the school than we found ourselves swept up in the popular activity of seeking grant money for a research project. The stiltedly scientific language of the grant proposal we drew up is revealing of how tempting it was, at the outset, to avoid facing our own anxieties about integration by taking refuge in a research project. The danger inherent in too much emphasis upon reading and research seminars was that we would withhold ourselves from a project that urgently required our active participation and sharing of ourselves, just as much as we expected participation from children and parents. We were most fortunate in obtaining financial support from a source which regarded the investment as payment rendered for a service, rather than as a grant for research to be produced.

Of course, any avoidance of what we had set out to do would only have increased our own guilt. But the dangers of these academic avenues of escape from psychological integration carried more serious threats in that they could have hindered our physical integration. In the course of processing our grant request a rumor began to circulate that we were doing a research project about Negro children. It was necessary to lay this rumor to rest quickly and with the least possible fuss. A Negro struggling for a sense of his own individual worth would not willingly cooperate with a school where his child's individuality might be secondary to a research project. (For example, the anxieties of Pamela's parents about their child's being used for research have been reported above.)[1]

[1]Whitney M. Young, Jr., Executive Director of the National Urban League and newspaper columnist, wrote in his weekly column in *The National Observer* (April 1, 1968): "My plan is for no more studies of Negroes this year. Think about it. Studying Negroes threatens to become one of the biggest industries in the United States. . . . Every university has its 'Negro expert,' usually white. Every foundation is swamped with requests for funds to study this Negro ghetto or that one. We've had studies of the 'souls' of black people, the 'pathology' of the Negro family, and others. . . . In fact the Negro-studying business has become so big that I'm afraid if we just end it quickly, too many people will be thrown out of work. I'd like to propose a study of white folks. After all, Negroes didn't create the ghetto, white folks did. The sickness of racial hatred is a problem white people have had to live with for years, without the benefit of anyone studying it. . . . What sort of sickness is it that makes a man fear Negro children going to his child's school? . . . let's hire Negroes to do the studies. After all, who knows the subject better than Negroes, who have had to live with racists for 400 years? White 'experts' have lived off studying Negroes for long enough; it's time to reverse the process."

2

STAFF MEETINGS

The Hanna Perkins School in Cleveland, Ohio is a therapeutic nursery and kindergarten for children with psychological
difficulties. The nursery and kindergarten classes each contain
fifteen children, and meet daily from 9:00 to 2:30. The mother of
every child has a regular meeting, usually weekly, with one of
the school's analytically trained child therapists. Psychoanalytic
treatment is available for those children in need of it. (Further
information about the school and its methods is available in the
recent publication, *The Therapeutic Nursery School* [1969],
edited by Robert Furman and Anny Katan.)

FORM

Six teachers and I comprised the regular attenders of the
hourly staff meetings, held three times a month for two years,
and thereafter twice a month. My functions were to chair the
meetings, serve as catalyst or consultant as needed, and to keep
the records. Since I also observed regularly in the school and
knew all the children I sometimes could add my own experiences
to those of the teachers.

The early dismissal of the children on Fridays and the comfortable informality of the school library gave us both a time and
a setting conducive to our work. We were free of the cares and
confinement of the schoolrooms, yet close enough to the events of
the week to allow profitable discussion of them. Visitors were
welcome and there was often one, rarely more than one, in attendance. They were the school's child therapy staff, or visiting
teachers, social workers, analysts, or psychiatrists.

Occasionally we had an announced agenda—a report or discussion of a published article or a recent lecture, meeting, or

movie attended by one or more of us. Sometimes we continued a special topic from one meeting to the next. Carryovers usually concerned educational approaches with the children (below). Sometimes a visitor from another nursery school reported on experiences in her school. (A few of these visitor reports have been included, and so designated, in Chapter 3.) Most of our meetings were discussions of recent everyday observations and problems presented by the children. At first we confined ourselves to the nursery children, but soon enlarged our scope to include the kindergarten.

A typical meeting would begin with an experience reported by a teacher. Generally the teacher's report led us into discussions which improved our understanding of and in turn our communication with both children and parents about racial differences. Occasional meetings never progressed this far, and the teacher's report might end up as "another one for your collection," even though we tried to de-emphasize the importance of records as an end in themselves. Sometimes there was not even anything for the collection. It was, of course, often difficult or impossible to understand the unproductive meetings. Was it that nothing of interest had taken place, or that unrelated events were more important? Or was it that our own resistances were collectively operating? We had to be patient and await future developments, and we had to be satisfied with never knowing all the answers.

TRENDS

In retrospect we can trace some general trends in our meetings. In the beginning our enthusiasm ran away with us. We tried too hard to notice too much. Worse, we sometimes acted wrongly upon what we noticed. Most of us sooner or later made ill-timed and tactless remarks to mothers and children, especially if they happened to be Negroes. For example, if a child made an obvious remark about his racial difference, we complimented him too quickly for his ability to talk about his brown skin, and we might even go further and hazard an interpretation of what he might be feeling about his color. Or we might flood him with factual explanations about racial differences. To his mother we might too enthusiastically report the child's remark and our own valuation of it as a good sign of developmental progress. We ignored the all-important fact that our relationships with new children and their mothers had not yet developed sufficiently to support more than the earliest overtures to the highly charged, highly personal subject of race and racial differences. Our rushed tempo came from our own anxiety, more than from the needs of children and mothers. We were rushing through defensive layers and laying claims to private areas in others' lives where we had not yet been invited to enter. The price of these beginning mistakes in timing and tact was high. Children and mothers defensively girded themselves for protection against us, and we in turn became discouraged and withdrew too much. Probably we were not even able to recognize adequately the heightened defenses which greeted our efforts, and as a result tended all the more to withdraw in discouragement. At least this seems a likely interpretation of a rather marked falling off in observations and enthusiasm after the first weeks.

Slowly, as the necessary relationships developed, as our anxiety lessened and our sense of tact and timing returned, we began to notice more, and children and mothers began to trust us more to use our observations well with them. We then went through a period in our meetings of collecting innumerable observations. Our discussions of them were confined mostly to evaluating their validity. Our conviction of their meaningfulness sometimes had to await repeated reports of the same observation, or the piecing together of a series of observations over a period of time, or the occasional bolstering effect of hearing similar observations made by our visitors from other schools. We were going through a necessary period of sharpening our powers of observation and gaining confidence in our skill. Once we had gained confidence in our observations we felt less need to report them in so much detail. With the passing of the first year or so the duplication of offerings for the "collection" slowly fell off. Thereafter our meetings seemed to settle into more even and predictable working-through sessions. Observations were less an end in themselves, and more a starting point for our working-through process. This steadiness, born of our own experience and growth, generally held up even through the inevitable changes in teaching staff and entry of new classes into the school. That the head teachers remained the same throughout our work was an important steadying influence.

Within the school's nonprofessional staff there also appeared a trend which might be accounted for by our increased concern for racial problems. We did not announce our meetings to these staff people, and our secretarial work did not involve any of the school's clerical staff. However, it is unlikely that our meetings remained unknown to them. With the kitchen staff the teachers sometimes discussed individual children with whom they had contact at mealtimes and during kitchen projects. If, for instance, a child's fear of going to the kitchen for the snack cart was based upon fear of the Negro staff, the teacher discussed such a problem directly with the staff. The trend we noticed was that there was more open discussion of racial problems related and not related to the children, between nonprofessional and professional staff. With this atmospheric change there appeared a more open expression of dissatisfactions from some of the Negro staff. We regarded their new ability to complain as a release of an interfering inhibition which had previously kept them in a second-class servile attitude about their work. Some of the Negro staff could see that we were constantly building and protecting our psychological integration, and we believe the more open expression of their own complaints was a healthy sign of their trust and approval of our efforts. But with some, the release of aggression was overwhelming and contributed to their withdrawal from the school. In one case the changed atmosphere seemed to contribute to a breakdown of defenses and a paranoid state.

A basic problem which we have not yet solved is the integration of all school departments. Our teaching staff has remained all white and our kitchen and housecleaning staff has remained mostly Negro. Only the clerical staff is integrated.

EDUCATIONAL CONSIDERATIONS

Many times we discussed how nursery and kindergarten teachers should teach children about race, racial differences, racial problems. There was general agreement that the age difference in the nursery school and kindergarten children made a considerable difference as to what the teacher could and could not do educationally.

In the nursery school many children, of all races, were still in need of working through some of their observations and reactions to racial differences first with their own parents. They needed their parents' permission and support for this development in themselves, it seemed. Some children and parents had not yet faced together even the facts of racial differences. Consequently the group educational approach to the subject generally had to be limited to simple verbalizations of obvious facts, and sometimes of feelings. Mostly this education took place in the story hour. The newer children's books, with stories and illustrations about children of different races, proved most helpful. (The pressing need for more of these books is well known.[1])

In our meetings we discussed how to make use of these books. One discussion concerned whether a teacher should mention anything about the fact that some of the characters in a particular book were shown in the illustrations as Negro, when no reference was made to this fact in the story itself. This led us into a discussion of what is denial, and of how young children can identify with a defense, like denial, in a teacher. If a teacher gives evidence to a child of never noticing difference in skin colors, of never mentioning it, then the child may do the same thing. In the process of building up his own personality he may identify with the defense of his beloved teacher and make this hampering de-

---

[1] See, for example, the excellent survey article by Nancy Larick, "The All-White World of Children's Books" *(Saturday Review,* Sept. 11, 1965).

fense a part of himself. He may deny both the actual fact of difference in skin colors and any internal responses within his personality to that fact. A personality constriction, rather than development, then takes place. But if the teacher is free to comment on racial differences, for example, in a book illustration, even when the accompanying story or its hearers have failed to do so, then the children can comfortably look at and talk about the illustration. Sometimes this paves the way for their spontaneous expression of their own reactions to the story and its illustration. Anyone who has attended a nursery school story session knows how intensely absorbing an experience it is for children, and how strongly they can identify with characters in a story. If race is not a taboo topic, the children can freely identify with white and Negro characters, with or without regard for the fact of their own skin color. If a child voices reasons for his choice of identification, he may also inform his teacher about some conflict he has about his own skin color. At this point education has wandered into personality development and the teacher must make a choice about what to take up in the group, what to do with the individual child, and what to pass on to the parent for primarily parental help.

In the kindergarten a somewhat more extensive and organized approach to the teaching about racial differences was possible. Even though some children had not faced the issue at all (especially true of those children for whom kindergarten was their first school experience), still it seemed that at five years of age they no longer were so dependent upon first working it through to some extent with their own parents. Their parents, too, were less apt to be disturbed by their kindergartners' reports to them of what they had learned at school about race.

Even so, we sometimes became too enthusiastic about unrealistic educational approaches. Once we considered a simple historical presentation about the life of the Negro in the United States. A wise kindergarten teacher quickly disillusioned us. Any lesson in history immediately introduced dead people, and the subject of death immediately ended the effectiveness of the lesson.

The topic of death stirred up such an overriding anxiety in that age group that it was impossible to discuss Abraham Lincoln's role as anything but a man who was dead. Why did he die? Will I die? Why did the man shoot him? Will I get shot? How do you bury people? etc. Nor would nonviolent deaths of historical figures be any less anxiety-provoking. True enough, a few children in our group had major problems with death in having a dead parent. But it was our experienced teacher's conviction that any group of kindergarten children would meet the same stumbling block about death in any lessons from history. Developmentally these children were at an age where oedipal death wishes figured prominently in their conflicts in life.

Another approach that we rejected was making a visit to another kindergarten class in Cleveland, where there would be more Negro children. We hoped to give our predominantly white group an opportunity to meet more Negro children. In one meeting we discussed the possibility of establishing a small correspondence with a class at another school and then having our kindergartners visit it. Reflection led us to realize how artificial and how impossible our plan was. For the children, who were just learning to write their names and a few simple words, it was an effort to write or dictate a brief holiday greeting to a parent, let alone a letter to a whole group of strange children. If the teacher were to write the letter, it would become too passive a learning experience. Transporting children to another class had its difficulties too. A short trip to a nearby duck pond was a major undertaking. A longer trip to a strange classroom with strange children would make impossible demands of a kindergartner's ego functioning. While he might manage some aspects well, the experience of racial integration would not really be achieved. At kindergarten age, children are still easily threatened by any new children as rivals, and are made insecure by unfamiliar school surroundings.

Story and circle times proved the best opportunity for group education. In circle time the children sat quietly in chairs in a circle for fifteen minutes and had lesson-discussions with a teacher, much as they would be doing in first grade the following year. A series of discussions was held about families all over the world, and children's story books were chosen to help tell about these families. We considered telling about different families in Cleveland, but decided against it. Instead, in afternoon activities, the children drew pictures of themselves in their families. While much of the unit aimed at teaching about relationships and responsibilities in families, the fact of racial differences came under consideration too. In their family drawings, and particularly in coloring themselves and various members of their families, the children openly revealed feelings and conflicts about their color and the color of their classmates. (Chapter 3 includes specific examples from these sessions.)

In both nursery and kindergarten, but much more so in the latter, two major events opened the door to, and in fact demanded, a group educational approach to the subject of race. One was the appearance of the National Guard in Cleveland to quell the racial rioting in July, 1966, and the other was the death of Martin Luther King, in April, 1968. These events will be considered separately in Chapter 3.

We spent surprisingly little time on questions of what words to use with the children. Very little abusive language appeared in the school. When it did, the teachers handled it decisively. When a child used "nigger" the teacher told him it was an unkind and teasy word to say to brown-skinned people, and she helped him to find better words to express his feelings and conflicts. Explanations about white, brown, colored, Negro, Oriental, Caucasian did not seem to cause us much difficulty. We had little inclination to hide defensively behind terminology. Words seemed easily and correctly available to express facts, both about skin and other racial differences, and about feelings.

Whenever we had Negro teachers from other schools visit our staff meetings, however, we noticed that our discussions were apt to center upon what choice of language to use with young children in helping them to sort out and understand their observations and feelings. To regard this preoccupation with words as all defensive would have been a serious mistake. Words, for these Negro teachers, many of whom had been raised in the South, were concrete carriers of strong racial feelings. To many, "colored" was a derogatory "adjective," recalling the humiliating signs controlling public segregation. "Negro" was a "proper noun" with a capital "N"—a proud word for a proud people. To others, "Negro" was too dangerously close to the corruptions "nigra" and "nigger" and consequently its usage was taboo. Most Negro teachers, and all their Negro children, shunned "black" as meaning a bad person.[2] In listening to these teachers, we could not help but gain respect for the power of their own word choices to convey to the next generation the wretchedness of their past history and their determination to secure a better future.

PSYCHOLOGICAL CONSIDERATIONS

While every aspect of our meetings could be described under this subheading, some specific psychological considerations deserve special mention.

A frequent question for discussion was how to make use of our observations. What should the teacher say to the child, to his mother or father? What should the teacher tell the mother to take to her session with the child therapist? What should the teacher avoid and leave entirely to the mother and child therapist? These questions were such highly individual matters that it is not possible to give specific and detailed answers to them. How they were answered in some individual situations will be illustrated in the next chapter. In the course of discussing them in our meetings we had many opportunities to review psychoanalytic concepts which aided in arriving at answers. We discussed adaptations, defenses, feelings, conflicts, and their relation to consciousness and unconsciousness in the child and in his parents. A few general conclusions can be drawn from this part of our work.

[2]This sentence is already out of date. "Black" is no longer generally taboo, and has come to convey a generally healthy defiance and pride. (See also footnote 2 in Chapter 9.)

There was never any indication for a teacher to compromise or sidestep the *fact* of racial differences with any child or parent.

In reporting a child's experiences concerning race it was sometimes better to accumulate several pieces of evidence of the child's awareness and interest before communicating them to his parent. Then the parent could better appreciate some developmental trend taking place within the child and make use of it in discussions with him. A daily report of a child's remarks about skin color or other racial differences was most apt to feel like a nagging criticism, especially to a Negro mother.

It seemed to us that an important task for the teacher, in talking with a child, was to help him distinguish reality from fantasy. A teacher could confirm that one child was born white, another born brown, and could correct the unrealistic but common fantasy that a child could change color.

The teacher could help a child distinguish skin color differences from shared human likenesses—feelings underneath the skin are the same in all of us. In doing so she promoted a child's discovery and exploration of the internal psychological world, both of himself and others.

In discussing a child's *feelings and conflicts* about color differences the teacher had to be guided not just by on-the-spot superficial observations, but by her greater knowledge of the child's development. It was almost never possible for a teacher to talk with a child about his feelings, anxiety, and conflicts about color differences unless the child's own mother and father could do so first. (See below for an illustration of what happened with one family when we ignored this principle.) For example, if a Negro child called himself dirty because he was brown, the teacher could correct him and sympathize with his obvious worry about himself. She could add that she would tell his mommy how he felt about his skin so that his mommy could help him with his worries about it. But the teacher would not yet attempt further discussion with the child about his feelings. If a white child called a Negro child dirty, the teacher could respond in the same manner. Hopefully, the child's mother, either on her own or after assistance from the child therapist, could discuss the child's expressed feelings and conflicts with him. If so, and if she could report her progress to the teacher, then she in effect gave teacher and child permission to work through at school what she had started at home. The next time the child expressed the same conflict the teacher could do more than sympathize. She could remind the child of what she knew he and his mommy had talked about. Mommy had told her that sometimes he did not want to be Negro because he thought brown skin was dirty. Further she might even offer not just reassurance but an interpretation, based upon the immediate circumstance. If the child had angrily messed another child's artwork prior to calling himself dirty, the teacher would tell him that he did not like himself and called himself dirty because of the mess he had just made and because he felt he had hurt his friend. It was not his brown skin that made him feel dirty. It was his showing angry feelings by messing Johnny's artwork instead of telling Johnny his angry feelings. She would encourage him to *verbalize* his angry feeling next time so that he would not have to act messy and then feel he was a dirty unlikable little boy. He would not have to think his nice brown skin was dirty and he could like himself much better. Here the teacher has done many things. She has helped to verbalize and resolve a self-esteem conflict, paved the way for verbalization of angry feelings, and cathected the distressed and unhappy child as a valuable, lovable, brown-skinned person with normal human feelings. But the teacher could do none of this if the child's mother had not first worked through at least some of the basic conflicts and feelings distressing the child. If the school took the lead, the mother felt lagging behind, left out, and resentful. She might also feel shocked by the child's confrontations from his school experience. The child was then apt to be caught in a loyalty conflict between mother and teacher. If the mother's defenses did not allow her to recognize any of the child's feelings and conflicts, then this loyalty conflict could be intense for the child. We have seen children caught up in loyalty conflicts to the extent of no longer wanting to attend school, even

though previous investment and pleasure in coming to school had
been great.

Sometimes the mother's defenses could be worked through
sufficiently in her work with the child therapist so that she then
became able to take the necessary lead in helping her child with
his own conflicts. This result depended of course upon the mother's own lifelong experiences and personality development, as
well as on her attitude toward the work with the therapist. Powerful and healthy motivation for some mothers was their unnar-
cissistic, maternal investment in their child's development. Particularly some of the Negro mothers were eager not to have their
children repeat their own early life experiences as victims of prejudice. This wish enabled them to identify with the aims of our
work and to resist unconscious forces in the direction of repeating
the past with their children.

Often the results of our work were limited and unfavorable.
When the child's conflicts about his color—particularly his aggressive conflicts—reactivated too painful conflicts in his parents, we had to accept the inevitable. The parents needed their
defenses and the child needed to exist in his own family. In order
to do so he might have to develop similar defenses, even though
these would interfere with his development and promote prejudicial attitudes. We could not help him at the price of threatening
the basic security of his home. To try to do so in order to satisfy
our own criteria of what is healthy development in a child would
in reality be an act of cruelty to the child.

Over and over we found ourselves dealing with certain conflicts, feelings, mechanisms which seemed especially prominent.
The whole constellation of anal phase conflicts came up repeatedly in connection with brown skin color. The problems of identifications, of aggressive reactions to being or seeing a Negro, of
lowered self-esteem, and of guilt constantly occupied us. These
will be considered further in Part II.

The problem of being unable to express anger openly and
directly was common in mothers of minority groups. They feared
explosive loss of control of their lifelong rage as victims of preju-

dice. Sometimes this common difficulty united them into complaining cliques, where aggression and excitement unconsciously reverberated. Much of our work at staff meetings had to do with the management of this recurrent development, and it was in just this area that we had our own greatest difficulties and fewest successes. At least one Negro child probably was withdrawn from our school partly because of our inability to resolve clique problems with the child's mother.

These cliques succeeded in segregating mothers and staff because mothers complained to each other about the school, but withheld complaints and sometimes *all* communication from the staff. (The complaints might be openly about racial issues, but more often appeared as displacements from this obvious underlying concern.) The cliques at times even succeeded in causing subtle splits within the staff itself, but a major accomplishment of our regular meetings was to hold staff splits to a minimum. If the confidential exchanges within the clique drew in the Negro kitchen, housekeeping, or clerical workers as clique participants, the problem became increasingly complicated.

What the Negroes were doing in their clique formations was to make the white staff the victims of their segregation—just as so often they had themselves been the victims. The result was that the staff experienced all of the conflicts of the victims. We were angry, powerless, and narcissistically wounded in our ineffectiveness, in the face of the clique establishment. And the Negroes, now the segregators, experienced an intolerable guilt. The situation was complex since this reversal did not replace but only added another layer to the basic conflicts inherent in us all, as black victims or white victimizers in our segregated society.

It is my impression that our greatest difficulties were caused by a mutual inability of white and Negro participants to face guilty feelings consciously, and a mutual tendency to defend against guilt with projections. The guilt of the white staff led to too much permissiveness with Negro, in contrast to white, mothers. One result was clique formation. Then the Negroes felt guilty. They tried to escape their own guilt by pointing instead at the white's guilt. "You ought to have Negro teachers on your staff," they criticized. True enough, of course. Often the white staff ceased to function effectively in the face of this all-too-true accusation. We accepted the accusation at face value, rather than realizing its major purpose *at that moment* as a defense. Then we became too apologetic, or sometimes too argumentative with the accuser. The result had to be that mutual segregation was increased, and guilt on both sides had to grow.

Sometimes it was effective if a white staff member could show a Negro mother that it would not be helpful if, just because she was a white person, she allowed her own guilty feelings to prevent her from doing her work. If she, as a teacher, could not report on a child or, as a therapist, could not discuss the child's development, then she could not be of any help, and ultimately the child's welfare would suffer. This approach often paved the way for a tactful interpretation (from the therapist) to the Negro mother that she was avoiding a painfully difficult reaction *in her child*, a reaction which roused her own guilt, by projecting her guilt to the white person. For the white person to accept the *real* part of the accusation undefensively—to acknowledge openly the white guilt—also set an example for the Negro mother. It helped her to face her own guilt consciously. The success of this kind of an interpretation depended absolutely upon keeping the child in focus at the center of the conflict. It was, after all, always some disturbing development *within the child* which led to these complicated mother-staff altercations. To get lost in the adult interpersonal conflicts would be to participate in a combination of defenses whose primary goal was to deny painful conflicts and feelings about race *in the child*. The child who is unhappy and angry about his brown skin and blames his mother for it stirs a sympathetic pain in his mother which can reduce her to a state of guilty helplessness.

The following incident illustrates many of the psychological aspects discussed in this section and how the staff employed the fruits of our meetings to meet them.

After some months in the nursery a four-year-old Negro child was beginning to progress from factual observations of racial differences to verbal expressions of feelings about these differences. The parents, who had strongly supported the child's factual observations, drew back in uncomfortable silence at the teacher's reports of the child's verbalization of feelings, especially critical feelings, about being brown. However, both teacher and therapist ignored these first defensive warnings in the parents. The teacher encouraged the new development in the child and one day made an interpretation. When the child expressed a fantasy of daddy changing color, the teacher interpreted that perhaps the child *wished* daddy would change color. The child responded with talk of daddy going away and never coming back. The child's tone and manner made it clear at that moment that this was an angry wish toward daddy. The teacher wisely chose not to interpret this second wish to the child. The teacher kept the mother and therapist informed, and the therapist attempted to discuss with the mother her child's emerging angry feelings about being Negro. (The mother had already worked through with the therapist some of her own resentments about being Negro and the therapist's being white.)

Meanwhile the child began to show an unusual reluctance to come to school, and asked the mother whether it was all right to "tell things" at school. Unable to find out what things, the mother responded with correspondingly vague reassurance. Next the child began to complain to the mother about not wanting to talk with the teacher about skin color.

At this point the child's mother impulsively let go of her own anger to a Negro acquaintance who happened to be passing by the school as the mother was leaving. The acquaintance had no official connection with the school as parent or employee, but nevertheless harbored resentments of her own about it. The child's mother had found a much-needed sympathetic ear for her angry complaint that our school put too much stress on racial *differences*, thereby promoting discrimination and putting prejudicial ideas into children's minds. The friend called another friend, who in turn called another Negro child's mother, who in turn called a white child's mother. With each transfer came a tremendous reinforcement not only for anger and excitement, but for the growing conviction that the complaint about the school staff's *teaching* of prejudice was indeed a fact. The mothers involved even began to discuss with each other whether they should withdraw their children from the school. At this point the white mother's guilt at her participation in this grapevine broke through and she confessed the whole chain of events to the child therapist with whom she worked.

To a sincere and dedicated staff the incident was a frightening warning signal. Not just our psychological, but our basic physical integration was threatened. Teacher and therapist shared their guilty feelings at having precipitated such trouble through their mishandling of the problems involved. An immediate meeting of the staff members involved was held. As a result the therapist of the white mother urged her to tell the two Negro mothers that she had confessed to us and that they should do the same. The "middle" mother did so, but maintained a protective detachment and denial. The first mother thought we had made a mountain out of a molehill, but then she did succeed in bringing her complaint openly and directly to the therapist. She said she felt that we emphasized too much the racial differences and *caused* feelings in children through our attempts to verbalize them. The therapist agreed that this might well be true and then presented a solution for the problem. The mother would have to do more of the work. It was rightfully the mother's place to take the lead in helping her child with feelings and conflicts about their race. We would continue to report our observations, but would be careful not to invade the child's feelings with our interpretations. The teachers would hold back any efforts to help the child work through racial conflicts which the schoolroom stirred up, until the mother had herself evaluated these conflicts and initiated help for them with her child. The mother ought to lead the way and keep *us* informed of her efforts. The mother was visibly relieved, but she was incapable of altering her inability to observe, let alone work through, the child's conflicts. Angry skirmishes continued to flare up, grapevines flourished, and correspondingly it remained very difficult for the *child* openly to express aggression about color.

This child's mother had good reason to be angry, having felt deeply throughout her life the effects of racial prejudice. Much of her anger she discharged in the service of worthwhile community causes, but these were not sufficient to relieve the ever-present fear of losing control of anger in the wrong place—with someone close and necessary to her whom she might hurt, in this case the school, its teachers, its therapists. This mother was devoted to the school and its staff, praised it publicly, and regarded it as the best possible place for her child to be. In time she came to view our strange attitudes about race benevolently and rationalized that she put up with some of our quirks because of the importance of her child's attending a first-rate school like ours. We in turn became less concerned with requiring a child to fit our own concepts of healthy emotional development (to relieve our white guilt!) without regard for overriding limitations imposed upon this development. While this child's verbal expression of the anger so obviously contained inside might please us, the threat to the parents would make life at home for the child impossible.

In retrospect it is surprising that we did not spend more time in discussions of the general subject of prejudice. The problem of clique formations, to specify only one area, might have benefitted from a more thorough consideration of the nature of prejudice. We recognized that racial prejudices have many common characteristics with all prejudices, but we seldom attempted to view our own work from the perspective of the general phenomenon of prejudice formation. This omission may reflect the fact that our major interest was in racial awareness and racial conflict in the prelatency child. According to our formulations (Chapter 7), this is a period of life in which prejudice does not exist, a period when prejudice formation is not yet a possibility.

In summary, our staff meetings were the backbone of our program. We doubt that integration could be actively practiced in a school like ours without a conscious, deliberate, organized staff effort to promote it. Any free-floating conscious interest in integration would all too easily succumb to unconscious resistances, so prevalent in our culture, against change and progress toward integration.

Physical integration, while an absolute necessity, does not automatically guarantee psychological integration. Our meetings were an effort to achieve this guarantee. They helped us to face and not to deny problems of racial difference and racial integration in young children, in their parents, and in ourselves.

3

OBSERVING AND WORKING THROUGH

"TO NOTICE IS TO BE NORMAL"

We never doubted that there would be many opportunities to observe children's spontaneous reactions to racial differences. We rightly expected that our major problems would come in how best to work through, or possibly not to work through, what we observed. Occasionally we had teachers from other nursery schools attend our meetings as visitors. They too were fully prepared to expect racial observations and reactions from young children and often contributed their own similar experiences. These teachers, so like ourselves, fitted easily into the spirit and content of our working sessions. But occasionally we had to remind ourselves that other visitors, especially if they were segregated from Negroes or from young children, were not at all accustomed to expect nursery and kindergarten children to be able to notice and react to racial differences. One day a visiting analyst expressed surprise at the children's astute perceptions about race and logical conclusions about them. Accustomed as he was to the perception of sexual differences in the very young, the perception of skin color differences had just never crossed his path. We found him a most interested and receptive visitor. Of course, when unconscious denial is operating in the observer, the children's perceptions, or at least their feelings about them, inevitably succumb to its obliterating effect. The usual form of the mechanism seems to be that children must be incapable of perceiving differences in skin color in order to assure the adult that *he* has not noticed any difference, and communicated his own observation and irrational feelings to the child as a prejudice. Or, as one of our teachers succinctly stated it, "To notice is to be prejudiced!"

A visiting white psychiatrist illustrated his own denial and his child's identification with his defense. He was pleased that his five-year-old daughter had no prejudice about Negroes and gave as evidence her apparent failure to notice the different skin color of her Negro classmate. In a vain attempt to tell her father an incident involving the Negro child, whose name she had "forgotten," the white child described many features of the Negro child—dress, size, etc., but *not* her skin color. Finally the father guessed correctly the child's name, but he too, like his daughter, never mentioned the obvious fact of the other little girl's being Negro. We would strongly suspect that behind the "forgotten" (repressed) name lies an already implanted root of prejudice. Will this white child grow up and say that it is hard to identify Negroes by name, as individuals, because they all look alike?

Most parents in our school soon came to share in our conviction that "to notice is to be normal." If they did not already have it, they acquired it from their children. One white mother, still new to the school, reported her shock when her five-year-old excitedly burst in on her with the news that some Negroes were moving into a nearby home. (As the mother already knew, they were to be the first Negroes on the street.) She did not think her child could be normal if he made such an observation. She was easily reassured and in time was able to work through her own shock and to welcome her child's Negro classmates into her home to visit without fear of what the white neighbors would think.

While most parents sooner or later accepted the fact of their young children's ability to notice racial differences, not as many could accept the feelings called forth by the observations. A family where father and mother were of different races took special pains to point out racial differences within the family, in passersby on the street, etc. But the observations had to serve denial of feelings. Their formula seemed to be, "To notice is to be *not* prejudiced." It was especially difficult for these parents to notice preferences and resentments in their children about their own skin colors, and to tolerate their children's comparison of their experiences with that of their different parents. The children's perceptual knowledge had to be used as a defense against the outbreak of aggressive reactions regarding race. To dislike one color or the other inevitably bordered upon disliking one parent or the other.

A great advantage of our observations is that they have been made within the natural setting of the child's life in an integrated school. They can be understood and worked through with the child in relation not just to the moment but to the total picture of the child's developing personality and school and home life experiences. They do not depend upon artificially created test situations. Valuable and necessary as such tests have been in establishing proof of the young child's percepts and feelings about race,[1] they run the risk of introducing complications, and even suggesting prejudices to the child. What is a three-year-old child to think is going on when an adult, a comparative stranger who serves no understandable purpose in his life, as parent or teacher, surprises him with a series of strange questions such as: "Which doll do you prefer? The brown one or the white one?" and then takes away the test dolls he has just given him, supposedly to play with? Potentially it is of much more help to the child when it is his teacher or his parent who has to stop and think what is going on when the *child* surprises *him* in showing a preference for a white or brown doll in his spontaneous play.

EXAMPLES

Only a small fraction of our experiences of the past few years, recorded in detailed notes of our regular meetings, can be selected for inclusion here. In the loosely organized presentation which follows the intention is to invite the reader to join our retracing from the more simple and obvious observations into the more subtle and complex activities of our integration efforts.

Simple Perceptions

These observations by young children of racial differences can be understood by any unprejudiced observer, without further interpretation. They do not require special knowledge of the

---

[1]An outstanding example is the work of Kenneth B. Clark (1955), whose research influenced the Supreme Court in its *Brown* decision.

child's life or of the school setting, and are offered here as simple direct evidence that young children are able to make such observations and will do so spontaneously if permitted the opportunity.

1. Joe is our youngest example. At two and a half years of age he was not yet in our school, but we knew of him and his family because Clark, his older brother, came to the school. Their parents were unprejudiced people who practiced integration in their work and in their social relationships. Their good example reflected in Clark's good relationships with Negro classmates. One day Clark's mother gave Andrew, a Negro boy, a ride home from school. Joe, a white boy, reached over and patted Andrew's face, exclaiming, "Dirty face!" Joe's mother explained to him simply that Andrew's face was brown, not dirty, and that some children were born with brown skin.

2. Barbara, a three-year-old white girl, had just arrived at our school. She went home and told her family, "There's a chocolate man at that school!" She was referring to Martin, a large five-year-old Negro boy. (Soon this little girl developed a friendship with Warren, a Negro boy who was also three years old. In two short years at our school this friendship blossomed into a love affair and plans for marriage.)

These earliest and simplest observations tantalizingly invite our further exploration. Joe and Barbara were already interpreting their new perceptions according to their own familiar experiences. Their simple observations of a brown skin color at once became linked with food and with dirt, and we must suspect here that the discovery—indeed the shocking discovery—of a different-looking child evoked an effort to explain and master the unfamiliar in terms of the familiar. It is not the mind of a prejudiced adult, but of a healthy developing child, which drew these potentially prejudicial conclusions about Negroes.

The following example illustrates an interaction between two children, based on their observations of racial differences.

Here, too, we can see seeds which, if fertilized, could grow into weeds of prejudice.

3.   Ken, a four-year-old dark-skinned Oriental boy, complained to his mother that a white boy in his class, also named Ken, was teasing him by saying that his skin was dirty.

Although Joe is our youngest example, the following observation, reported to one of the child therapists by a Negro mother, suggests a much earlier awareness of racial difference.

4.   A ten-month-old Negro baby was left for a few hours with a Negro mother as a babysitter. So far as is known, the baby was unaccustomed to white people. When a white visitor in the babysitter's home tried to hold the baby, she cried desperately. But she willingly, sometimes happily, permitted any of the Negroes in the strange household to hold and care for her.[2]

Additional examples, from older children:

5.   Emily, an almost four-year-old white girl, talked a lot at home about her new school. She dwelt especially on a boy whose name she could not remember, but identified, "You know, Mommy, the boy whose face looks like this." Emily slanted her eyes with her hands in imitation of Ken, the Oriental boy.

---

[2] See also Lasker's example of the year-old white baby, probably frightened at the first contact with dark-skinned Mexicans (Chapter 10). Since the manuscript of this book was completed another instructive example was reported to us by a European mother. When her child was twelve months old and past the peak of his stranger anxiety, her husband brought to their home for a visit a dark-skinned African student from a nearby university. There were no Negroes living in their European community and this was unquestionably the child's first contact with a Negro. At sight of the visitor the child screamed and shrank away in terror. The African man seemed accustomed to this greeting by European white infants. He reassured the mother that her child's anxiety could easily be relieved, asked her to give him the child's favorite toy, and then requested her to step aside. As he played with the toy the child gradually accepted him, went to him, and permitted the strange-colored man to hold him. On his many subsequent visits to the child's home, the African, who frequently brought a new toy for the child, was always greeted as a favorite visitor by the little white boy. It would seem that for the frightened baby his mother's reassuring acceptance of the dark-skinned stranger was communicated in her trusting handing over of his favorite toy to the kindly, understanding stranger. The child was helped to overcome his skin color anxiety and to follow his mother and his toy in his acceptance of the stranger.

6. Clark, a four-year-old white boy, was playing near Donny, an Oriental boy. Edwin, another four-year-old white boy who was a markedly atypical child, claimed in a strange affectless way that Donny had blond hair. Clark answered Edwin, "Oh, you silly! He's brown!" Donny appeared not to notice this exchange. The teacher then heard Clark mutter to himself, "And I like that brown!" Clark and Donny were good friends.

7. When Clark had to wipe chocolate cake crumbs off his face he whispered to his teacher, with his typical friendliness, "If Andrew had chocolate cake crumbs on his face you couldn't tell it because he is black." Andrew covered his ears to shut out Clark's talk.

8. Ted, a four-year-old white boy, had an obvious affection for Abby, a five-year-old Negro girl. Sometimes he lovingly said to her, "You're brown."

9. One day a white girl brought some foreign money to the kindergarten class. In the discussion which followed, Ted (five years, white) asked the teacher, "Do Negro people use the same kind of money that we do?" His inquiry was an honest quest for information and the teacher answered it factually.

10. A visiting teacher reported that two new white girls, sisters three and five years, entered a day nursery class where most of the children were Negro. The Negro children were fascinated with them, especially with the cute three-year-old, whom they wanted to touch. The frightened little girl backed away and her older sister comforted her, "Don't worry. I found out that it won't rub off!"

11. Another visiting teacher told us of a four-year-old white girl who was worried about a new teacher who would be joining her class. She asked her teacher not to bring in a brown teacher to help in the class. When the teacher asked why not, the child replied, "Because it makes my parents nervous."

12. Another visiting teacher told us of a white girl in her

nursery who told her mother she was going to marry a Negro boy in her class. The child's mother told her she could not do it and that she would have to marry a white boy. A week later the little girl told the Negro boy what her mother had said. She added that she had thought it over and was going to marry him anyway when she grew up. (This teacher, with vast experience in nurseries and day care centers, said it was her impression that by kindergarten age most children, Negro or white, had acquired the concept that they would not be allowed to marry someone with a different skin color.)

Defensively Disguised Racial Perceptions and Reactions

In the following examples the fact that a child has perceived and is reacting to something racial does not show at once upon the conscious surface of his mind. He has defensively hidden or disguised what he has seen and felt because it has evoked some conflict in himself which he does not want to be informed about.

As observers of the child we must now put forth a greater effort to comprehend what we are observing. If we do not invest this effort and merely join forces with a child's defenses, we ourselves will see only the outermost defensive surface which the child consciously communicates to us. Then we will be unable to appreciate that what we are seeing and hearing has anything to do with race at all. The effort required of us is that we try to empathize with the child's underlying conflict. Our empathic effort sometimes may be limited by lack of knowledge about the child's school or home life or his stage of psychological development. But even if we cannot know the content of the conflict, we can appreciate at least that the child *has* one under the conscious surface. As bystanders we can go no further. We have to trust our own empathy as sufficient and valid evidence for the fact that underneath the child's defense lies perception, feeling, conflict involving race. For a teacher or parent, however, it is sometimes indicated to go further—to attempt to remove the child's defense by interpreting it for him. (If the defense is a healthy adaptive one, no interpretation is required; in fact interpretation may work against adaptation by depriving the child of the healthy defense.) If the defense is interfering with the child's development and with his acceptance of racial differences, then its interpretation can be helpful to him. With the understanding from a loved person which interpretation brings, the child can give up his defense, and permit himself to face his own conflicts consciously. If we, as observers, are permitted to view this process, then we no longer need rely solely upon our own empathy as evidence of what the child has taken in and reacted to about race. The child himself provides corroboration of our empathetic hypothesis through his conscious verbal expression of his own conflict.

Sometimes an observer may confuse interpretation of a defense with instilling of a racial conflict into the child's mind. Of course, the person who interprets to the child must be careful not to make this mistake. Making interpretations to a child carries great responsibility. The interpreter's effort must be sufficient to aid the child to understand *himself* better; yet it must not interfere with and impose upon the child's own internalized conflicts and his own ability to work toward a resolution of them. Only a person close to a child, loved by the child, will be able to participate with him in this special way of assisting his emotional development. An occasional visiting observer to the child's school does not qualify for the job. Nor can the visiting observer hope to achieve the full conviction that child and teacher or parent experience as active participants. In the examples which follow it may well be that the reader will also feel a lack of conviction that some of them really do illustrate a child's perception and reaction to racial differences. Limitations in the reporting may be held partially responsible, but we also recognize that no amount of exposure to reports can equal actual experience.

Interpretations are included below whenever they were given to a child. It may seem in some cases that obvious interpretations were withheld. Tactfulness and timing may have restrained the teacher, or the observer may not have had the needed relationship with the child to qualify as an interpreter of his defense.

With the illustrations in this subgroup we have progressed more deeply into children's reactions to their perception of racial differences. Further, we will see in them many evidences of the children's tendencies to intertwine these reactions with their normal developmental, or more complex neurotic, conflicts. The interpretative work of teachers and parents has as its goal the *segregation* of developmental and neurotic conflicts from what the children see and feel about race. (See Part II for further discussion.) For example, the brownness of feces, regarded as dirty and disgusting by the child, gets distinguished from the brownness of his, or his playmate's skin. (See the example of Joe at the end of this chapter. This child has already been described in Example 1.) At two and a half years he called Andrew's brown face dirty. As Joe's development progressed he achieved a segregation of the two browns—BMs, which are dirty and discarded, and brown skin, which belongs to a friend who is kept and valued. Just before his fifth birthday Joe was observed by a teacher to come to the defense of six-year-old Andrew, who was being yelled at by some other children. "Don't you yell at that brown boy! He's my friend!" shouted Joe at his classmates.

13. At story times the children in the nursery are frequently dismissed for lunch one at a time and asked to point to a favorite character in the story illustration as they leave the group. One day they had had a story about a large litter of kittens, each one of a different color or combination of colors. Andrew, the only Negro child in the group that day, was the only child to point to the one all-white kitten in the picture as his favorite. The teacher knew that currently Andrew was feeling very dissatisfied with his brown color, but she wisely chose not to comment at this moment on Andrew's displaced expression of his conflict.

14. Harold, a four-year-old white boy, talked with Abby, a five-year-old Negro girl, on the telephone when she was at home with chicken pox. Immediately after the call he went into one of his excited, uncoordinated states in which he became confused and unable to express himself. He began naming all the Negro

and Chinese children and calling them all black. Then he wanted to know if he could turn black and get chicken pox. His teacher tried to reassure him with calm explanations that being Negro had nothing to do with getting chicken pox. Harold knew that white children, too, got chicken pox, but he seemed to equate it with changing to Negro. His teacher assured him that he would always stay his own color, just as Negro children kept their own color. She further told him that the teachers liked Abby just the way she was and they liked Harold just the way he was.

15.   A visitor to the school, who stayed only for a morning and did not know the children, reported the following incident. Fred, a Negro boy, wiped his hands on a black towel. One of the white girls told him he had gotten the towel dirty and he angrily denied it. The visitor understood it as each child's expression of their reactions to racial differences.

16.   When Ted, a white boy, soiled in kindergarten, he went into the bathroom to change his pants. Edwin, who knew of the soiling, went into the bathroom where he could see only Ted's legs beneath the closed toilet door. He insisted that it was Fred, a Negro boy, not Ted, who had soiled. The teacher corrected Edwin's strange mistake and reported the incident to Edwin's analyst. (For a related illustration, see the case of Edwin, an atypical child, described in Example 37.)

17.   One day Donny (Oriental), Andrew (Negro), and Clark (white) were all playing in the doll corner of the nursery. Clark suddenly stopped, looked around, and said of his two close friends, "Donny is a boy, Andrew is a boy, and I'm a boy—and what are we doing here!" Clark had given other indications of being threatened by any possible identification with girls. The implication seemed that his nonwhite friends might have been nonboy friends as well. The teacher, feeling that she might not have correctly guessed Clark's fantasy, said nothing.

18.   In kindergarten the children were listening to a story about Great Salt Lake. Ken, the dark-skinned Oriental boy, was

by now much more accepting of his own color, but the appeal of the story was too much for him at that moment. When he realized that a swimmer in Salt Lake got covered with salt, he jumped up and said, "Yeah! When you come out of that lake you're all WHITE!" The teacher busied herself with calming the silliness Ken had generated in the group, but did not attempt to take up this brief return of Ken's old conflict with him, particularly in a group setting. She knew he was making good progress in accepting himself as he was, and that he did not need her extra help at that moment.

19. When Lucy, a four-year-old white girl, returned from a southern spring vacation, deeply tanned, the children seemed stunned and many avoided her or just stared at her. Lucy herself appeared very unhappy about her tan, and her mother seemed almost ashamed of her changed child. The teachers regarded the silence and the ostracizing of Lucy as reasons for action. They explained to the children, individually or in small groups, how Lucy's skin had changed color, and contrasted it with Negro skin, which stays brown. The assurance, for every child, was that he would remain the same, keep his own color, and always be valued most for himself, just as he was. The teachers predicted the summer tans that many of the children would get. With this opening from the teachers the children began to make remarks about tan skin and brown skin. Fred would not have to go to Florida to get a tan because he was already brown. Ben, a blond fair-skinned boy, who was just about to go to Florida for a vacation, had a tantrum and had to be removed when the teacher remarked that he would get a nice tan, like Lucy's. (Ben had had an anal surgical trauma in the first year of life.)

20. When Bert, a five-year-old Indian boy, discovered that a cut was healing over with pink skin, he showed it to his teacher and she explained the pinkness as part of the healing process. Bert's reply was that he was going to cut off all of his skin and get pink skin. The teacher reassured Bert that she liked his skin just the way it was and that it would be sad if he had to go hurt-

ing himself just to try to change his skin to pink. She did not say anything about the known conflict Bert had about his skin being dirty, since she also knew that Bert's mother had been totally unable to face this conflict. (See Example 40 for a more detailed description of Bert's conflict and his mother's reaction to it.)

21. George, a five-year-old white boy, was a very excitable and anxious new child in the kindergarten. When he first saw Donny, an Oriental boy, he jumped up and ran about wildly, pointing to Donny and saying, "Big ears!" (Donny did have big ears.) When the second Oriental boy in the class arrived George yelled, "Hey! There's TWO Chinese boys here!" That George was shocked and scared by these different-looking children was confirmed by his typical excited reaction to any shocking, frightening event.

22. When five-year-old Paula, a new Negro girl, entered the kindergarten, Andrew, a Negro boy, excitedly called to Abby, also Negro, "Look! Look!" But then he and Abby totally avoided the intruder. That afternoon when Andrew was shopping with his aunt he whispered to a little cousin, "Let's get rid of all the brown people!" His aunt, who had no way of knowing that he wanted to get rid of the new child in his school, rather angrily asked him what color he thought he was, and he teasingly replied that he was going to be white.

23. Rosemary, a light-skinned five-year-old Negro girl in the kindergarten, was unable to express verbally her feelings about being Negro because they met with denial from her parents. She gave evidence of them at times in her attentiveness to stories and conversations touching upon racial differences. Perhaps she was showing her conflicts when she chose a vivid black and white zebra costume to wear for Halloween. One of our teachers, who had taught in Hawaii, recalled a Hawaiian child who had openly expressed the fantasy that a child born of white and Negro parents would be striped. A white visitor at the staff meeting where this incident was reported added to our feeling that our guess about Rosemary's costume was correct when she

told that her own child had expressed a rather similar fantasy—
that a child of mixed parents would be half white, half brown,
with the dividing horizontal line in the mid-abdominal region.[3]

24. Alice, a three-year-old Negro girl, was the child of a
mixed marriage. She showed many of her reactions about skin
color in her reactions to food. When a white child had a chocolate birthday cake, Alice would not eat it and she declared that
for her own birthday she was going to have an all-white cake.
She mixed her vanilla ice cream with chocolate sauce and repeated over and over, "White and brown make brown!"

25. Alice, now four years, was especially fascinated by the
daddy cardinal bird in a bird poster which the teacher was showing the children. There were many brilliantly colored birds on
the poster and the cardinal had not especially interested any of
the other children. The teacher's thoughts returned to Alice's
intriguing fascination, and later in the day the teacher suddenly
realized that unlike any of the other bird pairs shown on the
poster she had used, the mommy and daddy cardinals' colors
were very different.

26. In a group of three nursery girls Alice (four years) was
the only Negro. The children were making life-size tracings of
themselves, coloring them, and cutting them out. Alice, an advanced child and ordinarily a very skillful worker, reluctantly
began coloring her portrait, gradually darkening the skin to a
black color. Then she got very angry and refused to cut out the
portrait, as the other children were doing. The teacher verbalized for her the distress she felt at her own color, and Alice nod-
ded in agreement. But even before the teacher could comfort Alice, Dorothy, an especially empathic four-year-old girl, asked
Alice what the trouble was and offered to help her with her
work. Alice had angrily refused. At that moment, only the attention and comfort of the teacher suited her.

27. Stuart, five years and white, watched a Negro boy wash-

[3] In one of his speeches Martin Luther King declared that we do not need black power
or white power. What we need is "striped" power.

ing his hands. Stuart told the teacher that the other boy had "old hands." Stuart was new in the kindergarten and the teacher did not yet know him very well. She merely clarified that the Negro boy was Stuart's own age, but that his skin color was different from Stuart's because he was a Negro.

28. In kindergarten, Adam, a white boy, got into one of his loud, contagiously out-of-control states and began teasing Gerald, a Negro, calling him "brown." Andrew, swept up in Adam's excitement, seemed to forget for the moment that he himself was Negro as he joined Adam's taunts of "brown" at Gerald. The teacher stopped the teasing, reprimanded Adam and Andrew, and soon had to remove Adam to an area by himself, where he was accustomed to going until he could regain his self control.

29. In kindergarten two Negro boys, Andrew and Gerald, and a white boy, Dean, together had removed their socks and were excitedly comparing their feet. The teacher suspected that some covert sexual play might also have taken place, but was unable to confirm it.

30. Frances, a five-year-old white girl, was in the midst of an intense oedipal rivalry with her mother as a result of her strong affection for her father. Blocked in her verbal expression of hostility to her mother, and also in her excitement, she regressed to an earlier difficulty—wetting—and during the day she made many trips to the bathroom. During this stressful period in her development she began some solitary doll play. She would assemble all the Negro and white dolls together, angrily throw aside all of the Negro dolls, and then introduce a white father doll who went about kissing all of the white but none of the Negro dolls.

31. In kindergarten, Paula, a Negro girl, excitedly told the teacher she had taken her pants down because Helen and Jane, both white, had asked her to do it. "We didn't see anything. She's just like us. She's a girl, too," Helen and Jane said to the

teacher. The teacher confirmed the sexual likenesses, although the girls had different skin color.

But she also encouraged the children to ask questions, to verbalize rather than to show. However, the implied confusion about racial and sexual difference had already been acted upon and now did not gain any verbal expression.

32. A visiting teacher from a day care center told us the following incident. In their nursery there was a Negro boy whose last name was Black. None of the children had ever made any comment, although they knew the boy's full name well. When his father came to visit, the teacher greeted him, "Hello, Mr. Black." One of the Negro children in the room yelled a friendly admonishment, "Hey, Mrs. H.! What *you* said!" (This center was in the heart of the ghetto, where, at that time "black" carried a sinister connotation.)

33. Gerald, a Negro kindergartner, talked and joked about anal functions when he got excited and out of control. At these times he teased about making "white do-dos." Gerald still had occasional lapses in his bowel training, about which he felt very ashamed.

34. Paula, a five-year-old Negro girl, had serious emotional conflicts which led to neurotic symptom formation. One of her symptoms was stealing. (Stealing cannot be regarded as an ordinary manifestation of a developmental conflict in a child. If it exists to any appreciable extent, it is not a normal developmental reaction. Its persistence must always be regarded as an indication that a child's personality has had to resort to developing a neurotic symptom in its struggle to bind some overwhelming anxiety.) Paula consciously suffered from feelings of inferiority and could often verbalize them very clearly. But for her, verbalization was not enough to bring understanding and relief. Factors which were unconscious to Paula (especially the full extent of her penis envy) kept her inferiority feelings fixed and unresolved. In her need to compensate for these feelings she stole things from other children's cubbies, and secreted what she had stolen in her

own cubby. If her theft was discovered and she was confronted with the evidence of it, she strongly denied it, but looked very forlorn and guilty. Paula openly expressed much dissatisfaction about being Negro. She especially disliked her hair, often combed and fussed with it, and frequently compared it unfavorably to the long blonde hair of a much admired white girl. We were very familiar with this rejection of their hair by Negro girls, as we had invariably met it as a temporary developmental reaction in every Negro girl in the school. But in the case of Paula, these inferiority feelings about her color and her hair were channeled into the neurotic current in her personality. She secretly began to throw her combs away and to make up excuses about why she had "lost" her comb and why the teachers had to give her a new one from the school's reserve supply. She also took combs from girls whose hair she admired. (Her stealing was from both white and Negro children, though always comfined to girls.) A further complication had to do with Paula's shame and disapproval about her symptom, which she tried so hard to conceal and disown. It seemed that she unconsciously displaced some of this shame and disapproval of her neurotic symptom onto her Negro features, especially her hair and skin. Then no amount of help for her inferiority feelings about being Negro could reach the hidden reinforcements supplied to them from her shame and guilt about her stealing. In this complex set of developmental, neurotic and racial difference problems there was very little that the teachers could do. At least they could understand their limitation and not feel unduly frustrated at their own helplessness. They tried to limit Paula's stealing. They also tried to keep Paula's mother and her child therapist informed, and the therapist concentrated on preparing Paula's mother to recognize and accept her child's need for treatment.

Racial Perceptions Misused As Defenses Against Other Conflicts

The following examples are, in a sense, the reverse of those reactions to a racial perception which are defensively disguised because the perception evoked conflict. Here the children have used a racial perception defensively, to ward off some other conflict from consciousness. Consequently these are deceiving examples. They do attest to children's ability to perceive racial differences. Further, they may even *appear* to attest to the ability of a young child to develop a blatant, full-blown racial prejudice. But once again, the underlying conflict of the child must be recognized and *segregated* for him from the matter of race, by his parents and his teachers. If his "racial prejudice" is taken at face value and not recognized as defensive, such a child is in danger of getting himself badly rejected, because the defense he has unconsciously selected will be regarded as a most offensive one by most people. It is also one which will cause the child himself considerable guilt. (See especially the case of Ralph, Example 36.)

35. Donny A., a five-year-old white boy, was upset at the news that his mother was going to have another baby. In very untypical fashion he began to berate a Chinese boy, whose name was also Donny. He teased him that he was brown, and Donny B. insisted that he was not brown, but Chinese. Then Donny A. turned to Fred, a Negro boy, and attacked him by calling him brown. Fred was quiet and Donny angrily went on, "Your tongue is brown!" Clearly, in attacking a like-named boy Donny was berating himself, and in selecting Negro Fred's tongue to berate, he was berating his own at that moment. Ordinarily Donny A. was a very outgoing, friendly boy, who got along very well with Donny B. and Fred. The teacher tried to help Donny A. by telling him that his mommy had told her she was going to have another baby and she understood now that Donny was feeling very angry about the new baby. If he could *tell* his angry feelings about the baby, he wouldn't have to get so angry with his friends, and then he wouldn't have to feel angry about himself either.

36. Ralph, a white child almost four years old, had been in the nursery almost a year. His father had died when he was an infant. Margaret, a Negro girl not quite three years old, was new

to the nursery and still had her mother with her during much of the morning session she attended. At snack time one day Ralph became very provocative with Margaret and her mother, rudely calling them "brown" and exciting other children to do the same. A quick response by the teacher restored order, removed a seeming prejudice, and promoted a psychological racial integration for the entire snack table. Her familiarity with Ralph's life-long and current problems led the teacher to interpret in a friendly but firm manner that Ralph was teasing Margaret because he was missing his own mother so much just then, and he wanted his mother with him, just as Margaret had her mother with her. But if he couldn't have *his* mother there, he didn't want any other child to have a mother there either. Ralph was not a prejudiced child. He was a child with a great separation anxiety, and his misuse of racial differences was only one small version of how he presented his major separation conflicts. Several weeks later Margaret's mother withdrew her from the school. Ralph's guilt overwhelmed him. He loudly declared that Hanna Perkins ought to keep Margaret in the school and not let her leave. Shortly after this outburst he lost complete control, fell on the floor, kicking about and requiring a teacher to protect him from himself. "Margaret is stinky!" he shouted. Frightened and guilty Ralph greatly feared that Hanna Perkins regarded his own behavior as stinky and might not want to keep *him*. He needed much reassurance about it.

37. Edwin, a white boy aged four years, could be descriptively categorized as a markedly atypical child. He was bizarre, appeared unrelated to people or environment, engaged in repetitive solitary play, and made strange affectless pronouncements. One of these was a loud, "Nigger!" Sometimes he called out, about a Negro girl in the class who was often out of control and frightening to the children, "Abby is a nigger!" The teacher told him he could not say that because it was an unkind word and it made Abby feel sad. She encouraged him to *tell* what worried him about brown-skinned people, but he was too ill to be able to do so. His unprejudiced and very worried mother was extremely

embarrassed by her disturbed son's remark. At age five Edwin began psychoanalytic treatment, and in time his disturbance could be comprehended. At age eight Edwin was recalling with his analyst his first days of treatment. "Do you remember how I pretended the dolls made BM in their pants and I was washing it off in the shower? I used to play a lot with that Negro doll and wash it off." Edwin could tell now in words what had been going on in his initial bizarre play in the treatment. He himself, in his great anxiety, had been afraid of making BMs in his pants, getting spanked, and thrown out. To him the brown skin had represented an external version of his worst fears—losing control, getting brown BM all over himself, and getting thrown out like a BM. (Edwin had had a very traumatic separation from his parents in a hospital emergency room, at two years, in the middle of his toilet training and just after the birth of his sister.)

It is of interest that Edwin's use of "nigger" was one of the very few times that any of the children used derogatory terms to express perceptions and feelings about racial differences. When a child did use such a term, the teacher's response, as with Edwin, was to teach both white and Negro children that the remark was unkind and to help them to find other means of verbal expression of whatever concerned them at the moment. Sometimes she had to explain why the word was unkind. Grownups, who had never gotten over their worries about people whose skin color was different, used these words in a mean, unkind way, which made Negroes feel angry and sad.

In the above examples white children used perceptions of racial difference to defend against a conscious expression of other internalized conflicts. In the following examples both white and Negro children wrongly associated some unrelated characteristic or event concerning a Negro child with the color of his Negro skin. We found that both white and Negro children tended to make this displacement onto brown skin color especially in relation to out-of-control behavior and being sent away.

38. Abby and Martin were four-year-old Negro children who attended our nursery school in different years. Each had

overwhelming anxieties which often led to out-of-control behavior requiring their removal from the schoolroom as the only effective means of helping them to regain their control. Their removal was worked through as well as possible by the teachers, both with Abby and Martin, and with the other children. The children were assured of the reason for and the purpose of the removal, the protection and concern for the out-of-control child, and the child's return as soon as he regained control. But inevitably, it seemed, many children associated the disturbed behavior with the brown skin, and gave indications of expecting any brown-skinned person to behave in an out-of-control way. Abby was, for awhile, the only Negro child in her class, but in Martin's class there were other Negro children who did not have his difficulties with loss of control. It seemed that the realistic correction offered by the Negro children in control did little to alter the displacement. Nor did a white child's loss of control and removal from the group help very much in correcting the equation of brown and loss of control. (The reality corrections could not reach the unconscious forces at work in the children.) The Negro kitchen staff in the school had strong reaction formations against this childhood equation of badness, loss of control, and brown skin. They were less tolerant of "bad" behavior in the Negro children, and had higher expectations of them than of the white children, when the children went to the kitchen to help serve snacks.

39. When Margaret's mother withdrew her from school, many children associated her withdrawal with her brown skin. For a long time there was a general anxiety among both white and Negro children in the nursery that a Negro child might not be kept by the school. (When Brenda, a three-year-old white girl, saw Margaret several weeks later, while shopping in a store, the two girls were overjoyed. For Brenda, who excitedly reported this reunion in nursery school, it seemed more than a reunion. It seemed an assurance that Margaret was still all right, even though she had left our school.) The teachers worked hard

to correct such misapprehensive anxieties with realistic explanations, but the children did not seem satisfied. They needed to
hear them over and over. Although it had been the transportation arrangements that had failed in Margaret's case, the children seemed to feel that her departure had something to do with
her brown skin. (The staff, too, suspected that her mother had
withdrawn her because of a dissatisfaction with our approach to
problems of racial differences.) After Margaret left, a teacher
observed Alex, a four-year-old light-complected Negro boy of
mixed parentage who had been adopted by a white family, as he
played angrily with a Negro doll. "We don't like dirty babies
here!" he declared. He scrubbed the doll vigorously, saying,
"I'm going to clean you off!" Alex was a boy who had endured
painful separations and greatly feared being sent away or losing
those close to him. More than four months later, Alice, a Negro
girl also of mixed parentage, returned to school two days late following a vacation. Her late return had been planned before vacation and all the children knew that Alice was away on a vacation
trip with her parents. But Alex had obviously doubted the explanation of her absence. When she walked into the schoolroom after her prolonged vacation, Alex jumped up and down for joy,
shouting Alice's full name over and over, as though her return
were too good to be true. It is interesting that soon after this
event Alex introduced the first hints of his conflict about being
Negro. It seemed that he had to work through these school separations, as well as many others (his mother and the child therapist had worked well together for many months in order to help
Alex get some relief of his separation anxiety), before he could
face any conflicts about his color. (He began feeling the texture of
white children's hair, perhaps sensing that his different hair was
of some concern to his white mother. Later, while in a group of
four children, he said, "There are three white children and one
brown child in this group." In reality there were two white children, a dark skinned Negro boy and Alex. Alex was beginning to
inform us of his need to deny his own color.)

Complex Reactions

The examples in this miscellaneous subgroup are generally of a more complex order. They illustrate many of the points already brought out, but they tend to include more people in more complex interactions. Knowledge of the current school situation as well as of the many people involved is needed to comprehend these examples in depth.

40. Bert was a five-year-old boy from India. After he returned from a summer visit to India, he was observed to have acquired what amounted almost to a hand-washing compulsion. In fact, he and his mother had been caught in the outbreak of war, and living conditions had been very unstable and unsanitary. Their return to Cleveland, where Bert's Indian father had remained to work, was for a time in considerable doubt. During their stay in India Bert's mother had placed much emphasis on cleanliness, especially hand washing, in connection with eating. After their return to Cleveland, the mother, with the help of the child therapist, was able to clarify for Bert that the food in Cleveland was safe and that he did not have to wash his hands so much any more. Bert's "compulsive" handwashing lessened considerably. However, Bert's conflict about his own and his mother's color was also contained in his residual handwashing. When they passed a Negro on the street, Bert told his mother, "She's dirty! She hasn't washed!" His mother replied, "No, she can't help it," and rather anxiously tried to explain that her skin was not dirty, just brown. Bert replied that his mother ought to wash too. His mother was never able to give any response to this remark, finding her child's aggressive blaming of her for his own skin, which seemed so dirty to him, an unbearable confrontation. (See also Bert's wish to grow pink skin, described in Example 20.)

41. Fred, a three-year-old Negro boy, was still quite new in school and his mother was comforting him about the fact that she would no longer be in school with him the following week. After he felt reassured enough to venture away from her lap, Helen, a

four-year-old white girl, suddenly threw herself into Fred's mother's lap. Fred's mother was astonished but responded warmly to Helen. Helen's mother, nearby, seemed stunned. At the end of the school day, when Fred was excitedly running up and down the hall, Helen's mother said loudly to a teacher and within earshot of Fred's mother, "Is this the kind of behavior this school advocates?" In order to appreciate this complex situation one had to know of Helen's mother's early maternal deprivation, of her difficulty in sharing her daughter with anyone else, but also in mothering her daughter. Helen often seemed to provoke her sometimes-rejecting mother with a preference for Negroes, based very likely upon her attachment to a warm Negro maid in her home.

42. When Andrew's mother visited he teasingly misnamed all the paint colors, and he pulled up his shirt and stuck out his tummy. At this time he was insistent upon wearing only white shirts to school. He seemed to be provoking his mother to recognize how angry he felt about being brown. Soon after this incident Andrew showed his gleaming white teeth to his teacher and insisted that his teeth were brown. "White teeth are brown teeth!" he teased. When the teacher asked what he meant, he responded with the question: "Are there any brown teeth?" The teacher answered factually that all people had white teeth, regardless of the color of their skin. Andrew looked relieved and wanted to hear more. Then he asked, "Where's Edwin?" The teacher reminded him that Edwin was with his therapist in her office. "What's he doing there?" Andrew asked. The teacher repeated an explanation that Andrew already knew—that Edwin had especially big worries and needed extra help for them, more than his mommy alone could give him. Andrew declared that he had big worries too. The teacher could reassure him that she knew he was worried about his brown skin and assured him that his mommy would be able to help him with these worries. (His mother was in fact proving herself capable of giving Andrew whatever help he needed about this conflict, and there was no reason for a therapist to supplement or intervene for An-

drew.) Then Andrew began to talk about his mommy helping him by coming to visit more often. One trauma in Andrew's life was an early separation from his mother, which was repeated now in that she could not always transport him to and from school. It seemed that Andrew's conflicts about being brown and about his feeling that his mother rejected him and did not help enough were all mixed together in his mind.

43.   When a Negro-white couple visited the nursery school in the course of applying for their child's enrollment, none of the children appeared to notice or comment, although they were introduced, as usual, to the visitors, and the purpose of the visit was explained to them. A white mother, who happened to be visiting her child that morning, gulped visibly, but quickly recovered her composure and responded graciously to an introduction. (Later on she became genuinely friendly with this family and their children, and the families exchanged many visits.) After the visit of these parents Betty, a Negro girl, was observed to play with the dolls. She picked out Negro dolls to represent herself and her mother, but then could not decide whether she wanted a Negro man or a white policeman doll to be the father. (Both of her parents were Negro.) Betty resolved her dilemma by choosing *both* the Negro and white men to be her father doll.

44.   When an Oriental-white couple visited the kindergarten, prior to enrolling their child, the children were unusually quiet and unusually good, the teacher noticed, with relief. Ordinarily this particular class did not do well with visitors, particularly with visitors whose children might be entering the school. Two days later, when two white social workers, both women, visited the class, the children behaved as badly as they ever had done with visitors. The teacher wondered whether this was the "backlash" from the preceding visit.

45.   Bruce, a rather nonverbal three-year-old Negro boy, was just beginning to adjust to school without his mother, and to be able to stay for nap and afternoon activities by himself. One

afternoon the activity involved each child's drawing a picture of himself and coloring it. Bruce began drawing himself, beginning with his feet and working upward. When he got up as far as his hands he asked the teacher what color he should make them. The teacher encouraged him to look at himself and to make his own decision. He answered, "brown," after inspecting his hands carefully. He colored in his arms and legs very well, and also colored his face brown without difficulty, working unusually well all the while. When he got all the way up to his hair, he hesitated, then called to the teacher for help. "What color should I make my hair?" Three-year-old Brenda, a very black-haired white girl, called back, "Black! Just like mine!" Bruce was obviously pleased at Brenda's friendliness and at once colored his own hair black, thus completing one of his best pieces of artwork at school. But when Bruce's mother came she seemed very angry at the sight of the brown picture Bruce had drawn of himself. (She often tended to feel that her children were discriminated against because they were Negro.) She failed to appreciate the excellent work that the picture represented and began criticizing it. That she chose colors, especially, to criticize, seems to confirm that she was displacing from her real color conflicts. She told Bruce he was not wearing red pants, as in the picture, and Bruce was too disappointed and hurt to reply. The teacher explained that plaid pants had been too hard for Bruce to copy, so they had chosen just one color in the plaid pants—red. Then Bruce's mother complained that he had painted himself in mittens. In drawing his hands he had not attempted to make fingers, so now his mother tried to deny that the brown was Bruce's skin, in making it instead his mittens. At this point Bruce's older brother, standing nearby, joined in and jeered at Bruce's fine drawing. Poor Bruce was not through with the ridiculing, though. The next day, upon getting up from nap, four-year-old Phyllis, a white girl, took a look at Bruce's self-portrait pasted on the wall and exclaimed, "Yuck!" with disgust. Bruce looked very sad indeed. The teachers gave Bruce much help, and in time his mother, with the help of her child therapist, became more sup-

porting of her child's progress. The following example illustrates
some of Bruce's improvement, and a corresponding improvement
in his mother.

46. Three four-year-old white boys were busily building a
ranch with a bunk house for cowboys. Bruce summoned up a
newly found courage and asked the boys in a quite grown-up
manner to permit him to play too. Bill angrily rejected Bruce,
began to yell and to have a temper outburst. Recently Bill's
mother had been encouraging him to tell his angry feelings and
not just yell. Now the teacher did the same thing. Bill stopped
his yelling and told Bruce in a very angry voice that he did not
want him to play because there were no brown cowboys and
Bruce was brown. Then he told Bruce to get a Kleenex and blow
his nose, thereby emphasizing his concept of Bruce as brown and
messy. The teacher dealt first with Bill. She corrected his mis-
conception and told him that there really were brown cowboys
and that he should try to let Bruce play, especially since Bruce
had asked in such a grown-up and friendly way. By this time
Bruce had regressed to his old blank, uncomprehending, passive-
appearing state. The teacher now turned to Bruce and told him
she knew how hard it must have been for him to listen to what
Bill had said about his brown skin. She said that he must feel
very upset and angry about it. However, Bruce could not express
his anger to Bill, even with the teacher's support. He remained
blank, but several minutes later gave unmistakable evidence that
he had unfortunately turned his anger upon himself. He went off
to play by himself, built a building and then suddenly kicked it
down angrily. Again the teacher tried to help and reassure him.
She told Bruce it was sad that he had to destroy his own fine
building just because he was angry at Bill. She told him that it
was all right to be angry with Bill for not wanting to play with
him because his skin was brown. Although Bruce's mother had
not heard of this incident, she gave evidence of being in touch
with her son's conflict about himself. The next day, when she
was in nursery school, she saw that Bruce's nose needed wiping

and in a kindly supportive manner directed him to get a Kleenex and blow his nose. She told him that people wouldn't like to be with him if he didn't blow his nose and looked messy. Previously she had always wiped Bruce's nose for him.

Sometimes a single isolated observation about a child tells little or nothing about his reactions to racial differences. One can at best suspect that more is going on than meets the eye. But an accumulation of related observations convincingly portrays the child's underlying conflicts. The extended series of observations presented below, on each of four children, demonstrates this cumulative effect.

47. Abby was a five-year-old Negro child in the nursery. During a prolonged period when she was known to be very distressed about being Negro some of the following observations were made. She wanted to wear only white shoes and refused to wear her black shoes. She threw her chocolate cookies on the floor, refusing to eat them. She openly admired Jane's long blond hair, berated her own hair, and competitively offered her own pigtails to the teacher to comb out for her. When the teacher described a new girl who was expected to join the class as having curly hair, Abby eagerly asked, "Like mine?" She was visibly disappointed when she learned that the new girl was not a Negro. She took comfort in other Negro children, and was especially friendly with Ken, a dark-skinned Oriental boy. Abby liked to eat snow. When the teacher told her she shouldn't, she said it was white and all right to eat; only brown dirty things are not all right to eat. When chicken was served for lunch, Abby ate only the white, not the dark meat. For a long time Abby played house with two white girls. Always she had to play the part of the maid, until the teacher worked through with all three girls that each should have a turn at being mother or baby, as well as maid. Some time after Abby had left our school one of our teachers reported that she had turned up in the teacher's Sunday School class. A white child asked Abby and the only other Negro

child there if they were sisters. Abby replied matter-of-factly, "No, we're just colored."

48. Andrew, a three-year-old Negro boy, refused to color a picture of a workman black, and insisted upon drawing his picture on white paper. (The children were drawing pictures of the workmen at the construction site next to the school. One of the Negro workmen, whom Andrew much admired, had responded to Andrew's wish to grow up and be a workman with a friendly remark that when he grew up he would be something much better than a workman.) Andrew spent much time washing his hands and spreading the white soap suds lather all over himself. He refused to play with clay because it was black. One day he bent his fingernail back in what appeared to be a very painful position and sought the teacher's admiration of the whitened nail bed. For a while he would not go out in the sun because he was afraid of getting a tan.

49. Ken, a four-year-old dark-skinned Oriental boy, wanted to scrape his brown skin off. He sought out an unhappy Negro girl, Abby, as a favorite friend. The next year, in kindergarten, after working through with his mother much of his conflicts about his race, Ken gave evidence of being more comfortable and sure of himself, although remnants of the problem persisted. When the children were studying shapes, Ken replied to the teacher's request to identify a round object in the room, "Your eyes." The children immediately began a discussion about what shape Ken's eyes were. When Eileen then declared that Ken was black, he denied it and said, "I'm Chinese!" Later on he brought a book to kindergarten, wanting the teacher to read it in class. It was a good book about Chinese people, a book which explained that even though children looked different and had different skin colors, underneath their skin they were all alike and had the same kinds of feelings. (See also Ken's reaction to a story about Salt Lake; Example 18.)

50. Harold, a four-year-old white boy who suffered from a very low self-esteem, repeatedly appeared in our discussions. He

both identified with minority race children and rebelled against any identification with them, by ridiculing their racial traits. He tried to bolster his own esteem by belittling these other children, often in quite subtle ways. (As Harold's self-esteem later improved, we heard fewer reports of his conflicts about minority races.) Harold teased Ken, an Oriental boy, about having a dirty face. At home, when Harold's mother wanted him to look in the mirror to see that his own face was dirty and really needed washing, Harold at first refused to look. When he finally did look his mother noticed him pull up the skin around the outer corners of his eyes with his fingers. She noticed him repeat this again a few days later, and this time Harold confirmed that he was making Chinese eyes, like Ken's. Harold insisted, in front of Abby and Fred, that he had to wash the dirt off the Negro doll. Then he "pestered" the teacher to repeat her explanations about why a Negro was not dirty. On a walk in the park, Harold pointed to a passing Negro woman and asked if that was Abby's mother, knowing very well that it was not. (See also Example 14, illustrating Harold's equation of chicken pox, contagious illness, brown skin, dirtiness, and badness. Harold's fear of catching chicken pox also contained his fear of becoming Negro, and thereby confirming that his low estimate of himself was correct.) As Harold improved, he announced one day, after the teacher read a story about Hanukkah, "I celebrate Hanukkah because I'm Jewish." But in his shaky pride, he had to imply that Ken, the Oriental boy, could celebrate neither Hanukkah nor Christmas—that he did not belong anywhere. Ken retorted to Harold, "Well, *I* am Chinese!" with a matching show of pride.

REACTIONS TO CULTURAL CRISES

The Cleveland Riots

In July, 1966, during the last week of the Hanna Perkins school year, rioting broke out in the Hough area, the Negro ghetto of Cleveland. Four people were killed in the riots; many were injured; many fires were set and much property was destroyed. Two days before the end of the school term the National

Guard came into Cleveland and filled not just the Hough area but many of the city's main streets. Armed soldiers were omnipresent. Meanwhile, at school, there was the usual end-of-the-year confusion, sadness, angry outbursts, and regressions in reaction to the imminent separation. Should we try, in the midst of our own normal turmoil, to take on the city's turmoil too? At first the general reaction at our staff meeting was to back away from this extra burden. We were reacting with a denial and rationalizing it with the fact that there were only two days of school left. We tried to tell ourselves it was enough just to cope with the strong separation reactions the children were showing. But as we talked we were embarrassed at the transparency of our own excuses. We knew that we would be wrong to try to avoid what was happening in the city. We could at least try to give some simple factual explanations to the children and some assistance to their mothers, who would be having to talk with their children about whatever continued to happen in the city after the school closed. And in the short time available to us, we could at least try to counteract any tendency to deny the riots or the reactions of the children to this crisis.

In the nursery school, because of the reduced enrollment and the early departures for vacation, there were only five children in attendance. So we were top-heavy with staff, and it was easy to arrange an opportunity for every mother to discuss the situation at length with a teacher. Each mother knew in detail what had gone on in the schoolroom and how she might best follow it up at home with her own child after the vacation began. Most mothers had avoided all mention of the riots, but eagerly welcomed the help and example of the teachers. (One of the children who had left early for her family's vacation was a Negro girl of mixed Negro-white parentage. We were all thankful that this family could be out of town. Everyone felt the city's anxiety and felt that no Negro family in Cleveland was entirely safe, and that any Negro-white couple would be highly vulnerable targets for the riotous actions all about us. When this family returned in the fall, they too expressed the relief they had felt at being out of Cleveland during July.)

While we momentarily hesitated, Lucy, a four-year-old white girl, took matters in her own hands and announced in nursery school that she had seen the soldiers. She said her mother had told her there were people living downtown who were doing bad things and the army had been called in to help them to be able to manage better. Her mother said it wasn't war and that the soldiers weren't going to shoot anybody. They were in town to protect people and to stop people from shooting. All in all, Lucy's mother had done well, giving her child both a factual and reassuring account of the city's disturbed state. The one thing she had not explained—she herself was chagrined when she realized it later, while talking with the teacher—was the racial problem at the basis of the riots. She had said nothing about Negroes and why they had started rioting.

Fred, a four-year-old Negro boy, loved to play with soldiers. He became very excited when his mother pointed out the soldiers in town. She had not yet given him any explanation of their presence, but Fred indicated that he had some understanding of what was going on. He brought to school with him some Negro and some white toy soldiers. During his excited play he talked about liking the white soldiers best. He remained in an excited state, showing much reversal of affect in reaction to the teacher's explanations, and he succeeded in drawing the other boys into his excitement.

All of the children sensed the adults' anxiety, especially, it seemed, from everyone's self-imposed restricted movement throughout the city. Lucy's mother canceled plans for her to go to a play school the following month because the play school was too close to the extensive riot area.

The explanations which teachers gave children and their mothers in the nursery school were the same ones given in kindergarten (below). The nursery children had little to say in response to group or individual talk. We could only hope that as the stress of leaving school subsided their mothers would later be able to help them at home with their feelings and conflicts about the riots.

In kindergarten none of the fifteen children mentioned anything about the riots or the soldiers. This in itself was unusual for the kindergarten; it was more like the nursery school children's silence in the face of major external events. At circle time the teacher introduced the subject by asking whether any of the children had seen the soldiers in town. With that the dam broke and the usual fifteen-minute circle time had to be forcibly drawn to a close forty-five minutes later. No sooner had the teacher made her opening comment than George, a white boy, jumped up and yelled out, "Yes! And eight nurses were killed in Cleveland yesterday!" George was ordinarily a very anxious boy who reacted to his anxiety with explosive excitement. Just then he was under great pressure because he was about to move out of town and his separation feelings about leaving the school were intense. His family would be moving to Chicago, where eight nurses *had* been killed by a madman some weeks ago. Many children joined George in repeating the news of this terrible mass killing. It was apparent that most of them had heard about it when it happened and for days had said nothing anywhere about it.

The teacher was now faced with explaining two terrible events and she found that she had to take up Chicago before the children could listen at all to anything about the soldiers in Cleveland. The children already knew about death but they did not know about murder, as a real happening and not an unreal fantasy. The teacher tried to explain that the murderer was sick, that his thoughts and feelings and behavior were sick, and very different from the ordinary angry thoughts, feelings, and behavior of the children. She stressed the rarity of his condition. In the limited time available, and in a group session, it was impossible to cope with all the complex reactions going on. As the teacher tried to explain the Cleveland riots, some children repeatedly interrupted with questions about the dead nurses, the man who killed them, what would happen to him, etc. To some extent these children might have been trying to avoid the army in their own backyard, but such a defensive use of the Chicago murders was only a small part of their reaction to this crime. Two children in particular could not leave the subject of the Chicago murders. One was Ben, a five-year-old white boy, who was having constant trouble with his own angry temper outbursts when he could not control events in the world about him. (Ben had had anal manipulations and surgery during his first year of life.) The other was Paula, a five-year-old Negro girl. Paula's family had recently moved out of the riot area. They were the first Negro family to move to an all-white street, where they had good reason to anticipate that they would receive an unfriendly reception, even before the outbreak of the riots. Paula teasingly interrupted the teacher with comments about the dead nurses, or she whispered about the nurses to other children, as the teacher tried to discuss the Cleveland riots. Clearly, the Chicago murders were safer than the Cleveland riots for Paula at the moment.

At first only George acknowledged having seen the soldiers. Then Timothy, a boy of mixed Oriental-white parentage, volunteered that the soldiers were all around his house. Timothy's statement was true; he lived on the fringe of the ghetto. Gradually, other children told of having seen the soldiers and of hearing grownups talk about them. One boy, whose father was a social worker, said that his father "tried to help those people," the poor, angry Negro people who were rioting.

The explanation that the teacher gave was the following. There were places in Cleveland where many Negroes lived who were poor. They could not get jobs and did not have any money. They did not have enough food to eat, enough clothes to wear, or enough rooms to live in. For a long time many white people in our country had not liked Negroes and had not allowed them to get good jobs so that they could earn money and buy food and clothing. Nor had they allowed them to live in comfortable houses, in neighborhoods where the white people were allowed to live. This was not fair treatment of Negro people and now many people in the country, white and Negro, were trying to make things better, fair, for Negro people. The teacher went on to explain that the Negro people who lived in such poor conditions were very angry, as anybody would feel who had to live that way. Some of these poor people got so angry that they got out of control. They started to fight, to set fires, and even to kill people. The teacher stressed that the rioters were a very small minority, and most of the Negro people, as well as the white people, did not approve of the rioters being unable to manage their angry feelings. Most of the Negroes, even though they were very angry, wanted to stay in control and did not want riots, fights, and killings. The rioting did not mean that Negroes were bad people. White people, too, got out of control. The teacher also explained, as Lucy's mother had done, that the soldiers were in town to help the police to stop the rioting. They were here to help people to get back in control of their angry feelings so that they would stop doing bad things. She also reassured the children that the presence of the soldiers in town did not mean there was a war in Cleveland. She did not try to cover up the real anxiety of all the adults and acknowledged freely to the children that the adults shared their own anxious feelings. But the emphasis was on the effort that most grownups were making to restore order and to work in a peaceful and helpful way toward better living conditions and more friendly feelings between whites and Negroes. Most people in Cleveland were staying home at night, not going through the riot areas, trying to live quietly as the mayor had asked them to do, in order to help everyone in the city to get back in control.

The many fires in the city seemed of the greatest concern to the children. They could hardly contain their anxiety and excitement at the mere mention of them. Many reported how often they had heard the fire sirens throughout the days and nights of rioting. Ben said, probably quoting his parents, that the people who burned down houses were just hurting themselves. Some children talked about the police putting the bad people in jail. Many worried about whether their own houses could get burned down. Their anxiety about the impermanence of their homes was not new. All year long they had watched old apartment buildings being torn down on the street where the school was located, and the demolishing equipment had stirred many primitive aggressive anxiety-laden fantasies. (The open jaws of the wrecker were seen as the huge angry mouth of a monster which might gobble up the child's school next, or go to his street and gobble up his home.)

During the group discussion the teacher paid special attention to the problems Paula was having. She explained Paula's teasiness as caused by the fact that this talk was especially hard for Paula to hear. Thus she tried to elicit the other children's understanding of and support for Paula, and to limit their undermining of Paula's control through inciting her provocative teasing about the murders. She said that all Negro people in Cleveland were especially frightened right now. She explained that Paula had just moved away from the area where all the trouble was, and that hers was the first Negro family to move to a street where only white people had been living. Paula's family felt very worried about whether their new white neighbors would be friendly with them because of all the trouble now going on between white and Negro people in Cleveland. After the circle time Paula was very angry with everyone. She demanded that she be given toys, bikes, and anything at all that any of the other children were using. For the most part she rejected the teacher's efforts to understand and comfort her. Paula's family were extremely angry themselves, and no doubt struggling hard to maintain their own control in such tense times.

In the two days before school closed much had been accomplished. Facts had been explained and sorted out, from each other (the Chicago murders and the Cleveland race riots) as well as from primitive out-of-control fantasies. A tendency toward denial had been considerably diminished, and communication between children and mothers had been opened up, hopefully to be continued in later working-through processes during the summer vacation. The worst anxiety of the children, exemplified in their concern about the fires, was the out-of-control state of the adult world. How could they, as children, maintain control if the grownups, who were supposed to stand for control, could not control themselves? Had nothing been said to the children about the riots they might well have assumed that parents and teachers were themselves too frightened to talk about the crisis and consequently were trying to deny it. Probably they would in turn have identified with the adults' denial and made it their own defense. The discussion with the children established for them the difference between the rioters and their parents and teachers, who, though realistically frightened themselves, nevertheless were in control, *telling* their feelings, and working to help others maintain control.

For parents and teachers of very young children it is an extremely difficult task to explain real events of such horrible magnitude as these riots and murders. Once upon a time, when parents used to tell their children fairy tales filled with similar horrible happenings, parents and children together established for themselves that these stories were only fantasy and not fact. They joined forces in mastering their primitive instinctual anxieties stirred up in their relationship with each other, and discharged in the fantasies contained in the fairy tales. But when murders and riots are real, a distinction between fact and fantasy is much more difficult to achieve. The parent, even so, has to try to distinguish between the real events and the child's fantasies. Then the parent has to assure the child of every feature in the real world that is working to protect his safety and to restore control and order. He has to make himself an example of control and order in a world that contains murders and riots, and he has to assure the child of his parental ability to protect his child, both from the real dangers all about him and from the child's loss of ego control in the face of either his own fantasies or the frightening realities.

Many children were most relieved at the example of adult control—with verbalization of conflicts and feelings—set by teachers and parents. They had strong needs to distinguish their own childish angers from those of adult murderers, rioters, and assassins (see next section). They wanted to know that they would grow up to be adults in control. One boy, recalling President Kennedy's assassination, reassured himself with, "Oswald didn't have a school like Hanna Perkins to go to when he was little."

The Death of Martin Luther King

In April, 1968, on the first night of the school's spring vacation, Martin Luther King was shot and killed in Memphis, Tennessee. Ten days later, when school reopened, we returned, dreading the task of facing and working through this new disaster, but knowing that we would have to do it.[4] Denial was no longer one of our major problems.

Upon their return very few parents or children made any comment about the assassination. When teachers or therapists mentioned it to mothers, they learned that most of the parents had been profoundly affected by the event, but were largely denying the extent of its effects upon their children. In many instances the children had been the first to inform their parents of the news because the early bulletins of the shooting had interrupted their television programs. Almost all parents had given honest simple factual explanations of the event and had been generally reassuring to their children of the safety of their own families. Most realized that to their young children the most frightening aspect of the shooting was that a daddy could be killed. But what most did not realize was the extent of fantasy and anxiety stirred up in the children, not only in response to the killing but in reaction to its effects upon their parents. Some parents, both white and Negro, had withdrawn emotionally from

---

[4]The problem of explaining death and coping with reactions to it in young children cannot be fully discussed here. This subject was investigated by the Hanna Perkins staff in a series of four papers by R. A. Furman (1964a, 1964b), Barnes (1964), and McDonald (1964). For a publication addressed to nursery school teachers, see McDonald (1963).

An excellent account of a nursery school teacher's efforts to help her children comprehend this assassination and its consequences was reported by Louise Ellison (1968).

their children and in their grief had become totally absorbed in the extensive television coverage of memorial services and funeral events.

In the schoolrooms nothing at first was said about the tragedy. The teachers waited, trying to sense the proper moment to bring it up. Not only did the children fail to provide any immediate and obvious opportunities, but they failed to have much of anything at all to report about their vacations in general. What the teachers noticed, then, was an avoidance on the children's part of almost their entire vacation. They seemed subdued, perhaps even stunned, and had little to say. Questions from the teachers about what they had done on their vacations brought meager replies. The teachers' questions only dried up the general conversation—a most unusual response, when contrasted with the ordinary postvacation competitions to tell about trips, visits, etc. This, then, was the opening for which the teachers were searching. The teacher said to the children that she wondered if they weren't talking much about their vacations because something terrible and frightening had happened in our country during the vacation and they did not want to be reminded of it. Some children said that Dr. King had been shot, but beyond these confirming remarks they at first had little to say.

The teacher reviewed what had happened. She identified Dr. King as a man who was trying to make life better for everyone in this country by helping Negroes get better jobs and better homes, and by helping white and Negro people have more friendly and less angry feelings toward each other. She drew upon previous discussions with the children of race problems. She explained that some adults had not finished growing up in their feelings and were out of control in their anger with Dr. King. Some white people did not want to share with Negroes and did not want Dr. King to help Negroes. The man who shot him must have been very angry at him, and he did not know how to manage his angry feelings. Some children specified that he was a white man. Most children were frightened by the fact that the man had escaped and could kill more people. To this the teacher had to agree, but she tried to reassure the children that the police were working very hard to find him and to prevent further shootings. It was very difficult for the children to realize that the teacher could only guess about why the man had done the shooting, since nobody knew who he was and nobody had had any chance to talk with him. The children were also very concerned about what would happen to him when the police caught him. The teacher explained that he would be fairly treated and given a chance to tell why he had done it, but that he probably would have to stay in jail a very long time.

Along with their concern for the assassin was a strong sympathy for the King family. The children spoke of how sad his wife and four children must be, of how angry they must be at the assassin. They were sad for the children, and many could openly say that if their daddy died, or if Dr. King were their daddy, they would be very sad. The teacher joined the sadness, but also reassured the children that after a while the sadness of the King family would stop hurting so much. As for Dr. King himself, there were several questions about what death is, and a review of the facts about death. But the anxiety that such an important man could be vulnerable, or that they themselves would become vulnerable upon entering the adult world as it is now, was not so easily voiced. (Today a boy's anxiety about having to grow up, become a soldier, go to Viet Nam, and get killed has spread downward in age, even into the nursery years. When, in addition, men in their own country are assassinated, the developmental task of becoming a man can look quite impossible to a little boy.) Some children thought Dr. Martin Luther King was a king and wanted to protest that a king cannot die. Interestingly, although all of the children spoke of him as Dr. King, nobody confused him with a medical doctor.

There was a great concern among the children about the extensive rioting throughout the country following Dr. King's assassination. Some of the older children remembered the Cleveland riots and the soldiers who were in town at that time. The anxieties about these national riots were dealt with by the teachers much as they had been two years ago during the Cleveland riots. However, this time the teachers were fortunate in being able to point to a reassuring local example of control and order. Many of our children had met the city's new Negro mayor, Carl Stokes, and they knew of his children. They had been very interested in the election, six months earlier, which had brought Mr. Stokes into the mayor's office. After the assassination almost all of the children had seen the mayor in a televised church memorial service for Dr. King. The camera caught him during the singing, tears rolling down his cheeks. At first the children were uncomprehending and frightened, but in time they could accept and identify with the mayor's adult example of grief for his personal friend. The teachers could also point to Mr. Stokes's efforts to prevent rioting in Cleveland. They explained to the children how he was out in the city every night encouraging people in the potential riot areas to stay calm and in control. His work was effective and Cleveland was one of the few large cities where no riots occurred. Once again, in a time of national disorder, small children needed concrete evidence of adult forces at work to restore control.

In the nursery school the reactions were generally taken up on an individual basis. As usual, in kindergarten the work with individual children supplemented group discussions which the older children were more capable of sustaining. Individual reactions, observed in the nursery school and in the kindergarten group, follow.

Nursery School. Bill was a four-year-old white boy who had had an inhibition in the verbal expression of his aggression. He defended himself against angry feelings with a reversal of affect and a babbling confusion in his speech. Now he was just beginning to verbalize directly and distinctly his angry feelings. Bill talked a lot about Martin Luther King. He referred to him as the man who shot himself, and the teachers corrected this fantasy. It was not clear whether Bill thought King had shot himself, or whether he was trying to tell a thought expressed by some of the kindergartners—that if they had been the killer, they would have been so angry at themselves they would have killed themselves. Bill seemed to be practicing his new-found ability to verbalize, as well as to be trying to sort out all his confusion about the assassination. He must have been garbling many of the quotations he heard on television. "War is wrong." "Put down your gun and march!" "They buried him. I know what that is. They put him in the ground." But then he talked of having seen Dr. King on television after he had seen the body put in the ground. In seeing the taped replays on television Bill thought he was seeing Dr. King alive, that he had come back to life, or else that he had not really died. He went on, "Martin Luther King was stupid. He should have stayed at home." And later, "I just don't like brown people!" The teacher tried to help him understand that what he did not like was to experience the anxiety which the death had caused. On another occasion Bill said angrily to four-year-old Negro Bruce, "I know where you got that baseball jacket [which Bill admired]. Martin Luther King gave it to you." When the teacher told Bill's mother how strongly he was reacting at school to King's death, his mother was amazed. She reported that he had seemed oblivious to it at home, in contrast to his seven-year-old brother who talked constantly about it.

Alex, a four-year-old adopted boy of mixed Negro-white parentage, responded to the general talk about King's death with the comment, "Ralph's father died, a long time ago." (See below for a report of Ralph.) During the preceding vacation Alex had been very anxious when any member of the family was out of his sight. After the shooting he just wanted to sit on his father's lap. His mother found it hard to reassure Alex because her husband was active in the civil rights movement and she sometimes feared for his safety.

Charlotte was a four-year-old white girl whose father had just moved away from her home prior to the parents' obtaining a divorce. Charlotte missed her father and was also very angry at him for leaving. In the midst of the talk about Dr. King Charlotte announced, "I'm glad Margaret isn't here! She kicked me under the table and I didn't like her!" Margaret was a Negro

girl who had started school with Charlotte, and whose mother
had withdrawn her after several weeks. The teacher assured
Charlotte that Margaret had not been sent away because of
Charlotte's anger at her. Nor had she been sent away because of
her color. Just how Charlotte was telling of her father's departure, Dr. King's death, her concern about brown-skinned people,
and her own angry feelings was not too clear. (See also a report, below, of Dorothy, her sister.)

Ralph, a four-year-old white boy whose father had died
when he was an infant, was very wild upon his return to school
after the vacation. The teacher asked his mother whether she
thought Dr. King's death could account for his disturbance. It
was her impression that Ralph, unlike her older two children,
had not paid much attention to this event. But at the teacher's
suggestion, and with the aid of the child therapist, Ralph's mother talked about it with him. At school Ralph then talked a great
deal about the assassination. He said he didn't believe Martin
Luther King was dead and he wanted to see his grave. Ralph had
been saying exactly the same thing about his own father, and his
mother was in the process of finding her courage to take him to
see his father's grave. She did so, soon after this incident. When
Ralph got wild at school, he shouted: "Don't kill me . . . don't
kill me . . . I'm gonna' die!" (We thought he was entering a
developmental stage of oedipal guilt for his father's death.) With
Alex, a Negro boy, he was very teasy and threatening. "I'm gonna' color you brown!" he said, starting after Alex with a brown
crayon. Alex panicked and pleaded, "No, don't do that!" It
seemed that Alex sensed Ralph's implication. Brown people got
shot and killed. (See also the case of Bruce below, for a further
report about Ralph.)

Ruth, a four-year-old white girl, asked how she could marry
Bruce, a four-year-old Negro boy, because his skin was brown.
Ruth might have been trying to join the talk then going on about
Martin Luther King. But the teacher, filled with the urgency of
our times, and perhaps sensing the significance of her answer for
Alice, nearby, whose parents were Negro and white, replied to

Ruth that when she grew up she would fall in love and marry and the color of her husband's skin would not matter to her. We knew that Ruth's mother would not have taken kindly to this explanation, but we never heard any follow-up about it. Perhaps Ruth wisely chose not to confront her mother with the teacher's remarks and maintained a judicious silence at home about her plans for marriage.

Upon his return from vacation Bruce, a quiet four-year-old Negro boy, had been quite unmanageable during naptime and had had to be removed the first two days. On the third day at naptime the teacher played a record which had on it, "My Country 'Tis of Thee." When Bruce heard this song (which had been sung at King's funeral) he bolted off his cot and shouted out, "A father got killed!" A general pandemonium broke out in the nursery school. Ralph, whose father was dead, got completely out of control, required most of the teacher's attention, and had to be removed. Meanwhile, Bruce was at last able to find his own control, once he had verbally discharged his anxiety. The teachers later tried to point out to both Bruce and his mother how helpful it had been that he could at last *tell* about it when something was bothering him. Interestingly, Bruce's mother narrowly focused on his nap disturbance as having been caused by another child's hitting him and making his nose bleed. Bruce had indeed had a slight nosebleed at naptime, but it was spontaneous. Nobody had hit him. Bruce's older brother, Gerald (see below) had reported that their mother was sad and her nose bled when Dr. King died. The mother did confirm her own nosebleed, which she did not connect, other than in time, with the assassination.

When Alice, a very popular four-year-old Negro girl, returned late from her spring vacation, many children were especially overjoyed to see her. Although they had been told that she was away with her parents and would return a few days late, some seemed to doubt that she would ever return. While no child verbalized it, we thought that they feared for her fate as a Negro. (We also suspected that the children thought Alice would disappear at vacation time, just as Margaret, a Negro, had done at the time of an earlier vacation.)

Kindergarten. In the kindergarten Emily, a six-year-old white girl, appended the teacher's description of Dr. King as a man who helped Negroes. She said her mother had told her that he helped white people too. The teacher agreed. Dean, a white boy, named all the Negroes he knew—all of the children and the kitchen staff—and said they were very sad. Clearly, Dean himself felt sad, too. Harold, a white boy, asked if Mrs. King was a Negro. Emily thought the assassin might kill himself. Andrew, a Negro boy, volunteered that he *would* kill himself if he had been the assassin.

Many children were much affected by having seen on television the mayor of Cleveland crying in church. Gerald, a five-year-old Negro boy, drew a very good picture of a church. His mother doubted the teacher's hunch that it could have anything to do with all the church scenes on television. However, she herself had been glued to her television set, probably too distraught to notice how much her two little children were absorbing of the entire event from the television screen. Gerald said his mother had cried and had gotten a bloody nose when Dr. King died. Then he got out of control and lost in fantasy about the assassin —"a bloody monster." He got the other children to roar with laughter at him. On the day of King's funeral he had drawn his mother into a battle with him. Gerald's mother had wanted her children to watch the funeral. She felt it gave them a point of reference for what a funeral was all about—a point that would help them in the future when their grandparents or their parents died. She was always very anxious about matters of health in her family.

Henry, a five-year-old white boy, obviously quoting his parents, said they were the only family on their street to put out a flag. His mother joked grimly with the teacher that she supposed they would find a cross burning in their yard some night. Gerald overheard this talk about a flag, and later asked the teacher, "*Who* put out a flag?" It was hard for Gerald to believe that a white person had put out a flag and felt as sad as did the Negro people. Gerald had often shown hints of his dissatisfaction with his own color and his wish to be white. He seemed genuinely grateful that a white person would like a Negro enough to be sad at his loss and to put out a flag for him. Gerald needed this concrete evidence, in addition to verbal expressions of friendly feelings from white people.

Dorothy was a six-year-old white girl, whose father had just left home because the parents were getting a divorce. (She was Charlotte's older sister.) Dorothy talked of how sad all the people were that Martin Luther King had died and how everybody was praying that he would come back to life. Here Dorothy seemed to be confusing the wish for the return of her father, the assassination, and the religious Easter story of the resurrection of Jesus. Like her younger sister, Charlotte, Dorothy focused her aggression upon a Negro girl. She complained to the teacher that she didn't like Jean, a Negro girl in the class. At home she asked her mother whether she had to like *all* Negro people, and now she quoted her mother's negative answer as authoritative permission to dislike Jean. We wondered what mechanisms were at work in these two sisters, who turned their aggression onto Negro girls just then. Did Negro stand for bad fathers, who deserted their children as Dr. King and their father had done? Did having brown skin mean being angry and rejecting? Did they themselves reject the bad, brown-skinned, angry Negro girls as their father had rejected them, and did they unconsciously identify with these bad brown girls, in their search for an explanation about why their father no longer wanted to be with them? We did not know the answers.

After the first group discussion in kindergarten Roger and Stuart, both white, excitedly charged into a nursery school teacher at outside play time, asking her to guess what they had talked about in circle time. Stuart gave a confusing account of someone who worked for his father (a civil rights worker) who had gotten shot at and wounded. Such a shooting had in fact taken place some months earlier. King's murder rekindled Stuart's old anxieties that his father, too, might get shot and killed. Roger confessed that once he had thrown a match on the floor at home and started a fire.

In a discussion group later in the week, in kindergarten, the subject of Dr. King's death came up again. Milton, a white boy, said he didn't feel sad because he didn't know him. Andrew felt *mad,* but changed it to sad when other children disapproved of his anger. (Andrew's mother had herself felt very angered by the killing, and she told how Andrew went about their home angrily hitting magazine pictures of Dr. King and the events surrounding the assassination. Andrew was no doubt expressing his anger at an incident which had so upset him and his family. But he may also have been identifying with the killer of the Negro father, in the midst of his own oedipal conflicts. Recall his earlier threat to kill himself if he had been the assassin.)

Dean said that he was going to visit Nicki. "I called her up and she is all right!" This was the first reference in some weeks to Nicki, a teacher who had moved away to California in the middle of the school year. She had been much loved by the children and they missed her greatly. Now Dean was revealing his fear that Nicki, in a place farther away than Memphis, might also be dead. Several children joined in a discussion about Nicki. The assassin had given a dangerous reality to their angry murderous fantasies of wishing Nicki dead because she had left them.

Some parents and children persisted in avoiding and denying the assassination. When one white child's mother heard that the teacher was going to discuss the assassination with the children, she reluctantly gave her permission, and then added, "But you aren't going to talk about color, are you?"

FROM THE COLOR OF THEIR SKIN TO THE CONTENT OF THEIR CHARACTER

There emerges from the observations reported so far a strong impression that the ability to recognize and accept racial difference is not inborn, but rather one which has to develop within the child. Further, it appears that this "racial" development is

frequently a close traveling companion for any active developmental current in progress within the child's personality. Conflicts about race and a succession of other developmental conflicts
for a while intermingle, only to part company as their resolutions
lead to a separation in their pathways. A discussion of this developmental progression will be postponed to Part II.

The brief case histories presented here are offered as clinical
demonstrations of how individual children confronted racial
conflicts within the context of their progressing personality development. Each case presentation comes from the cumulative
experience of teachers and therapist with a child and his parents
throughout (and sometimes beyond) his stay at the Hanna Perkins School.

In his famous "Dream" speech Martin Luther King, with
eloquence and economy of expression, charted the normal developmental route toward mature racial adjustment. (See the quotation at the beginning of the book.) People must progress from
judgment of each other by the color of their skin to judgment by
the content of their character.

Three Case Histories

Joe A. was the child of white parents who had wished to live
in an integrated neighborhood and had moved to one before Joe
was born. Mrs. A. was helpful to her children by making friendly relationships with people of different racial backgrounds. She
was also helpful by responding to her children's comments on
skin color differences in an appropriate way according to the
child's age.

The following series of examples shows how Joe, with his
mother's help, was able to progress in his understanding and
mastery of skin color differences according to his stage of drive
and ego development.

When Joe was two and a half years old he accompanied his
mother as she drove her older son, Clark, and his Negro classmate, Andrew, to school. Until then Joe had seen Andrew only at
a distance. Now, as he sat next to him in the car, Joe leaned over

and touched Andrew's face, saying, "Dirty face." In recalling
the incident Mrs. A. said Joe's remark had taken her by surprise.
She had not expected Joe to notice racial differences so early. She
said she had had to curb her impulse to speak sharply to Joe out
of her worry that he had hurt Andrew's feelings. Instead she told
Joe quite simply that Andrew's face was brown, not dirty, and
that some children were born with brown skin (see Example 1).

At three and a half years Joe entered our nursery school. It
took him several months to progress to playing comfortably with
other children because his fear of being overwhelmed made him
too controlling of others' activities. (The fear of being overwhelmed and his defensive need to be in charge derived largely
from the abdominal surgery he had experienced at age twenty
months.) In these early months of school Joe busied himself with
his own activities, but all the while he watched with interest and
admiration the group play of the bigger boys. As he neared his
fourth birthday Joe at last became able to enjoy some give and
take in play with other children. At about this time the teacher
asked a small group, including both Joe and Andrew, to paint
pictures of themselves as gardners holding tools, for a garden
mural. Joe, like the other children, greatly enjoyed this project.
He painted his portrait of himself with brown skin, just as Andrew, his Negro friend who was one of the older boys he so much
admired, had painted his skin brown.

Several incidents shortly before Joe's fifth birthday illustrate
his growth in relationships as well as his progress in mastering
feelings about skin color. Increasingly, he valued Negro children
as individuals in their own right. Joe's mother had been working
with him to help him master his marked anxiety about sexual
differences. (His abdominal surgery had the aftereffect, in the
phallic phase, of intensifying Joe's castration anxiety.) At home
Joe told his mother that Bruce's zipper was unzipped and he had
seen Bruce's penis. Bruce was a younger Negro classmate. Joe's
mother, in tune with her child's current phallic conflicts, had the
feeling that Joe was asking her whether Negro boys have a penis
the same as his own. Although Joe did not specifically verbalize

this question, she volunteered that he might be wondering about it and assured him that all boys, Negro and white, have a penis. In the same week, following Mrs. A's clarification that Negro boys and white boys differ only in skin color and not in sexuality, the teachers observed two instances of Joe's regard for Negro children. Joe was overheard talking with Bill, a white boy. Joe was telling Bill with obvious warmth about the brown-colored friends he played with at home. Then Joe turned to Alex, a light-complected Negro boy, and inquired whether he, too, had any brown friends at home. A few days later Joe, still in the nursery school, became alarmed when he saw the bigger kindergarten boys yelling at Andrew, now a kindergartner, in the outside play area, which the two classes sometimes shared. Joe called forcefully to the older boys, "Don't yell at that brown boy! He's my friend!"

In the anal phase of his development Joe could have settled upon his initial conclusion that brown skin is dirty skin. In the phallic phase he might have concluded that not only girls were different from himself but that Negro boys, too, were different. In this phase he might have developed a disparaging attitude toward Negro boys as not measuring up to white boys—in effect, as being castrated. Mrs. A.'s simple, honest, direct explanations, reassuringly given, prevented any such confusion between skin color and drive conflicts. Joe did not have to reject and avoid Negro children as either dirty or castrated. He was free to develop individual relationships with them, based on their human personality traits rather than upon their skin color.

Jean B., a medium-brown Negro girl, was unable to work through any of her conflicts about her color. When she left the school at the end of kindergarten, she seemed well on the way to a fixed denial of her thoughts and feelings about people's color differences. She needed this defense, for reasons which will become apparent.

Jean came from a good home. Her parents, both Negro, loved her and took good care of her. Mr. B. was a successful small businessman, and Mrs. B. helped in the family business. Jean, a very intelligent child, was precocious along many lines of ego development. She played well with other children, but she was also a much infantilized child. Her aunt, who helped in her care, still bathed and handled her as though she were an infant. She fed the child whatever Jean wanted whenever she wanted it. She also slept in the same bed with Jean until, with the help of the therapist, arrangements were made for Jean to have her own bed. Jean was weaned from the bottle by the age of one and a half, and her toilet training was accomplished easily at an early age. The family never observed any sexual curiosity or other signs of Jean's sexual development.

Jean was never permitted to express any unpleasant emotion, such as sadness, anger, or anxiety. For example, when she reacted with a defensive excitement (teasy, provocative, silly behavior) to the news that a favorite teacher would be leaving the school, her mother punished her by spanking her. For reasons of her own, Mrs. B. was unable to tolerate and empathize with the child's underlying sadness and anger at the teacher's departure. Jean's family also did not tolerate any expression of sexuality. When the teacher discovered Jean trying to peek at the boys in the bathroom Jean went to a corner and hung her head in shame. She told the teacher that her aunt would say she was a bad girl. (Jean's fear of her aunt's disapproval belies the home report that she had never displayed any sexual curiosity.) Another example illustrates the threat Mrs. B. felt at the school's attempt to accept and understand the children's feelings. When the teacher reported to the mother that Jean had expressed sadness and guilt at school because her hamster had died, Mrs. B. became angry with both Jean and the teacher. She said this incident was none of the school's business and Jean should not have told it.

In order to adjust to what was expected of her at home Jean needed to develop a denial that would protect her from expressing any disturbing thoughts and feelings. Sometimes this denial took the deceptive form of a self-sufficient ability to look after herself. At three years, when she entered another nursery school where mothers were expected to stay with the children for the first three days, Jean, turning passive into active, sent her mother home on the second day, saying she did not need her any more. When Jean's denial failed her she lost all control of her feelings and became a demanding, dawdling child, with temper tantrums and a low frustration tolerance. It was only in these infantile ways that her feelings found an outlet. Jean's personality thus contained many pregenital fixations. The main manifestation of her sexual excitement settled upon bathroom play with a white girl, who was much like Jean in that she too had a strong unresolved penis envy. In Jean's case her envy was enhanced by the alternation of stimulating play and disdainful rejection on the part of two older brothers.

Mr. B. introduced the problem of color with the therapist by reporting Jean's question about a very light-skinned relative who lived in their home. Jean had asked her parents, "Is she white?" Mrs. B. had answered this question with a long and detailed factual explanation about skin pigments. At the end of the speech Jean, evidently more confused than ever, repeated her question, "Is she white?" The mother evaded the issue and it was dropped. With the therapist Mrs. B. expressed her philosophy that Jean must learn that people are what they are, regardless of color. She was eager to protect Jean from the aggression of the outside world toward Negroes. In spite of her child's direct question about the white-skinned relative, Mrs. B. expressed her doubt that children really notice or are curious about color differences. She implied that if the school did not encourage them, the children would not notice color difference, and would not be disturbed by it.

The family history which the parents then revealed to the therapist made Mrs. B.'s need for her own defenses more understandable. There had been a number of Negro-white marriages in her family. The white relative about whom Jean inquired was a product of one of these marriages. She was conspicuously white in an otherwise Negro family. She also played a major role in the upbringing of Jean's mother. Mrs. B. recalled her own experiences as a child, living in a Negro neighborhood, of being teased and abused because of this white-skinned relative in her home. It was the confusion of not being accepted by either the white or the Negro race because of this one white member of the family that led to much of Mrs. B.'s bitterness and denial about racial differences. Now, as a mother, she could not respond to her child's curiosity about skin color differences in their own home. Efforts of the skilled and experienced therapist to work through the mother's denial proved futile. The therapist recognized that Mrs. B.'s need for this defense had to be respected and not unduly threatened. Not only the therapist, but also the husband intuitively bowed to this need. Unfortunately, this left Jean stranded with her own color conflicts. They could not be approached, at the risk of threatening her basic security in her home.

While observations of Jean's color conflicts could be made only infrequently at school, there were nevertheless unmistakable signs of them. She neatly colored with white chalk the small, well-formed face of her self-portrait, but she scribbled with brown crayon the huge, grotesquely asymmetrical body of the portrait. At a time when Jean might be expected to show some strong feelings about skin color she sometimes hid her face awkwardly between her legs, pulling up her white sox as though to hide behind them. (The teacher observed one other Negro girl who developed this same habit.) When Negro twins visited the school Jean was unusually teasy and provocative in the classroom. When Martin Luther King was killed Jean displayed no reaction and she appeared to ignore the class discussion about the death. Nor could the teachers help her to enter into it. To the staff Jean was conspicuous in being the only Negro child to maintain such a detachment from Martin Luther King.

It will be noted that Jean had to deny both sexual and color curiosity. What is unknown is the extent to which these two sets of conflicts became confusingly intermingled for Jean as a result of her denial.

Judd C., a moderately dark-skinned Negro boy, was referred

to our school because of his immature behavior in another nursery school. He was hyperactive and always needed to be the center of attention. At the time of referral Judd's parents were unaware of the fact that their son had any conflicts about his skin color. Since Judd was one of the first Negro children to attend Hanna Perkins School the staff, lacking experience, at first joined in this denial. But in the school setting Judd soon made it transparent to all that his strong feelings about his brown color led to the major conflicts in his life. The school program and the coordinated work of the therapist with the parents enabled Judd to achieve a considerable mastery of his color conflicts.

Judd was a tall, well-coordinated, intelligent boy. He was an only child, who lived with his parents in an apartment building. Mr. C. worked at two jobs. Both parents had high standards for Judd and put great stress on proper behavior and intellectual accomplishment. Judd's early development was generally precocious, partly through his innate abilities and partly through his mother's influence (e.g., bowel training, begun at four months, was completed at twelve months). When Judd expressed curiosity about his mother's body she chose to answer his questions by showing herself undressed to him on one occasion and giving him proper names for sexual organs. He never displayed any curiosity thereafter. Nor did he masturbate after his mother once observed him doing so and told him that he might hurt himself and he would not get another penis. Later it was learned that during his training to urinate in the toilet the toilet seat had fallen on him and bruised his penis. Although the parents did not feel it to be very effective, spanking was sometimes used as a disciplinary device. Judd displayed some accident-proneness, particularly when he did not meet his own high standards for himself. During his preliminary visit to Hanna Perkins he fell and cut his knee. He tried to deny the accident, rejected any help from his mother, but did allow the teacher to wash his knee and put a Band-Aid on it.

At school he tolerated frustration poorly. He reacted with whining, shouting, crying, or aggressive behavior. He was often silly and inappropriate. He was very anxious about making friends and he would rush from one child to another, begging each to be his friend. Sadly, his overbearing tactics resulted in more rejections than friendships. Judd especially begged the only other Negro child in his class to be his friend, and he was very hurt by this boy's rejection of him. (The other boy often insisted that he himself was not a Negro, and he rejected Judd because he was.) At home Judd announced his color problems to his mother by telling her that the other children at school teased him about being brown and dirty. (One of the boys he most wanted for a friend was a child who often joined in a mutually stimulating excitement with Judd. At other times this same white boy rejected Judd and called him dirty. The white boy was a soiler.)

Judd's parents at first refused to believe that his report of the teasing at school could be an indication of his own conflicts about his brown color. But with the help of the therapist the parents were able to accept the evidence and then they began helping Judd with his feelings about his color. First, however, Mrs. C. had to work through her own conflicts about her relationship with the white male therapist. She began by testing the therapist's stand on the gross injustices in Cleveland about restricted housing for Negroes. It took many sessions before she could accept that the therapist was "unprejudiced after five o'clock," especially on this matter of housing and integrated neighborhoods. Mrs. C. also had to work through the loyalty conflict she herself felt; to want what a white person had (housing and jobs) would be to harbor a disloyalty to her own race. It was the therapist's conviction that this essential part of the work was the turning point of the entire case. Only when it was reached did meaningful work on Judd's problems, and particularly on his color conflicts, become possible with Mrs. C. When Mrs. C. was finally satisfied that the therapist's views were sincere and unprejudiced, she then revealed that she had been taught as a child never to argue with a white man and just to do whatever he says. Following this revelation Mrs. C. was much more able to be an active coworker than an outwardly compliant, inwardly rebellious adversary of the therapist. Even so, the color difference between herself and the therapist remained an active theme needing re-current working through during their contacts.

The parents' efforts with Judd at first took the form of persuading him to be proud of his African heritage and brown skin. (This work took place several years before the appearance of "black pride" as a cultural development among American Negroes.) As the therapist observed, Judd's mother tried to "brainwash" her child out of his obvious, though not yet verbalized, wish to be white. The parents were pleased when their efforts did enable Judd to defend himself better at school against taunts about his color with a calm explanation that he was brown because of his African descent.

The following lengthy quotation from the teacher's record describes some of the teacher's work with Judd:

> The teacher began to help Judd see his behavior in relation to his feelings about being colored. As he increasingly got children angry with him and then felt hurt and mistreated, we told him that the only reason we could see for his wanting people to feel sorry for him was his being Negro. We wondered why he would feel sorry about that. The other children began to be more open in referring to his color and Judd showed more appropriate feeling to these incidents, though not necessarily at the time they occurred. He was very sad at times, sobbing out, "Play with me! Play with me!" He began to show some direct aggression and, in the context of a game, bit the boy who teased him most. He became furious with the other Negro boy when this boy maintained his denial of being a Negro. Judd indignantly reported this denial to his mother, but then came up with a surprising reverse denial. Nobody is really white, Judd told his mother. There are just little differences in shade.
>
> As the subject of his color came into the open and he began expressing his feelings more directly, there were areas of improvement in Judd's general behavior. He did better creative work with more enjoyment. He had more calm, constructive periods during the day and seemed more in touch with his feelings as they related to his behavior. We began trying to help him see when rejections were the result of his own behavior or other circumstances and had nothing to do with his being brown, and to help him express feelings appropriately when he was being teased about his color. This effort continued throughout the entire kindergarten term, and it was only near the end of the year that Judd could sometimes make this distinction for himself.
>
> The negative reactions of the other children greatly intensified after

Judd hurt his finger very badly in a frightening accident at school. They seemed to see him as both damaged and dark. One child tried to bite the injured finger. There were many more directly negative remarks. Judd was told he was dirty, his teeth were brown, and that he smelled. The boy who soiled led this attack and told Judd that he didn't like anything brown. Judd, who had been talking more with his parents, replied in a positive, dignified way, "I think my color is nice."

On other occasions, Judd expressed what he expected from others since he was Negro. "Nobody likes me," he said. "They don't like my face because it's brown and I come from Africa." He changed the words of a familiar song to, 'Honey, you can't love Judd." He rejected other children, e.g., "I hate X, he can't be my friend because his skin is too light." These incidents led to a discussion of differences of skin color on a reality level with the whole group. This was done mainly through our discussions of people of other lands, where physical differences came up as a natural part of the subject and could be related to their direct experiences. To Judd, we interpreted that he must be angry at all of us for being white.

The fact of his being Negro affected Judd's relationship with the teachers as much as his relationship with his peers. In his first weeks at school, Judd seemed to accept teachers easily. As already mentioned, he did not seem to miss his mother and he came readily to the teachers for help, approval, and attention. While he appeared to listen to us and accept what we said, he had a blank look and we never felt as though we were really reaching him. In addition, Judd behaved toward us in a blatantly seductive manner—rolling his eyes, wiggling his hips, and winking deliberately. The total effect was of a bizarre attempt to ingratiate himself. In what seemed a continuation of the struggle with his mother, he tested all rules; but when he was restrained and restricted, his extreme sense of outrage at being hurt and victimized clearly were part of the color issue. As he got closer to these feelings, he began to verbalize his anger at us and to provoke physical fights. The issues were created out of ordinary school routines. We began pointing out how he tried to be the exception and misuse being brown, stressing that rules were for everyone. Again this was a very slow process and it was only near the very end of the year that Judd could at times accept the consequences of his behavior and not attribute everything to rejection. When he injured his finger, Judd gained a new focus for his expression of anger because he blamed a teacher for the injury.

The injury to his finger, referred to in the teacher's record, brought several major conflicts into the open. It was a self-inflicted injury that occurred at a time when Judd had many troubles. A close relative had died. His apartment building had been robbed twice. The other Negro boy in his class was scheduled to leave the school to enter first grade (the day after Judd's injury) and Judd was convinced that the child was being expelled for bad behavior. He feared the same fate for himself. At home his mother was insisting upon closed bedroom doors, as a result of her work with the therapist, and Judd had expressed strong disapproval of this new policy. Just prior to his injury Judd had hit another child and had been talking back and trying to fight with the teachers. Then, in a game of hide and seek, Judd cheated and peeked out from behind a door. When the teacher told him to stop peeking, Judd angrily slammed the door and accidentally caught his finger in it, cutting it almost to the bone.

At the emergency room, where his mother joined him while his finger was sutured, Judd could not look at the injury and feared that his finger had been severed. It was hard for him to believe that he could have inflicted such a serious injury upon himself, and in his guilt he told his mother that one of the teachers had done it. A week later, when the stitches were removed, Mrs. C. was shocked at how bad the cut looked. She latched onto a chance remark of the doctor's that it was hard to understand how a child could have done this to himself, and she, too, began to believe Judd's story that one of the teachers had slammed the door on him.

For several weeks following the accident life became nearly impossible for Judd and for the school. Mrs. C. distrusted the school, implying to the therapist that the teachers were covering up for the guilty teacher. Judd insisted upon the teacher's guilt. At school he became violently angry. He often provoked his removal from the group and he often openly and without any provocation attacked the teachers. Once again, the teacher's record tells the story:

> It was in these upheavals and their aftermath that we saw Judd struggling with his feelings about being no good because he was brown. He raged, "I hate you! I want to kill you! I wish you were dirty and raggedy too!" He said he hated school and wanted to go home. His lip trembled when he was reassured that he was a good boy, that anyone would have trouble

with so many difficult feelings, and that it is harder to have brown skin than to be white. Much later he said that he hated himself and that when he felt that way he hated everyone else too, even his pet bird. He didn't want to be brown and he didn't want to be white either. He said he had decided to be a little animal.

Two things happened to bring Judd's period of extreme distress to an end. First he confessed to the therapist working with his mother, during one of the therapist's school visits, that he had indeed slammed the door on his own finger. He explained he had lied about the cause of the accident because he feared his mother's anger. (However, he was not able to give a convincing confession to his family until after he had left the school.) Second, the confession enabled him to bring his loyalty conflict between the teachers and his mother into the open. One day he asked his mother if he could go home with a teacher (not the one he had accused of hurting him, but one who had been especially empathic to his angry feelings about his color). To his amazement his mother was not angry with him for expressing such a preference for his teacher. The teacher did not refer to any wish that he might have to be white but merely said to him that perhaps sometimes he wished she were his mother. At home Judd told his mother that he *wanted* to be white and then said, "Now you've found out my greatest secret!"

These two developments made it possible to work through Judd's color conflicts about being Negro. In the working-through process he was able to make use of both his parents and the school staff. The general level of his schoolwork and his behavior improved greatly. However, he still continued at times to injure himself and to provoke other children. A most important accomplishment for him was his growing understanding that the children then rejected him for his behavior, not his color. In time he gave up his two "outcast" friends among the children (one of them was the soiler who had teased him about being brown and dirty) and instead became a friend of the group of children whose functioning was the healthiest. As Judd said, "They are intelligent. They don't act crazy like the others." As the school closing date approached Judd felt strongly that he was being rejected because of his color and he dreaded transferring to an all-Negro public school. Sadly he asked the teacher whether Negro children play the same as white children. (In his apartment building there were no playmates at all for him. His only playmates were at school, where he was now the only Negro child in the class.)

The injury to his finger had exposed Judd's intense castration anxiety. Mrs. C. was able to respond to his diffuse fear of body injury by telling him that all boys his age sometimes have big worries about losing a part of their body and that they fear especially that they could lose or hurt their penis. They have that special fear because when a little boy first sees a girl undressed he usually thinks she has lost her penis and this wrong idea frightens him. She reassured Judd that he could not lose his penis and clarified for him that girls had never lost a penis. As sometimes happens when a mother gets productively engaged in helping her child with a developmental conflict, Mrs. C. now recalled an important detail of his early history. It was a detail which helped to explain both to herself and to Judd a specific origin of his castration anxiety. She remembered at this point the incident when the toilet seat had fallen and bruised his penis.

In first grade at public school Judd made an excellent adjustment and received very good grades. As a result he was transferred to a "major work" class for children of superior ability, and, fortunately, this transfer brought him into an integrated classroom. Both Judd and his mother kept contact with the Hanna Perkins teachers during the next few years and reported his good progress. Mrs. C. continued her work with the therapist through Judd's first grade year. It was during this year that Judd finally made his full confession to his family about the injury to his finger. In an overly stimulating game with his uncle Judd got upset, "fell apart," and slightly injured himself. At once he blamed his uncle for the injury. His mother recognized that Judd's affect and his projection of guilt repeated exactly the situation at the time of the school injury, and she pointed out this similarity to Judd. Judd then confessed that he had really been peeking behind the door at school when he wasn't supposed to. He said he "knew" nobody but he, himself, had slammed the door on his finger, but he had the "thought" that the teacher could have done it to him. He "thought" it because he was so frightened that his mother would get mad at him and bawl him out. He said she often got mad when he tried to tell her something. There was much discussion of the event for the next several days and Mrs. C. reported that she found Judd very difficult during this period—to the point that she thought he would need psychiatric treatment.

As Judd achieved an acceptance of his own color and no longer felt so threatened by his secret wish to be white, the relationship between him and his mother improved considerably. His mother described it, "It's like when you first meet someone and don't like them, but when you get to know them you do like them."

Judd demonstrates the relationship of his skin color conflicts to his self-esteem and his conscience development. The prematurely imposed toilet training, with its standards for cleanliness, promoted the development of harsh superego precursors, with a turning of aggression upon the self, reflected both in Judd's accident proneness and in his lowered self-esteem. As Judd came to resent and depreciate his skin color this racial conflict joined forces with the unresolved anal conflict, still strongly reflected in his teasy, messy interplay with his mother. In that he blamed his mother for his unwanted skin color, his angry resentment of her grew stronger, and in turn his guilt about this anger led to further injuring of himself and lowering of his self-esteem. He accepted as fact about his own skin the soiler's projection onto him of his own dirtiness.

In addition to the anal phase roots of his color conflict, Judd also demonstrates the interplay of color and castration conflicts of the phallic phase. In his heightened castration anxiety following his injury, Judd hurled a combined threat to the people he accused of injuring him and not liking him. He wanted to kill them and he wanted them to be brown—"dirty and raggedy," like himself. It appeared that Judd equated as inferior qualities being brown, being dirty, and being injured (castrated, feminine). (Recall also his feminine flirtatiousness with his teachers when he first entered the school.)

The three children selected for inclusion in this section demonstrate many facets of the complex problems arising from differences in skin color. Joe, a white child, was able to develop a realistic appraisal of brown skin as a different, but neutral, quality in his friends. (This development closely paralleled his progression along the developmental line, "From Egocentricity to Companionship," described by Anna Freud in 1965.) The working through of his successive reactions to children of a different color almost certainly contributed to his maturation in all of his relationships—to people of all colors. He could embark upon this healthy developmental course because he had the example and support of his unprejudiced parents, who chose to have their children grow up in an integrated neighborhood. Joe's prospects for growing up free of racial prejudice seem good.

Neither Joe, nor any other white child in the school, ever expressed a conflict about why his skin was white, in contrast to all the Negro children who struggled with why their skin was brown. It seems that no white child, recognizing himself to be in the favored majority, felt any need to work through any conflict about why *his* skin was different. Unfortunately, it was only the minority race child, not the white child, who sensed himself as different. In this unbalanced situation, "different" inevitably meant "inferior." No white child came to grips with any conflict about why he should regard his own skin color as "not different" —as the expected and superior color. It would be better if a balanced state of integration faced white children with an active conflict about harboring such an unjustified sense of superiority.

Jean, a Negro child, developed a strong denial of feelings and conflicts about skin color differences. As a result of walling off this segment of her mental life from consciousness, her personality acquired a superficial shallow quality. Jean was almost always friendly and likable, but too often her feelings were unavailable in her relationships. In her denial Jean seemed to be short-circuiting any step involving the judgment of people by their skin color. Had she been able to go through this step it seems likely that she then could have achieved more meaningful relationships with people of all colors, based on her judgment of them as people. Indeed, the example of Jean, and by contrast the example of Joe, suggest that judgments about skin color are a necessary and normal developmental step that must be worked through on the way toward mature judgments about people based on character content. The prospects of Jean's growing up free of racial prejudice seem in doubt.

Jean needed her denial in order not to threaten her mother's denial. At the root of the mother's need to deny skin color reactions was her childhood experience of her intense loyalty conflict about the "white" member of her family, rejected by both Negroes and whites. Jean's mother's difficulty is similar to the special conflicts we have observed in children of racially mixed marriages. These children have the extra complication to work through that to express preference or rejection of one skin color is to express preference or rejection of one parent over the other. It takes both a strong marriage and individually strong parents to withstand the pressures introduced by these special conflicts of the racially mixed child. The child's aggressive feelings about his own color in relation to the color of one parent may be narcissistically wounding to the rejected parent. The parent's retaliatory anger at the child can then make it impossible for him to empathize with and help the child. Even if one parent is less narcissistically vulnerable and more able to help the child with skin color conflicts, he may not be able to risk doing so for fear of the disturbance it will produce in the differently colored parent. The child's anxieties then succeed in introducing a rift between the parents. The consequence is that the child senses the rift he has caused and becomes fearful of the omnipotence of his own anxiety and aggression.

Judd, a Negro child, seemed to make good progress in mastering his skin color conflicts, and, as in the case of Joe, the prospects for his growing up free of racial prejudice seem good. His parents differed from both Joe's and Jean's parents. Unlike Joe's parents, they came to the school unconcerned about the importance of an integrated setting for a child so young as Judd. Like Jean's parents, they had a denial of their child's already-established racial conflicts; but unlike Jean's family, they were able to give up their denial and to give Judd the active help and support he needed in facing his own feelings about his color. Judd then did some sorting out of both his anal conflicts about dirt and his phallic conflicts about castration from his conflicts about his skin color. He also worked through his loyalty conflict between his white teacher and his brown mother. Of special interest in Judd's case is the focusing of all of his conflicts upon a current traumatic experience—the accidental self-injury to his finger. It is apparent that conflicts about color can invade not only ordinary development drive conflicts, but any and every corner of a child's life experiences.

In this chapter more than fifty clinical examples of racial reactions in young children have been presented. They are examples widely varied both in content and complexity. The cumulation of clinical experience which they represent offers a basis for further discussion as well as theoretical consideration. It will be the purpose of Part II, "Theory and Practice," to attempt this discussion and theoretical consideration.

PART II

THEORY AND PRACTICE

To serve as the prototype for all others, there is one basic developmental line which has received attention from analysts from the beginning. This is the sequence which leads from the newborn's utter dependence on maternal care to the young adult's emotional and material self-reliance—a sequence for which the successive stages of libido development (oral, anal, phallic) merely form the inborn, maturational base. The steps on this way are well documented from the analyses of adults and children, as well as from direct analytic infant observations.

—ANNA FREUD
*(Normality and Pathology
in Childhood,* 1965)

4

SKIN COLOR ANXIETY

Racial prejudice is only one of many forms in which a prejudice can appear. All forms of prejudice have certain common characteristics in the mechanisms which form and maintain them (see Chapters 7 and 10). The uniqueness of a particular prejudice is usually marked by the superficial manifestation of its content (racial, religious, etc.). In our work we have been especially interested in the unique features that not only contribute to the formation, but determine the special selection, of a prejudice with a racial content.

According to our findings it is especially the difference in skin color which is at the root of a racial prejudice. Other distinguishing features of racial differences, although important, are secondary. Part II will explore the nature of the anxiety aroused by a different skin color, and the relationship of this anxiety to the successive stages of libidinal development—the "inborn maturational base" (Anna Freud, 1965). From this base the effect of skin color anxiety upon the developmental line of object relationships will be investigated. Racial prejudice is, after all, a problem in object relationships. These explorations in turn will lead to some conclusions about the sources within the personality foundation from which racial prejudice can spring forth. Since our clinical material ends with the beginning of latency, we can say very little about the manifest condition of racial prejudice. It is our impression that a racial prejudice cannot develop before latency.

Nowadays children first discover the existence of different races at many different ages. The sensory capability to make this discovery, dependent upon visual perceptual development, exists well before the end of the first year of life. Hopefully, as our racial integration progresses, the age of discovery for all children in our society will approach the age at which it is first possible to make it.

The discovery will be profound, at whatever age it is made, because it will be first and foremost a discovery about the color of the skin. The skin is an organ establishing body identity throughout life. Less well known is the fact that in the first year of life the skin figures prominently in the beginning establishment of a psychological identity. Any observation of a basic difference in this organ invites the obvious comparisons of body identities and, for reasons which I hope to make clear, less obvious but equally important comparisons of psychological identities.

Other features of racial difference ordinarily make a secondary impact in relation to the primary observation of the skin color difference. If these secondary features come to assume a *primary* importance, the suspicion is that they do so defensively. The differently colored skin may have to be denied, and the conflicts about it displaced onto some physical feature defining a part rather than the whole body image of the different person. Such a substitution of the part for the whole adds to the difficulty of recognizing the whole personality, the individual human identity, of the differently colored person.

Today it is especially his full identity as a human being for which the Negro is fighting. He does not want to be regarded, or to have to regard himself, as a black object; he wants his status as a worthwhile human being whose skin is dark. The frightened white person opposes the Negro for a similar reason. He feels the Negro to be a threat to his identity as a human being with light skin; he fears becoming demoted to a white object. To have contact with dark skin threatens the worth of his overvalued light skin. One important reason why interracial contact generates this kind of anxiety is that the skin may never have sufficiently relinquished its early role in identity formation. Then integrity of personality, of human individuality, remains too attached to an external body attribute, instead of progressing inward to the personality itself as the prime guarantor of one's stable, worth-while, and unique human identity. This arrest may be the result of disturbances in the earliest stages of psychological identity formation, or it may not be an arrest at all but rather the end result of a regression from unmastered later developmental conflicts.

THE SKIN AND ITS IMPORTANCE IN PERSONALITY DEVELOPMENT

The skin is an organ of great significance to personality de-velopment, especially during the first year of life. Like the mouth, the skin of the infant is strongly invested with his drive to live and develop, and in turn the skin acts as a major organizer of this driving force. In the neonate, skin sensations merge with other sensations "so that they are 'sensed' by the neonate as a unified situational experience with the character of 'taking in,' of incorporating" (Spitz, 1965, p. 72). As sensations from various perceptual organs become discriminated the skin continues to play an important and more specific role as the transmitter of the mother's warm and loving stimulation of the infant. Through his mother's handling the infant develops his earliest awareness of his own value, as well as of the value of his relationship with his mother.

In the latter part of the first year the skin outlines for the in-fant his first awareness of his own body boundaries, separate from those of his mother. His developing ego thereby acquires a first sense of his own separate body identity, and simultaneously the ego achieves a first mental sorting out of the self representa-tion and the representation of the mother. This mental internali-zation of body separateness promotes the necessary beginning of a separation of the personalities of mother and infant. At first this new discrimination of the infant's own body and his own rudimentary personality must be very tenuous. Normal fluctua-tions between states of merging with mother and states of being aware of the separateness from her must go on for some time and the process must be a very vulnerable one. The mother's actual presence or absence is an obvious influence upon it. But any kind of stress, internal or external, can cause a return to the state of a merging reunion with mother for the *defensive* purpose of once again being one with her. The sense of body boundary is lost as the skin takes in, or reincorporates, mother so that mother and infant once again feel a sharing of the same body limits. At the same time the newly formed "mental skin" between self and object representations temporarily disappears.

After the first year the importance of the skin in further development of the personality recedes as other drive and body developments push forward. The child's drive to live and develop, the libidinal drive, detaches itself to a large extent from the skin and mouth and becomes invested in motor development and anal aspects of the digestive process. Nevertheless, the skin remains a libidinally invested organ throughout life. This is most evident, normally, in the sexual foreplay of the adult; and, abnormally, in some perversions, notably certain forms of fetishism and transvestism.

This picture of the role of the skin in personality development during the first year is the one hypothecated by psychoanalysis. In psychoanalytic shorthand, the mother's libidinal cathexis of her infant through her ordinary loving handling promotes the infant's own libidinal cathexis of his skin. This satisfying erotization of the skin, along with oral and other gratifications, contributes to the infant's healthy primary narcissistic cathexis which forms an essential core for his later personality development. In the latter part of the first year a body ego develops as the infant begins to recognize and accept his separateness from mother, and the earliest separations of self and object representations within the mind become differentiated. With the separation from her the infant begins to cathect his mother with his own drives and feelings. This first cathexis of a person recognized as not part of himself marks the beginning of his ability to form object relationships.

When circumstances in the first year interfere with the ordinary libidinization of the skin—e.g., excessive or aggressive skin stimulation, lack of a mother's loving stimulation, severe eczema, orthopedic casts—both a disturbance in primary narcissism and in the earliest steps toward a separate identity formation may result. Instead of a primary sense of well-being, there arises a primary sense of pain and anger. Normally, the child's budding ego strives for the recognition of separateness from mother and the beginning establishment of inner, separate self and object representations. But disturbances which produce a state of painful tension, a state of anxiety, interfere with this normal progression and may tend to bring about a fixation or a regression to the safety of a merger with mother. It may be that in these disturbed states the skin retains or reacquires its earliest psychological significance as an incorporator of the mother. The merger may be one of physical contact, if the mother permits and encourages it, or it may be limited to a psychological merger, where only the "mental skin" between self and object representations ceases to separate and instead incorporates the object with the self.

When an anxiety is specifically induced by abnormal skin sensations complications arise. In his actual body care, the child may necessarily be too little or too much handled, and this handling may become associated with strong and painful skin stimuli. As a result the mental separation of his self representation from the representation of mother may be too quickly or too slowly and incompletely achieved. Then the child's sense of separateness will be insecure and remain a vulnerable spot in his development. The skin may retain its early function of incorporating the mother, or it may also, under the influence of painful handling, become the focus for rejecting the mother. Later in life anxiety may revive the conflicts contained in these primitive developmental interferences. Disturbances in body image may result, with corresponding disturbances in both self and object representation. Anxiety may lead to a surrendering of a part of one's own identity for the sake of a safe reunion with a mother figure, or it may lead in the opposite direction of defensive rejection and too great an independence from any person threatening, as a mother figure, to revive the painful conditions of the early relationship when mother and child were not yet distinct and separate. Then the sense of body and personality separateness is preserved, but at the expense of rejecting an acceptable and even a needed object relationship.

SKIN COLOR ANXIETY

To recognize that another person has a different skin color can never be a meaningless discovery. The early and lasting psychological importance of the skin is such that this discovery must always have great import. Many factors will shape the effect of the discovery. The child's age and level of personality development are important. So are the circumstances in which the discovery is made—the child's own mood and ego state at the time, the emotional climate in his environment, the other people present, the amount of help he is given in comprehending the surprising reality. If the skin has acquired special meaning for him, e.g., through a skin disease, this too will influence his reaction to his discovery.

Whatever the particular internal and external circumstances may be at the time the child discovers skin color differences, the discovery must come to him, like *any* discovery of a body difference, as a disturber of his equilibrium and therefore as a generator of anxiety. It is not so easy, however, to describe or define the content of this skin color anxiety.

The earliest time at which the child is neurologically capable of observing skin color difference is somewhere before the end of the first year, or even the first half year of life.[1] But the infant probably cannot associate as a distinct human attribute a skin color observation about another person before he reaches the stage of the eight-month stranger anxiety. A different skin color

---

[1]The cones of the retina are present and well developed by the age of three months, although the central portion of the retina is not completely developed until the end of the fourth postnatal month. Studies of infants suggest that the sensation of color—red, yellow, green, or blue, as distinct from grey—may be perceived by the age of three months. The same studies demonstrate that from the ages of six to fourteen months color becomes an increasingly effective stimulus. Red, yellow, green, and blue are probably distinguished as distinctly different sensations by twelve months, and unquestionably by fifteen months (Staples, 1933).

has no meaning as such during the period of the "smiling response" which Spitz (1965) has described as occurring from two to six months. The "smiling response" is a universal development, occurring in all races. (See Spitz, 1965, Table III, p. 87.) The "sign Gestalt" eliciting this response is a human face, or a mask of a face, presented straight on, smiling, and in part or entirely in motion. Spitz calls this Gestalt a "preobject," indicating that the infant is not yet capable of discriminating another person as separate from himself, loving him, and being loved by him. Spitz comments, "Not only the child's mother, but anybody, male or female, *white or colored* [my italics], can at this stage elicit the smiling response if he fulfills the conditions required by the privileged Gestalt which acts as a trigger for the response" (p. 89).

After the age of six months the smiling response disappears. The infant reserves its smiles for mother and other familiar persons and no longer responds with smiles to a stranger. By the age of eight months not only does the infant not smile at a stranger, but he greets him with unmistakable signs of anxiety and he rejects him. He may cry or scream, look away from the stranger or hide his face behind his clothing, and throw himself face down in his crib. This reaction, which Spitz calls "the first manifestation of anxiety *proper*" (p. 156), is commonly understood as a disappointment that the stranger is not mother. It does not come about as a reaction to an unpleasant experience with a stranger. It is rather the result of an internal development within the child, indicating a new capacity to recognize mother as a separate person and his own special love object.

It might be difficult to distinguish during this developmental phase of stranger anxiety what, if any, portion of the child's anxiety is aroused by the specific quality of a new and different skin color displayed by a stranger. Perhaps the skin color is still an irrelevant observation for the eight-month-old infant. A remark made by Spitz (1965) suggests a possible approach to an investigation of the earliest response to skin color difference, as separate from separation anxiety.

A word of advice is in order: if one wishes to observe the phenomenon of
the eight-month anxiety—and to experiment with it—this should not be
done in the mother's presence. Where manifestations of the eight-month
anxiety are mild, the mother's presence will suffice to make them quite
inconspicuous whereas in her absence they will show up unmistakably [p.
156].

If a person of new and different skin color is presented to the
child, during the period of stranger anxiety, but in the presence
of his mother, what reaction would he demonstrate? Would his
responses to like-colored and differently colored strangers be distinguishable?

There are a few observations which I have reported in Chapter 3 (Example 4, including footnote) which suggest that there
may be a specific response of anxiety to a *differently colored*
stranger persisting beyond the usual period of stranger anxiety.
It is my impression that the significant recognition of skin color
as a distinct human attribute probably begins during the period
of stranger anxiety, when the child becomes capable of discriminating his first love object. Then, as stranger anxiety recedes, a
specific skin color anxiety becomes distinguishable and persists
for awhile beyond the period of stranger anxiety. The duration of
this period of overt skin color anxiety would have to be determined by infant observations during the end of the first year and
the beginning of the second year of life.

The earliest meaningful observation of skin color difference
thus appears to occur, given the opportunity, toward the end of
the first year of life. It is an observation which is made while the
skin is still an organ of dominant libidinal importance, although
this dominance already may be subsiding. In the latter half of the
first year the observation comes at a time when ego functions are
either still very primitive or not yet in existence. The child is just
beginning to develop his first sense of his own identity, body
appearance, body boundaries, separateness from mother. He is
also beginning to distinguish who in his environment is mother
and who is not mother. In the midst of these developments we
can only try to surmise what the infant's anxiety at the discovery

of a new skin color would be about, and give it words which the child himself is not yet capable of assigning to it. The strangely colored person, so different in overall appearance from himself, his mother, or other strangers must create a confusion about many of the recent achievements his primitive ego has tried to secure for itself. Looking at the new-colored person he might feel, "What is that?" "What does it have to do with me?" "Or with my mother?" "Will it change me?" "Will it change my mother?"

The infant's skin color anxiety may also have roots which go deeper than the stage where loss of the object is the developmental danger (as reflected in stranger anxiety). These deeper roots reach back into the first half year of life, when skin libidinization played a major part in the basic integrity of the infant's existence. The developmental danger during these earliest months is commonly conceived of as a fear of disintegration. The visual discovery of changed skin could regressively recall skin experiences from an earlier period when the importance of the skin depended more upon tactile, kinesthetic, vibratory, and temperature sensations than upon its visual presentation. The infant might fear not only visual but also *physical* contact with a strangely colored person as a threat to his libidinal gratification and in turn as a threat of disintegration. In his infantile world the libidinal gratification in skin contact has never come from skin of such a color.

These primitive skin color anxiety reactions must be regarded as healthy responses to a disturbing new perception. Under favorable circumstances the primitive ego of the child can be expected to master the anxiety and as a result to gain a greater familiarity with the object world, an improved sense of his own body image with an added dimension of body color, and a strengthening of the ego itself. If circumstances are unfavorable, the anxiety may be too great for the ego to master. If the child's mother is nearby at the time of the discovery, her loving presence can provide the emotional security the child needs when the strangely colored person temporarily plunges him into a strange world. As his mother accepts and approves of the stranger, so in time can he. If the child is given ample opportunity for a visual exploration of the stranger before being handed over to him for any physical contact or care, he can experience his skin color anxiety in the best timing and dosage. (See Chapter 3, footnote 2.) But if the infant first meets the strangely colored person in the absence of his mother and in the midst of a frightening physical contact, the disturbance both to his ego and his drives may overwhelm him. For example, the infant who awakens in the night to find his mother gone and himself in the arms of a strangely colored babysitter may associate the frightening experience not just with the absence of his mother or with strangers in general, but with the color of the stranger's skin. The potential danger in such an experience is that it sets up a preverbal, affectively disturbed ego state as a prototype of what it is like to have contact with people of the stranger's skin color. The soil gets its first fertilization for future prejudice.

For the infant who is raised biracially, the awareness of different skin colors inevitably comes during his first year. His discovery comes in relation to his sorting out of his own body appearance and limits, as separate from his caretakers, and in sorting out their separate colors. He may have to work harder to establish his own identity in that he has to secure his own color identity, as different from parents, or a servant who cares for him. If he is unable to achieve his own color identity, the anxiety aroused by awareness of the different color of a loved person may foster a regressive tie to this person where, in their oneness, their disturbing color difference no longer exists. The child's own self representation then is insufficiently discriminated, particularly in regard to his own separate color identity.

The discovery of skin color difference made during the first year of life is in a sense a phase-appropriate discovery. It concerns an organ, the skin, at the time this organ is at the height of its libidinal investment. The discovery also comes at a time when the ego is most intensively preoccupied with its evaluation of the skin and its sensations as it establishes body boundaries and a sense of body image. For the ego to be challenged with skin color.

discrimination, as part of the total assessment of the infant's own skin as his body boundary, adds to the thoroughness of the body evaluation. Another dimension, that of body color, is actively discriminated and established as a part of the self representation. This kind of discrimination cannot be made so clearly unless an actual confrontation with a skin of a different color initiates it.[2]

The perception of the new skin color and the total external and internal experiences associated with it become important memories of the first year of life, to be stored in the unconscious regions of the developing personality. Rediscoveries of skin color difference made in later developmental phases inevitably will reach back toward these earliest memories. If the child has not

[2]Phyllis Greenacre's remarks (1958) on identity and the sense of identity are especially helpful. "The term *identity* has two significant faces—an inner and an outer one. It means, on the one hand, an individual person or object, whose component parts are sufficiently well integrated in the organization of the whole that the effect is of a genuine oneness, a unit. On the other hand, in some situations identity refers to the unique characteristics of an individual person or object whereby it can be distinguished from other somewhat similar persons or objects. In one instance, the emphasis is on likeness, and in the other on specific differences. . . . The *sense* of identity, or awareness of identity involves comparison and contrast—with some emphasis on basic likenesses, but with especial attention called to obvious unlikenesses. . . . But in general a sense of identity involves some relation to others and has a socially determined component, with a degree of observation both by the person himself and/or through another person. Even for the individual, his inner sense of himself is not enough to produce a sense of identity. His self-image, based as it is on a fusion of implicit, but generally not clearly focused awareness of his own form and functioning with his wishes as to how he would like to appear and to function (forerunners and derivatives of identifications and ideals) forms the core on which his sense of his own identity is built. But this core, in so far as the fusion is relatively firm, is comparatively muted and stable. *The sense of the self-image is maintained and perhaps vitalized by the continual redefinement which accompanies comparison and contrast with others*" (pp. 612ff.; my italics).

In a recent televised discussion held by leaders of Cleveland's Negro community, some of these men talked of the need for the Negro to "internalize his blackness," and to reject any "white" conceptions of himself. The social implications of this advice, good and bad, were far-reaching. But I believe this fundamentally realistic advice must come from an intuitive understanding of an important infantile development. In the formation of his self representation a child must internalize his skin color as a discriminated identifying characteristic of his body image. This internalization of skin color has the best chance of becoming amalgamated into the personality if it can begin in the first year, as part of the child's normal body image development. The longer it is delayed the less secure will be the amalgamation into the unconscious foundations of the personality and the greater the restriction to the superficial region of consciousness. Then, in adulthood, a conscious effort to be black (or white) can only partly compensate for the missing or confused skin color facet of the unconscious body image laid down in the first few formative years of life.

had any opportunity to make such a discovery during his first year, then he has no such specific early memories concerning skin color available to be reactivated. However, the later discoveries cannot be expected to occur in isolation from the oral phase and the earliest ego and drive developments involving the skin. The first discovery of skin color difference, at any age after the first year, can be expected to hark back and to be affected by the memory traces of the innumerable constellations of "skin" experiences during the first year of life.

As stated above, the content of "skin color anxiety" is not easy to describe or define. Its earliest roots lie in preverbal experiences. As the discovery of color difference is made and remade at later developmental stages, these early roots are tapped, and simultaneously successive developmental layers become superimposed so that the nature of the anxiety becomes increasingly complex. The state of drive development, structural development, and—in our society especially—the state of narcissistic development, all come to have a bearing on the nature of skin color anxiety.

In the anal phase our observations demonstrate that brown skin color is equated with brown bowel movements and dirtiness. The child reacts to the brown skin according to whatever his reactions may be at that developmental point to dirtiness and to his BMs. In two-and-a-half-year-old Joe, for instance, there was no note of criticism when he touched Andrew's face and called it dirty (Example 1, Chapter 3). Rather, his attitude was one of curiosity, of wanting to touch and explore, and perhaps enjoy. But five-year-old Gerald's repeated joking about "white do-do's" reflected his low self-esteem about his own brown color, which he consciously rejected and regarded as dirty (Example 33).

In the phallic phase the skin color difference and genital difference can become confused, so that castration anxiety and skin color anxiety now take on complex relationships to each other.

Of fundamental importance to the child will be the relation of skin color to the state of his narcissistic evaluation of himself.

Here his parents' attitudes are determining factors. If his mother has an unrealistically low or high esteem regarding her own color, then the child's own self-esteem, as well as his valuation of people of other races, will also be unrealistically distorted.

In all phases the child's structural development is significant. The capacities of his ego to perceive, to evaluate reality, to tolerate anxiety roused by differences, to form fantasies, to employ age-adequate defenses, all affect his mastery of his discovery. Another very important factor will be the help his ego is given in comprehending the reality of his perceptions. If the child is not yet verbal, this help is given by the mother's loving reassurance of him and her acceptance of the strangely colored person. If the child has acquired verbalization, his parents can tell him the facts about different-colored skin—that it is simply a different-colored skin that some people are born with; that it is inherited from their parents; that it is a lifelong trait that never changes in anyone; that inside the skin the strangely colored person is indeed a person, with thoughts and feelings just like he himself experiences. In addition to being told these facts, he also needs an opportunity to tell his fantasies about his perception, and to have the help of an adult in correcting their unreal aspects in order that his mistaken anxieties can be relieved. For example, he may need to be told that the different skin has nothing to do with cleanliness or dirtiness, masculinity or femininity, disease, etc.

The significance of specific color has relevance for skin color anxiety. The meanings of colors to children can be manifold, and adults place great stress upon the early teaching of colors to a child. A small child who knows his colors unfailingly wins the admiration of the adult. Andrew, a three-year-old Negro boy in our nursery, in a stage of rejecting his own brown color and being angry at his mother for not perceiving his distress, greatly embarrassed his mother at school in front of his teachers by misnaming all the colors she had taught him so well (Example 42).

In a multiracial society the mastery of skin color anxiety becomes an important developmental task of childhood. When successfully carried out it contributes to total personality development, as the child sorts out the reality of skin color differences, detaches other irrelevant developmental problems, and comes to value himself as well as others for their personalities without being disturbed by differing skin colors. When the child is unable to master the anxiety produced by the strange skin color, he cannot see the skin—either his own or another person's—realistically. He fixes upon a confusion of skin color with other developmental problems, and he cannot value a person for his personality because of his inability to recover from the impact, the anxiety, repeatedly produced by contact with the strange skin color.

Skin color is the most striking distinguishing feature of racial differences, the one which produces the greatest visual impact. However, other racially different features are also important. For example, the difference between Negro and white hair is well known to stir reactions in both races. An especially intriguing racial difference is one in which the organ of perception itself appears altered, as it does to the Negro or white person in viewing the Oriental eye. In spite of their fascination with Oriental children's eyes, none of our children ever questioned whether Oriental children see in the same way that white and Negro children do. This question would seem a most natural and logical one for a child to ask. One of our teachers speculated that in "slanting" their eyes in order to appear Oriental, other children might be "trying out" what it would be like to be Oriental. (She aptly described it as a step on the way toward empathy.) In the "trying out" they might be discovering for themselves that Oriental vision is no different from the vision of their own race.

THE VISUAL IMPACT

In our society, which still has so far go to in the mastery of the visual impact caused by racial difference, Negroes are repeatedly the victims of the shock of the white people. A Negro hunting for a house in a white neighborhood knows it well. When a racially mixed (white and Negro) couple visited our school as part of their application for their child's admission, a white mother stared and gulped in her momentary shock. Her eyes alone were not enough to take in what she saw; she had to breathe and swallow it as well in her attempt at instant mastery (Example 43).[3] A white latency girl, long a friend of her family's Negro handyman, suddenly surprised him one day by holding her arm next to his and exclaiming, "Joe! Look! We're a different color!" A pregnant mother, whose husband was of a different race, found herself frequently and tactlessly confronted by speculations about the sex of her unborn child. Here the suspicion is that the anxiety, in anticipation of the shock at the new baby's unknown skin color, has been defended against by displacement to the baby's unknown sex. (See the observations of Robert Coles, reported in Chapter 10.) The common white reaction that all Negroes look alike is based upon an attempt to deny the visual shock of a different skin color, and a fear that to perceive the skin clearly is to come too close to it. The denying white person does not want to touch with his sight what the little white nursery school girl, fearing that the brown color would rub off on her, did not want to touch with her hand (Example 10).

It was not unusual for Negro parents to report vivid recollections of shocking discoveries in their own childhoods. Several reported being overwhelmed as very small children at the sight of the dead body of a close member of the family, at a funeral home or church. Several also reported the shock and hurt they experienced as children when white friends suddenly shunned them. These shocking rejections often came at the beginning of a new developmental phase—the onset of latency (going to school) or puberty (beginning boy-girl parties).

It was impressive, during our work, how often we found Negro parents expecting and preparing their children to be vis-

---

[3] This woman's child had a symptom closely related to the normal behavior she displayed here. When he was in a state of separation anxiety, he had to gulp in food and air, in an effort to regain the lost object. For him the psychological process of introjection of the lost object still depended upon a concomitant physical process of incorporation.

Recall also an opposite behavior in Freud's (1918) well-known case of the Wolf Man. He was compelled to breathe out when he passed a frightening crippled person in the street, in order to ward off a respiratory incorporation which could lead uncontrollably to an identification with the frightening person. See also an example quoted by Lasker (referred to in Chapter 10).

ually shockproof. A child might be taken, for instance, to a frightening museum exhibit, instructed about it in advance, and then expected not to experience any anxiety at the frightening sight. If the child did show anxiety, the parent was apt to deny its manifestations. The local dinosaur skeleton in a nearby museum was a favorite choice for such a toughening experience. All that got toughened was the defensive crust of consciousness against the overwhelming anxieties of the inner affective and fantasy life. The potential richness of thought and feeling was forced out of consciousness and defensively walled off in the unconscious mind.

In another society it is the white man who becomes the victim of the Negroes' shock in the discovery of white skin. For example, a member of the tall, proud African Masai tribe is reported to have given white people the disdainful label of "skinless ones." A recent magazine article[4] quotes Dr. Robert F. Thompson, a Yale University authority on the Yoruba people of Nigeria, who described the visit of a white person to the Yoruba as follows: "The Yoruba feel that white skin in unfortunate, but they are very polite, so if they happened to have an albino child, they would bring it out, to put you at your ease by showing that it could happen to anyone."

A COMPARISON OF TWO DISCOVERIES: SKIN COLOR DIFFERENCES AND SEXUAL DIFFERENCES

Psychoanalysis discovered long ago the importance for personality development of a universal childhood experience—the discovery of the difference between the sexes. Reconstructions from adult analyses, child analyses, and direct observations of children have confirmed beyond any doubt the momentousness of this experience. It is of interest here to compare this well-known and thoroughly explored childhood discovery with the discovery of skin color differences. Both are visual discoveries and both *normally* evoke anxiety about body differences, in *all* children, regardless of sex or color. Why is it, then, that castration anxiety

[4]*The New Yorker*, November 9, 1968 (from "Talk of the Town").

is so well known and accepted as a normal occurrence while skin color anxiety is not generally recognized as a normal anxiety and goes unnamed except when it takes a pathological deviation from its normal course and then is named prejudice?

A cultural explanation contains some truth but serves primarily a defensive purpose. It is true that in our society it has been possible for some white children to live in ignorance for far too long a time of the existence of other races, but it is not possible for boys and girls to live in ignorance of the existence of the opposite sex. It is also true that strong and irrational reactions within the culture to racial differences are introduced and offered for identification to many children very early in their lives. A white child whose parents hate Negroes has generally internalized this attitude as his own even before he goes to public school. A white child whose parents deny their conflicts about Negroes by avoiding all contact with them and in effect denying their identity as human individuals will early profess the same racial attitudes proffered by his parents. The Negro parent who hates white people communicates his hatred, similarly, to his children. Today the cultural reactions to which children are exposed are so compelling that they can easily be used to deny what young children themselves bring to the discovery of skin color differences. If the reality of a child's own reaction to color difference is presented to an advocate of childhood innocence and cultural guilt, this advocate misinterprets the child's reaction as an inoculation from the culture. He answers the claim for the reality of the child's own internal reaction by explaining it away as the prejudice of the observer, projected into the child. Similarly, an absence of any overt reaction to racial differences in a child is used as evidence in support of an absence of parental or cultural prejudice. In reality the child is identifying with the parents' and the culture's denial. This denial of the innate mental life of the child— of his normal ability to observe, and to react with anxiety, conflict, feelings—resembles the denials of childhood sexuality which greeted psychoanalytic explorations into psychosexuality.

Underneath the cultural explanation for the failure to recognize a normal skin color anxiety, in contrast to castration anxiety, lies an intrapsychic explanation. I have already alluded to this explanation in considering the difficulty of describing and defining skin color anxiety. Castration anxiety, in contrast, can be quite specifically described and defined. The contrast has to do with the different body organs involved in the two discoveries, and with the difference in the development of the personality structure, particularly the ego, at the different times when these organs—skin and genitals—reach the height of their libidinal investment during childhood. It may also have to do with the timing of the discovery in relation to the peak period of libidinal investment in the organ in question.

The discovery of the difference between the sexes may be made *before* the child enters the phallic phase of development. If so, and if the experience does not occur in traumatically frightening or stimulating circumstances, the child's ego generally protects itself by denying the reality of the observation. The drives are still largely attached to the functioning of the gastrointestinal tract and the child may draw his sexual discovery into the sphere of his digestive developmental conflicts, but for the moment genital sexuality ordinarily has relatively less claim upon his psychological structure and function. Then, as the child enters the phallic phase, he rediscovers, or else discovers anew, the difference between the sexes, and the discovery now comes under the dominance of the libidinally invested sex organs. By the time he has reached this level of development his ego has come more under the influence of reality and denial is on the wane as a useful mechanism of defense. It no longer protects him from what his ego now comes to know must be accepted as a part of reality— that the world contains people whose sex organs differ from his own. The resulting anxiety is a specifically focused anxiety about sex organs and sexual identity. Conflicts become specifically sexual conflicts. Many other aspects of personality development and identity formation are by now securely enough developed that they need not be drawn into these sexual conflicts.

The intense investment made in the sexual discovery under

the impetus of the phallic phase (and its corresponding oedipus complex) comes relatively late in the development of the rudiments of personality structure. A great deal of structural differentiation has already occurred. Global, diffuse reactions have become narrowed and specific. Verbalization is available for specific expression of sexual conflicts. Further, the resolution of the oedipal sexual conflicts with the parental objects during this phase draws together the last organized structure to be formed within the mind—the superego.

The discovery of the difference in races, in skin color, *cannot be made before* the period of development in which the skin is at its height of libidinal investment, since this period begins at birth. It may not even be physiologically possible to make this discovery until the peak of libidinal investment in the skin has passed, toward the end of the first year. Often it may be made long after the skin has yielded to other organ systems its position of libidinal dominance. The sexual discovery can be held in abeyance by the ego until the phallic phase of development; the skin color discovery cannot be held in abeyance to await the arrival of a skin dominance. Either it comes at a time when the skin is highly invested and the ego functions are barely developed, or else it comes *after* the skin (oral) phase and *reawakens* the invested memories of this early period. Skin experiences during the first year are global, diffuse, not even restricted to a separate self representation, let alone a separate, specifically conceptualized and excitable body organ. Anxiety, too, is a global, ill-defined experience, rather than a narrowed-down and specific event attached to specific verbalizable conflicts. Verbalization (secondary process thought) is not available at the time skin experiences have their greatest meaning in life. Other ego functions are primitive or undeveloped and the ego is relatively helpless when confronted with states of tension and anxiety.

Skin color anxiety stirs reverberations of this psychological state of affairs during the first year of life. It throws a vague uncertainty upon the old accomplishments of the primitive ego functions which established the earliest self representation, the earliest sense of identity, on the basis of a particular skin color. In this threatened disruption of one of the foundations of identity the newly experienced skin color anxiety reaches back as well to the primitive states of global tensions and anxieties of the first year, when the undeveloped ego often was powerless to defend itself and bring a sense of relief from these states.

Unlike castration anxiety, skin color anxiety concerns a preverbal period, whose memories will never be capable of returning to consciousness. These early memory traces and the conflicts and tensions they contain are deprived of the resolution and discharge consciousness offers in the form of secondary thought processes and verbalization. At best only remote derivatives of the early identity confusion, of its attendant anxiety and the ego's primitive defensive efforts reach consciousness. In their journey toward consciousness these derivatives may be further obscured by displacements of later developmental conflicts onto the skin identity conflicts.

The end result is that skin color anxiety often goes unrecognized and thus it fails to achieve its status as a normal developmental anxiety about body differences. The consequences could be serious. To deny or to consider pathological a normal, necessary developmental anxiety makes its realistic resolution more difficult for the child, and he may seek a solution along a neurotic or characterologically disordered pathway.

5

SKIN COLOR ANXIETY
AND THE STAGES OF
LIBIDINAL DEVELOPMENT

Many advantages accrue to the child who grows up in a racially integrated environment in the first few years of his life. Under favorable circumstances the skin color anxiety he experiences leads, through comparisons and contrasts, to a sharpening of his own sense of identity as well as an improved awareness of the identity of others. As discussed in the preceding chapter, the child acquires an added dimension of body color in both his self and object representations.

Racial integration can also promote a child's libidinal development. Inevitably, skin color anxiety intermingles with anxieties generated during each successive stage of drive development, and consequently skin and drive conflicts converge. A conflict about skin color takes on oral, anal, or sexual qualities; conflicts about oral, anal, or sexual developments become shaded with skin color anxieties. The thoroughness of the ego's resolution of any conflict is always promoted when the ego has an opportunity to work through the presentation of the conflict in as many versions as possible. The task facing the ego of the racially integrated young child is *to resolve and to segregate* his conflicts about skin color and his conflicts about his drive development. In the coming together of these two sets of conflicts *during* the formative stages of personality development, there is mutual gain for the resolution of both because of the additional challenge they present to the ego to accomplish their resolution and segregation. For example, both skin color anxiety and castration anxiety are better mastered when a child resolves his unrealistic anxiety that to have dark skin is to be castrated. (Fred denied his brown color in order not to be like a Negro girl, during a stage of heightened castration anxiety when he had to dissociate himself from anyone feminine.)

Not only does the racially integrated young child gain in the buildup of the foundations of his personality, but he gains an equally valuable head start toward its future expansion. Through resolution and segregation of skin color and drive conflicts he has removed potential focal points for the growth of later prejudices. The problems of object relationships and prejudice will be considered further in Chapters 6 and 7.

The present chapter traces the overlapping and the sorting out of skin color anxieties and developmental drive anxieties. It brings together psychoanalytic theories and findings about personality development and the clinical examples drawn from our work and presented in Chapter 3. As already acknowledged in Chapter 1, our experience with an integrated group of children suffers from its narrowness. Nevertheless, the observations we have made do not lack validity on that account and no apology seems necessary in drawing almost solely upon them here for purposes of bringing together theory and practice. Indeed, it seems unwise to do otherwise. We cannot stretch beyond the limitations of our own practical experience to try to establish any kind of "controls" or universality for our findings and formulations.

Many additional approaches to the problems of racial difference and personality development readily come to mind. Of value would be observations of other age groups—especially of children in the first three years of life and in early latency, observations of children in other cultures, and psychoanalytic findings from both children and adults in treatment. The expectation of such additional sources is that they would provide the much needed verifications, clarifications, and corrections of our own work.

SKIN COLOR ANXIETY AND IDENTITY DISTURBANCE

It is difficult to find clinical examples of undisguised skin color anxiety. An explanation for the hiddenness of this anxiety has already been proposed. Its preverbal root, its disturbance to the body image, and in turn to the earliest stages in identity formation of the individual, tend to make the anxiety a diffuse one and to place it out of the reach of consciousness and verbal expression. The few examples available of children nearing the end of the first year of life suggest that intermingled with, and perhaps persisting for some time after, the period of stranger anxiety there is an anxiety aroused by the sight of a stranger with a different skin color (see Example 4, and footnote 2 in Chapter 3). Further observational data of this period of life are needed. *Perhaps* the little white girl who sensed, and probably shared, her younger sister's anxiety that the brown color would rub off is another good illustration (Example 10)—"perhaps," because we do not know what her accompanying fantasy might have been. Was the brown color already an unwelcome dirt stirring up anal stage conflicts and threatening their recent mastery? Or might it have aroused even earlier, less discrete, anxieties of a poisonous substance, ingestible through the skin? We just do not know, but underlying such oral and anal conflicts is the suggestion of a skin color threat to identity.

There is Harold, whose confusion about the stability of the skin color of both himself and the Negro and Oriental children, precipitated by a Negro child's chicken pox, openly expresses a skin color anxiety, with its threat to identity (Example 14). There is also George's visual shock at the Oriental children (Example 21). It contains an unmistakable anxiety, but for him anxiety typically became covered over in the excitement and loss of control it produced. Other examples where the skin color difference produced or encouraged an excitement and loss of control (Examples 28, 38) suggest an undisguised skin color anxiety, but it would be a mistake to confuse the excitement, particularly its defensive aspects against the anxiety, with the basic anxiety itself.

It seemed that the anxiety produced by a differently colored skin came closest to the surface, as an identity threat, when in reality someone's skin actually underwent a change. A good example was Lucy's spring-vacation sun tan (Example 19). This phenomenon, so familiar and often so welcome to adults, was foreign and frightening to Lucy and her classmates. In the reporting this example has been greatly condensed. The questions and concerns about Lucy's darkened skin went on for days. Furthermore, this experience was duplicated several times with other tanned children, and with each new class of children. The anxieties of the children about tanned skins contained little evidence of confusion with ordinary developmental drive conflicts, as they so often did in relation to a child whose color was different, but reliably stabilized in its difference. Here the *change* in color in another person drew forth the more basic anxiety of the possibility of body change in oneself. Nor was the anxiety confined to one of *body changes*. The bodily changed child was looked upon by other children as a child with a *changed personality* as well, a frightening stranger to be avoided. Both white children and Negro children reacted with fear of exposure to the sun because they did not want to get a tan and have their skin turn darker (Example 48). They feared nobody would know them, remember them, and love them if their body changed. At this young age, individuality of personality is still closely tied both to one's own body image and to the loving support of mother, of others in the family, and of familiar teachers and classmates. To experience a total change in exposed body covering and to be unrecognized by the all-important loving objects can for a child result only in the loss of a sense of both body and personality identity. Lucy reacted with some regression in her well-developed ego skills, and, in a sense, she seemed temporarily out of touch with her old prevacation self.

The change produced in the skin by disease has already been mentioned and an example cited of its arousal of an identity disturbance (14). There are, of course, many illnesses where a changed skin color is a significant symptom. Changes in the skin are also important in aging and in dying. Stuart's confusion of a Negro child's hands with "old hands" especially intrigued us

(Example 27). Whether the difference in color of the front and back of the Negro hand had something to do with Stuart's confusion we do not know. Nor do we know what personal experiences, with aging people or with Negroes, he may have been drawing upon in judging the Negro child's hands as "old." It must be remembered, too, that normally by the time a child reaches kindergarten he has made the association of "old" with death, the ultimate destroyer of identity.[1]

THE ORAL PHASE: INTROJECTION, PROJECTION, AND DENIAL

There are two aspects of the oral phase of development and skin color anxiety to be considered, in addition to the problem of early identity formation, discussed above. One is the expression of skin color conflicts as oral conflicts. The other is the use of primitive oral phase mechanisms in the face of skin color anxiety. (In Chapter 6, I offer the speculation that these mechanisms may persist in connection with racial conflicts because skin color anxi-

---

[1] The changed appearance of the skin in death is often the focus of the anxiety aroused in the living at the sight of the dead. A mother who, with her children, witnessed a near drowning at the beach, dwelt upon the dark blue cyanotic color of the swimmer as the feature most disturbing to her children as well as to herself. In the sudden collapse and death of a man performing at the piano for friends it was his blue color in death that fixed the onlookers' attention and seemed to underscore the irrevocableness of what had happened. After his death his friends recalled his pale white skin as the one sign of ill health which he had not succeeded in concealing from them.

The reaction of the artist, Claude Monet, to the death of his young wife, Camille, is a poignant illustration of fixing the color of the skin in death. "And when he contemplated Camille at daybreak on her deathbed, he noticed—in spite of all his grief—that his eyes perceived more than anything else the different colorations of her young face. Even before he decided to record her likeness for the last time, his painter's instinct had seen the blue, yellow, and grey tonalities cast by death. With horror he felt himself a prisoner of his visual experience, and compared his lot to that of the animal which turns a millstone." (John Rewald, *The History of Impressionism.* New York: Museum of Modern Art, 1961, pp. 431-433.) This great Impressionist painter was momentarily turning his artistic preoccupation with light and color to a defensive purpose to protect himself from the full and immediate impact of his overwhelming grief. A recent biographer, writing of the time of Camille's death, makes the following comment about Monet, "Beneath Monet's 'objective' naturalism lay not only a suppressed Romanticism but an even darker spirit. There may even be a deep-seated psychological significance in the elimination of black from his palette. When life seemed unsupportable, he saw 'everything black.' He associated darkness with death and had been afraid of it ever since the days of his military service in Algeria." (William C. Seitz, *Monet.* New York: Harry N. Abrams, 1960, p. 29).

ety has its deepest root reaching down into the oral-skin libidinal phase of development.)

First, the mechanisms. Introjection and projection are the earliest of these mechanisms; a later, though still primitive, mechanism to be considered is denial.

Introjection and projection are very early mechanisms which prevail before the ego is sufficiently developed to appraise objectively the real world. They represent the infant's efforts to acquaint himself, bit by bit, with the external world and to build up a division between it and himself. Very simply, he ingests the world, gives it a trial taste, and keeps inside himself, as part of himself, what he likes, but spits out, rejects as not qualified to be part of himself, what he does not like. Thus he begins to build up separate inner representations, both of himself and of the external world. As the ego develops an appreciation for reality, these early building methods, which operate without any regard for reality, give way to more advanced "realistic" mechanisms. The pleasure-pain principle yields to its later modification, the reality principle. The division between inner and outer reality then becomes governed by reality, regardless of any associated pain or pleasure. A good "grip on reality" becomes the best insurance against a resurgence of "prereality" uses of introjections and projections. That is, to know what exists externally in reality and not within, to know whether it is familiar or new, and to tolerate the tensions that come with its being unknown and/or painful, all insure against a loss of *realistic* boundaries between external and internal. Further they insure against an *unrealistic* reconstruction of boundaries according to pleasurable and painful, or good and bad qualities. How and where the boundary between external and internal is drawn is, of course, crucial to an individual's sense of identity.

If a confrontation with a particular reality is not merely strange, in a rather neutral way, but instead presents some frightening feature, the child finds himself confronted as well with his inner anxiety. In this situation the building mechanisms of introjection and projection can acquire their first *defensive* uses, through the efforts of the child's ego to cope not just with the strange reality but also with the inner anxiety it arouses.

The discovery of a new and different skin color is not a "neutral" strange experience, but one which arouses a skin color anxiety. The ultimate relief of this anxiety depends upon the child's acquiring some comprehension of the reality facing him. For the preverbal child this comprehension must be communicated through reassuring feelings shared with the mother, or her substitute (see Chapter 3, footnote 2). For the verbal child, the realities about different skin colors must be reassuringly explained to him. The child himself will have almost no way of defining for himself the strange external reality, without this outside assistance. If, then, he has no way of gripping onto reality, he can easily fall back upon a primitive restructuring of the world as he prefers it to be. In doing so he discharges his anxiety, but it is at the high price of settling for a distorted view of reality. Qualities from within are projected outward, irrationally, and the strange object, now in familiar, less frightening dress is accepted or rejected accordingly. At first the division of inside and outside is simply according to pleasure and pain. Later, as superego precursors develop, it is also according to good and bad. If the child's skin color anxiety is intense, there will be a large defensive component in the use of these primitive mechanisms and he may become fixed to their usage, unable to shed them for more advanced, more realistic mechanisms as his overall development proceeds. Of course, if he receives no realistic explanations about skin color, he is not given any realistic grip against these primitive mechanisms. And if loved adults also use these same mechanisms to cope with their own skin color anxiety, the child's use of them is further encouraged through identification with these adults.

Some of our examples of first or early confrontations with skin color differences illustrate various steps in the children's efforts to deal with the new and frightening reality. Two-and-a-half year old Joe and three-year-old Barbara (Examples 1 and 2) do not appear openly anxious. But they cannot tolerate the unknown, and each makes a pronouncement about the strange Negro child which makes the stranger familiar. (In their pronouncement they are also making a bid to the grownup for some helpful information about the strange reality!) Joe declares that Andrew is dirty and Barbara declares that Martin is chocolate. In the case of Joe we do not sense any displeasure as yet in the quality, dirty; indeed his reaching out to touch Andrew's face suggests an effort to take in Andrew with his hand. Barbara makes it clearer that she means to ingest the stranger, in calling him chocolate, a food she probably likes. Thus Barbara gets rid of her anxiety and gains a yield of pleasure for herself. (While we can assume her "engagement" to a Negro boy two years later was based on a much more realistic appraisal of this boy as a friend, as well as upon her oedipal development, still the initial pleasurable reaction to the "chocolate" boy must have proved a favorable foundation for her later relationship.)

Emily, almost four years old, both took in and rejected the Oriental child who so much impressed her when she started school (Example 5). She imitated his facial appearance but rejected any memory of his name. However, in her conscious imitation she was already in control and trying to comprehend reality, rather than making the frightening external object familiar to herself in an unrealistic way.

The little girl who assured her younger sister, "Don't worry. I found out that it won't rub off" (Example 10), appeared to be protecting herself and her sister from an unwanted and fearful incorporation, through the skin, of a strange and frightening discovery—the brown skin of a Negro child. Her protection came through her remarkable research and correct appraisal of reality, and she was well on the way to understanding that brown skin is just different skin, no more and no less.

Ken is a white child who illustrates a persistent use, perhaps already amounting to a fixation, of projection to cope with his skin color anxiety. (This conclusion cannot be drawn solely from Example 3, but from the school's acquaintance with Ken.) He felt threatened by an Oriental child with the same name as his own. He warded off a dangerous introjection, with its threat of identification with a like-named boy, and projected onto the other Ken the dirtiness he did not like in himself. To identify with the other, dark-skinned Ken, was to become dark-skinned, and to white Ken, dirty.

Andrew presents an example of a more advanced mechanism (Example 7). He covered his ears in order not to take in what Clark was saying about brown cake crumbs not being visible on Andrew's face. Andrew appears to be trying to *deny* the real fact of his own unwanted brownness. We know that in his dislike of chocolate, brown toast, and other brown-colored foods he was much under the influence of the pleasure-pain principle and attempting to ward off any introjection of a quality he did not want included in his self representation. But in covering his ears, he gives evidence of having progressed to a better awareness of the external world, and the fact of his own brownness. He does not disown his color by, for example, calling Clark brown or dirty. That is, he does not fall back on a projection which would totally disregard the reality of his and Clark's different colors. Instead he tries to maintain his denial of his own color and covers his ears not to hear any reminder of it. The mechanism of denial implies an awareness and unconscious acceptance of what in reality exists, although one might wish it did not.

Two white children, Clark and Ted (Examples 6, 8), who had progressed far beyond their initial confrontation with skin color anxiety, openly declared their liking for the brown skin color of their Negro friends. These white boys had acquired an aesthetic appreciation of the beauty of brown skin. Primitive introjections, projections, and denials did not appear much in their behavior in relation to their brown friends. These boys appeared to have mastered their skin color anxiety, to have achieved acceptance of the reality of differently colored skin, and to have distinguished it as but one feature characterizing a friend. It would seem that the support of the loving object relationship with the differently colored child in each case favored the development of a realistic appraisal of the object by the child's ego.

In contrast, Jane, a blond girl much admired and envied by all the Negro girls, remained frightened of the brown-skinned children, tried to avoid them, and rejected holding their hands in group hand-holding games. For a long time she was reluctant to go to the kitchen for the snack cart, and her fear seemed to be of the Negro women who worked in the kitchen. As she developed, Jane became a very good little girl, and goodness and whiteness became equated. For her, especially, the dark people represented badness and out-of-controlness, and she protected herself against any introjection of and identification with these "Negro" qualities by avoiding contact with Negroes.

A self-evident example of a child using introjections and projections to cope with his skin color anxiety is Harold (Examples 14 and 50).

The confusion of skin color anxiety with developmental experiences and conflicts of the oral phase is illustrated in several examples. As mentioned, Barbara's chocolate man brings brown skin and food together (Example 2). All of the Negro children at one time or another expressed strong likes and dislikes for food, based solely upon its color (Examples 24, 47). Sometimes these food disturbances were diagnosed—both correctly and incorrectly—as allergies. When the diagnosis of allergy was incorrect, it tended to fix physical illness both as a substitute for and a defense against anxiety and conflict.

That skin color conflicts can arouse an aggressive reaction experienced on a primitive oral level of development is illustrated in two examples. Andrew, in a state of anger at his brownness, provocatively projected his brown color onto his gleaming white teeth (Example 42). Then he seemed to become frightened that his teeth could really turn brown. Perhaps as a punishment for his aggressive thoughts and feelings about his disliked color, the prized white teeth, the instruments of his oral aggression, would turn brown. The teacher's reassurance was not enough for Andrew. So great must have been his conflicts and anxiety about his aggression that he declared he needed special treatment for them, identifying his needs with those of an atypical boy, recognized by all the children as a boy with severe problems.

Donny A. experienced a strong aggressive reaction to the news that his mother was going to have another baby (Example 35). He was unable, without help, to give it direct verbal expression and appraisal according to the reality principle. Instead he discharged his angry, rejecting feeling for the new sibling upon innocent friends, at the same time using their different racial characteristics as pegs upon which to hang his projections of his own badness. Donny B., with his Oriental skin, was brown and so was Negro Fred's tongue, he declared. Here brownness is bad and dirty, and suggests an association with aggression in the anal phase. But anal conflicts are also transferred to the oral zone, and the tongue, the instrument of oral verbal aggression, which Donny cannot control, is also declared dirty.

If oral conflicts and skin color conflicts are not resolved, the consequences can be manifold. Various forms of eating disturbances, based openly or covertly upon food colors, may persist. Related disturbances in object relationships can also persist. For example, it is obvious that Donny's aggressive impulses, experienced largely on a regressive preoedipal level as oral and anal phase reactions, caused a temporary disturbance in his object relationships with his Negro and Oriental friends. Should he, for whatever reason, have ceased to develop and to recover from this state, he would very possibly have had to become an adult with a racial prejudice.

THE ANAL PHASE: NARCISSISM, CONTROL, SEPARATION

In our experience these topics have so many interconnections in relation to racial reactions that it would be an artificial isolation to try here to consider them separately. It is also our experience, again admittedly very limited in scope and skewed in selection, that the critical overlap of racial, skin color, conflicts with inner developmental drive conflicts occurs in connection with the anal phase. It is a temptation to declare that a pivotal parting of the ways of these two conflictual currents ought to occur in relation to anality, and as close in time as possible to the anal phase itself. This parting of the ways must be brought about through the resolution and mastery of skin color and anal conflicts. It is also a temptation to declare that anal phase conflicts, even if they do not significantly outweigh other drive determinants, are the critical organizing forces of trends that can develop into later Negro-white prejudices (see Chapter 8). But without a broader experience these declarations must remain unmade. Instead, what follows are statements of our own impressions and convictions, rather than universally established facts.

Naturally, individual and social customs concerning toilet training and the prevailing racial climate in a society greatly influence the associations between anality and darkness of skin color. But aside from environmentally induced connections we are inclined to believe that there is inherent within a child a natural tendency to make such connections himself, *if* he has had the benefit of exposure to differently colored people.

The basic and normal skin color anxiety, whether or not it is experienced for the first time in the anal phase, comes as a threat to body image and the earliest foundations of identity, built up during the oral phase. The anxiety arises at a threatened *loss of identity*. In the next phase of development, the anal phase, a new loss treatens. It is the *loss of a body content*, the feces, and this loss becomes a new focus for anxiety. The child must lose a part of his body, and at the same time build further, rather than lose as well, his recently acquired sense of identity. In the course of control and mastery of this newly sensed anal loss the child goes through many complex conflicts. He must devalue his brown feces, reject them as a needless part of himself, yet not devalue or reject himself. Here he is greatly dependent on the example of his parents' own healthy narcissistic evaluation of themselves, as well as upon their valuation of him, his body, and his personality. Through an identification with his parents' attitudes toward themselves and through their loving support of him, the child promotes and maintains his own necessary narcissistic investment in himself. If a parent feels that his skin color makes him inferior, his like-colored child will also feel inferior about his own skin color. The narcissistic problem can become more complicated when parents and child differ in skin color. A separation from parents during this stage readily leads also to narcissistic devaluation. The child feels the separation as a rejection for his dirtiness, for loss of control of anal impulses. Indeed the developmental danger situation which puts its stamp on all of the events of the anal phase is the child's fear of the loss of the love he receives from his love object.

During this stage the child begins to develop a new set of values and primitive judgments (superego precursors) in which clean is good and valuable, and dirty is bad and valueless. Commonly, "brown" temporarily becomes a *bad* color and anything brown gets rejected as of no value. The easy regressive displacement of this set of anal conflicts to the oral zone and to brown-colored foods is well known. It is so common that it must be regarded as a normal temporary regressive step in anal phase development.

"Brown" becomes a color symbolizing all anal stage conflicts. It becomes equated with forbidden anal pleasurable excitements, as well as aggressions. It represents to the child a visual reminder of the ego's actual or threatened loss of control over anally tinged feelings, as well as over anal contents. When his ego control fails, the child himself can feel totally bad, worthless, and rejectable, and his sense of identity can suffer a loss.[2] For a time during this stage, a child feels that the best guarantor of his successful ego control is to dissociate himself entirely from the color, brown. Just to see it may stimulate his innate anally centered drives beyond his ego's newly developing ability to control them. To ingest brown—orally, in his food, or dermally, through anything or anyone brown or dirty touching his skin—is even more dangerous. Such a taking into himself of the bad color can result in an identification with a bad, out-of-control, dirty person. The establishment of such a self representation would be at the expense of his parents' love and approval, so vital to support of both body and personality. For these people he wants to be good, clean, and in control.

[2]Edith Jacobson (1964) has pointed out the rich feelings of identity that come with successful ego actions. Failures—in this case, a failure in ego control—correspondingly must lead to impoverishment of identity sensations.

It should come as no surprise that the anal phase "brown," so readily spread from feces to everything brown, can brand the skin color "brown" with its special markings. This branding brings with it, of course, the whole constellation of anal phase conflicts, displaced onto the darker skin shades. Here two important questions arise. First, of what significance is the child's own skin color? Second, of what significance is it whether or not a child has had the opportunity to meet someone with a different skin color?

The actual color, or shading, of a child's own skin makes no difference at all in his anal phase conceptions of a relatively dark skin color as dirty, bad, worthless, and indicative of loss of control. Our examples abound with both white and nonwhite children who react to brown skin on this anal basis as dirty (see Examples 1, 3, 15, 16, 18, 20, 28, 30, 33, 35, 36, 37, 39, 40, 42, 45, 46, 47, 48, 50). It is the color of the child's feces, not his skin color, which brings on these reactions. Gerald, a Negro boy, seems to be stressing this fact that it is the color of the feces, not the skin, that is of primary importance (Example 33). In his frequent talk of "white do-do's" can be sensed his wishful fantasy for a white skin, as though with such skin he could produce good, clean, valuable, controllable, white bowel movements, and thereby escape the overwhelming (for Gerald) developmental conflicts of the anal phase. Gerald still soiled occasionally and he was easily provoked to states of anal excitement and loss of emotional control. Ted, a white child, symbolically posed a question about the color of brown-skinned people's feces, based on the universal unconscious symbolic equation of money with feces, when he asked whether Negro people have the same kind of money as white people (Example 9).

It is of great significance for his development whether or not a young child has had an opportunity to discover that other people have skin colors which differ from his own. As discussed previously, in the oral developmental phase the discovery of a different skin color aids him, through the contrast, to evaluate his own color and to include it as a definitive aspect of his own body image. In the anal phase there is a new gain to be had from the experience of racial integration. So long as a child knows only his own skin color his attention is not drawn specifically to it as a distinctive feature about both himself and other people. He can continue to take his color for granted and all too easily isolate it as an irrelevance to his development. The advantage of knowing people of another color is that it adds a new dimension to the child's anal phase development. At the very time when he is normally busy discriminating and evaluating all the browns in the world in relation to the color of his feces, the discovery of a different-colored skin—whether the child is white or not white— forces him to work through this color discrimination in yet another and very important focus. Now he must detach skin color, both his own and others, from the color of feces. In doing so he must also detach other qualities he comes to attribute to feces, from people—himself or others—whose skin reminds him of feces. The success of his efforts leads to a parting of the ways of anal conflicts and reactions to racial difference. Feces, he discovers, have no more and no less importance for Negroes than for white people. The child's success also leads to a gain in his valuation of himself,[3] and in his valuation of the personality, the identity, of the differently colored person.

The more and varied the opportunities presented to the ego to work through the anal developmental conflicts, the more secure will be their mastery. It is normal and advantageous to development in a multiracial society that a child of any color has the opportunity to go through a period of confusion about skin color and fecal color during the anal stage of his development. Bringing these two *realistically unrelated* matters together at a time when the ego is busiest with problems of color, cleanliness, control, and valuableness is phase appropriate. Through their overlapping they can gain a realistically worked-through separation. In this working-through process the racially integrated toddler has an opportunity to establish for himself a foundation for future good racial relationships. If he succeeds, he will be in less

[3] See footnote 2 (p. 127).

danger in later life of contaminations creeping in from anal
phase conflicts unconsciously stirred up by unresolved skin color
anxiety produced at the sight of a different race.

As for problems of narcissism, it is especially concerning
them that we are aware of the limitations of our clinical experience. In Chapter 1 I referred to the qualities of character evident
in Negro families who brought their children to our therapeutic
school. Many held high ego ideals, and for some these ideals contained the unconscious goal of becoming white. The very unreali-
ty of this goal made it a constant abrasive to their self-esteem,
and led to an impoverished narcissistic investment in themselves.
These people projected onto their children their aspirations, but
they offered their children for identification their diminished self-
esteem. A mother who felt her Negro child to be inferior because
of his color could not succeed in investing him with enough unambivalent love and admiration to support his own healthy narcissism sufficiently. Many times we observed an unconscious
communication from parent to child, condemning one or another
of the child's Negroid (or Oriental) features.[4]

The lowered esteem at being a darker color was distressingly
painful, not only to a child himself, but to anyone who knew the
child and tried to help him with it. The pain always seemed so
tenacious. Andrew, who probably worked through his conflicts
about his color as well as any of our Negro children, needed endless support and reassurance of his self worth (see Examples 42,
48). On his first school vacation, at three years, he thought everyone else was in school and only he had been excluded—ultimately, for being different, Negro. When he left the school three
years later the departure was very painful for him and he again

---

[4]In a contrasting social scene, this communication of inferiority from parent to child
was sometimes a fully conscious process. In *Children of Crisis,* Robert Coles (1964) describes the deliberate efforts of Southern Negro mothers to teach their preschool age children that they must accept a position of fear and inferiority toward whites, for their own
safety and survival. Some of these mothers managed, however, to teach their children the
difference between an appearance of inferiority as a defense and the reality that they were
not in fact inferior people. They taught them that God had specially selected them as
strong people, capable of enduring suffering, for an ultimate gain, known as yet only to
God, Himself.

felt specially excluded, even though now he could understand better that his whole class was graduating and leaving.

We never lacked for illustrations of this narcissistic conflict. Sometimes it seemed that all roads led to Rome; everything in a minority child's life led to his dark color and the narcissistic difficulties it brought him. The activity of making life-size self-portraits almost always revealed narcissistic disturbances associated with being brown (Examples 26, 45).[5] Doll play and playing house did the same. Abby accepted the white children's asking her to be the maid, and easily demonstrated her feeling of inferiority in this position (Example 47). Paula, a Negro child with a fully formed neurotic disturbance, relentlessly confronted not only the adults but also the other children, with her severe impairment of self-esteem and her aggression to herself. (See discussion included in the report of Example 34.)

Closely associated with a lowered self-esteem is the defense mechanism of turning aggression upon the self. Andrew frequently would hit himself in despair when he did not meet his own high standards of performance, particularly when he was in a state of inferiority about his color. Bruce at first had seemed oblivious of his different, brown color. But as he became more able to face the fact, his distress about it became evident. When another child rejected him for his color Bruce was silent, but later kicked over his own building (Example 46). These children were at first unable to defend themselves against aggression directed at their skin color because they accepted the cruel pronouncement of other children about their color as realistic judgments. The rightful anger they should have felt for the child who insulted them they instead turned upon themselves, blaming themselves for being the wrong color. Where the equations, brown = dirt = feces, prevailed so strongly, the Negro child was trapped. To be angry at someone threatened his loss of control of a seemingly useless feeling; to lose control would be like soiling,

[5] See also Chapter 3, *Children of Crisis,* in which Coles gives many examples, accompanied with drawings of this same narcissistic difficulty in the Southern Negro children he observed.

being dirty, and losing more ground in his battle to maintain his healthy narcissism. By turning this aggression to another child back upon himself the Negro child gave himself what he regarded as a deserved punishment and rejection. He grabbed the reins and took charge of his own rejection. In doing so, the Negro child also made an appeal to his attacker to befriend him, on the basis of their mutual rejection of brown skin. Were the Negro child to settle for this mechanism as a character trait, his ambivalence toward his own color could never be resolved and he would become a Negro with a prejudice against Negroes.

Bert, the Indian boy who planned to cut off his own skin in order to get pink skin (suggested by his pink healing wound), demonstrates yet another version of aggression turned upon the self. His siege of compulsive hand washing also contains this mechanism (Example 40).

Another mechanism used by the minority child who felt himself to be inferior was a passive-into-active rejection in anticipation of being rejected. This mechanism disrupted object relationships because it was often responded to with a reciprocal rejection from the white child (or adult!). The darker child then could interpret the reciprocal rejection he received as the one he anticipated in the first place, and a confirmation of his feeling that he would be rejected for his color. Since his own passive-into-active mechanism operated unconsciously the minority child could not see his own part in provoking the rejections he repeatedly experienced—not for his color but for his behavior.

The passive-into-active mechanism also had as its goal the bolstering of self-esteem through a lowering of esteem for the object. Esteem was not yet an independently measured quality but one which depended upon a teeter-totter comparison with another person. The dark child acted too important, or too busy, to have time for the white child. This need to insure self-esteem at the expense of esteem for another is sometimes met in connection with events of the anal phase. A child who has recently mastered toilet training, but whose mastery has not yet survived the test of time, can be very scoffing toward a younger untrained sibling or playmate. For that matter, an older untrained child, with his unavoidably low self-esteem, can be more scoffing toward a younger trained child, in his anxious efforts to reverse his appraisal of their relative values.

Ken, the Oriental kindergartner, presents a wonderful example of what happens when there is a release from the state of lowered self-esteem through a fantasied fulfillment of the impossible ego ideal (Example 18). With a sudden burst of infectious elation, he dunked himself in fantasy in the GREAT Salt Lake and in a miraculous rebirth he came out WHITE! The sudden release of tension between his white ego ideal and his berated brown body image expressed itself in a joyous overflow which the entire class seized in identification. Ordinarily only the white children who themselves suffered from a pronounced state of lowered narcissism identified with the lowered self-esteem of the nonwhites. (See, e.g., Harold, Example 50.)

A most interesting variation of the narcissistic difficulties of a minority child was presented by Charles (Chapter 1), who at three years already bore a charisma, if not yet any accompanying signs of inflated narcissism. Unfortunately we never had an opportunity to get to know Charles because his mother withdrew him after his first visit.

It was always gratifying to see signs of good self-esteem and spontaneous pleasure in themselves in these minority children of dark color, who had to work so hard to achieve a prevailing affective state which many a white child more or less took for granted. Many of our minority children did achieve such a state, but over and over we found that every new conflict, related to their skin color or not, could throw them back to a lowered esteem about their color. New children entering the school especially stirred up their feelings of being worthless and unwanted, particularly if the new children were white.

We do not have any examples of nonwhite children expressing a genuine liking for white skin, independently of any jealous, covetous feelings and lowered esteem for their own skin. We have many examples of genuine friendships which dark-colored

children shared with white children, but their liking for a particular classmate never got expressed as an unambivalent acceptance of the color of skin which they themselves could never have.
There are two striking examples (6, 8) among the white children
of a liking for the brown skin of their friends for its aesthetic
quality. With both Clark and Ted their liking was based on
friendship, but these two children seemed especially responsive
to the natural beauty of their brown-skinned friends. They never
professed a wish to be brown themselves, but their realization of
the problems of being in a minority (a realization which most
children had) did not prevent their appreciation for the physical
beauty of their nonwhite friends. How much farther advanced
were these children than most white adults in our society!

Separation anxiety can have many determinants, from many
developmental levels and many different kinds of personal experiences. In our clinical experience we found that no matter what
the individual developmental or traumatic focal points for the
separation anxiety, the dark-skinned child revived it, for *all* of
the children. Darkness of skin meant little value, easy discardability. No matter what the major content of the child's separation
anxiety, this lowered worth and discardability were based upon
anally derived qualities of dirtiness and loss of control. Ralph, a
white child who had had very traumatic losses during his first
year, long before his anal phase, came to regard Negroes as bad,
dirty people who deserve rejection (Example 36). Edwin's traumatic separation during his anal phase fixed for him the equation of Negro with dirtiness and being thrown out (Example 37).
Alex, an adopted Negro child, displayed his suspicion that he
had once been rejected (and could be again!) because of what he
considered his dirty color (Example 39). Still another form of
separation conflict was presented by Donny, who had wishes to
get rid of the new sibling he was about to acquire. He labeled his
aggressive impulses brown and then "threw them away" by
means of projections. He probably feared that he himself could
be thrown away for harboring them (Example 35).

When a Negro child did lose control of his behavior, or actually soiled, it seemed that *all* of the children associated it with

the child's brown skin and many expressed strongly ambivalent feelings about getting rid of dark, bad, out-of-control children (Examples 36, 38, 39). When a Negro child in reality left the school, all of the children seemed to fear the child had been expelled, and some of the younger ones seemed to feel that the discarded Negro child might not even exist any more (Example 39). The Cleveland riots and the death of Martin Luther King (Chapter 3) brought out in many children strong feelings of the vulnerability of the Negro to destruction. The separation of Dorothy and Charlotte from their father, through divorce, was associated by both girls with the death of Martin Luther King, and both girls expressed strong feelings of dislike for Negro girls. They appeared to be warding off an identification with these dark-skinned girls whom nobody (no father) would want to stay with. They also hinted at their anger at their father for leaving them, by identifying his loss with the loss of a man with the skin color they degraded—Martin Luther King.

To a small child, in or recently through his anal developmental phase, his major concern in life has been a separation of himself from his feces, and all the conflicts that emanate from this body loss. The main developmental danger for him during this period has been his fear of losing the love he receives from his love object. If he experiences any extended separation from loved and loving persons during this stage, he easily feels totally abandoned—unwanted and discarded, like his feces. Whatever his color is in reality, to have a brown skin would confirm his worst fears that he has no value, no control, and is just a dirty person to be left, flushed away like his feces, and forgotten about.

As the anal phase recedes, the racially integrated nursery school child is completing his segregation of brown feces and brown skin. Anal conflicts ebb away and new sexual conflicts flow into consciousness with the oncoming development of the phallic drive. This next new tide of drive development will once again draw into its currents the problems about racial differences. But the successful segregation of drive and race during the anal phase will have established an important precedent upon which a similar segregation during the phallic phase can be continued.

THE PHALLIC PHASE AND THE OEDIPUS COMPLEX

The events of this phase lead to the final structural differentiations within the personality. With the resolution of the sexual conflicts in relation to the parents, the superego, the last major structural unit to be formed, coalesces into an integrated group of functions. It is during this phase that a final parting of the pathways of skin color conflicts and inner drive conflicts must occur. This is not to say that they will never overlap again in later life, as internal and external events lead them to do so. But this is the last developmental phase in which skin color conflicts can achieve a segregation from drive conflicts *during* personality structuralization.

At first it might be expected that the bulk of our clinical examples would contain illustrations from the phallic-oedipal period of development—expected, because our culture seems to place so much stress on sexual dangers and conflicts as an important basis for our current racial problems. All that can be said is that our experience does not conform to this expectation, although with the addition of a kindergarten to our school some years ago we are now much better able to follow children through their entire phallic-oedipal development, and even with some into their early latency development. Perhaps our observations are limited by our skill as observers. However, in the atmosphere of our school it would be difficult for childhood sexuality to succumb to denial; and, in fact, observations abound of ordinary sexual development, unrelated to skin color. Again, we do not know whether other nurseries and kindergartens would duplicate our findings or not. But aside from environmental influences and limitations, an explanation for a lesser number of phallic, as compared to anally, tinged racial conflicts may lie within the personality development of the child. (Of course, developments belonging to one phase can overlap with or be displaced upon another, so that anality and phallic sexuality can appear together or as defensive disguises for each other.) The significance of the anal phase and skin color differences has already been stressed. By the time the child has reached his sexual development his ego development has progressed far. Through a better ability to think logically and to appraise and discriminate reality he may now be less inclined to confuse skin color anxieties with other conflicts. The sexual difference and the skin color difference do not *in reality* suggest so much in common to his phallic-phase ego as did his "brown" anal conflicts and his "brown" skin color anxieties to his less developed anal-phase ego.

There is still another possible explanation for our findings. Children in our school received much assistance in achieving a separation of skin color anxieties and drive conflicts. As a result, by the time our children were well into the phallic phase, skin color conflicts had already gained a significant segregation from drive conflicts, especially with respect to the critically important anal phase. By the time they reached the sexual phase of their development many of these children had achieved an advanced stage of psychological racial integration. They knew each other as friends and had resolved many of their infantile conflicts about each others' skin colors. With this foundation they entered the sexual phase with the best possible protection against gross invasions of skin color problems into sexual problems.[6]

[6] As a corollary of this point of view it might be expected that an opposite environment, one which supported segregation of the races and avoided helping children with their racial conflicts, would greatly foster an unrealistic link between sexual and racial conflicts. The Southern writer, Lillian Smith, offers an eloquent confirmation of this speculation in her book, *Killers of the Dream* (New York: Norton, 1949). The following passage (from Part Two, Chapter 1, "The Lessons") is an excerpt from her lengthy account of the Southern child's racial-sexual conflicts:

"By the time we were five years old we had learned, without hearing the words, that masturbation is wrong and segregation is right, and each had become a dread taboo that must never be broken, for we believed God, whom we feared and tried desperately to love, had made the rules concerning not only Him and our parents, but our bodies and Negroes. Therefore when we as small children crept over the race line and ate and played with Negroes or broke other segregation customs that were known to us, we felt the same dread fear of consequences, the same overwhelming guilt that was ours when we crept over the sex line and played with our body, or thought thoughts about God or our parents that we knew we must not think. Each was a 'sin,' each 'deserved punishment,' each would receive it in this world or the next. Each was tied up with the other and all were tied close to God."

Still it is likely that even the best of preparations during the anal phase does not, and should not, establish a complete, final segregation of color and sex. For a child to work through, *during* his phallic-oedipal phase of sexual development, that skin color differences have no significance in regard to sexual differences is important. It is the final and necessary step, during the formative years of personality development, in the separation of inner drives and race. During this period the developmental danger situation is experienced as a fear of bodily injury, a fear which is rooted in the child's castration anxiety. As skin color anxiety once again intermingles with a developmental danger, the child's task in achieving their separation is specifically to distinguish these two anxieties—to recognize what is skin color anxiety and what is castration anxiety. As he does so he eliminates displacements between skin color differences and sexual differences.

We found that the problems of sex and skin color seemed greater for Negro than for white children. Their narcissistic inferiority about their dark color readily blended with narcissistic sexual conflicts. In this developmental phase, inferiority, dark skin, and femininity became equated. Fred went through a marked period of avoiding girls, giving evidence that he regarded their condition as contagious. He expressed open contempt for them, and at the same time he denied that he was the same color as a Negro girl in the school. That Fred himself was a well-coordinated and active boy with a strong innate masculinity probably helped him greatly to overcome whatever inferiority he felt about his color, based on his equation of it with femininity. The Negro girls, on the other hand, had more difficulty. Being both dark and feminine was experienced by them as a double narcissistic wound during this developmental period. New white boys entering the school were especially hard for the Negro girls to accept.

Just as narcissistic conflicts about skin color, from the anal phase, carried over to the narcissistic conflicts of the sexual phase, so did conflicts about skin color and being out of control. The dark skin continued to stand for lack of control and excitement, now on a more openly sexual level. Often, of course, it was impossible to sort out sexual and anal determinants in children's excited states centering around a dark-skinned child. In fact, the dark skin provided a link between the two developmental phases, and facilitated an equation between sexual impulses, dirtiness, badness, and loss of control (Examples 28, 38).

A curiosity about whether a Negro girl's genitals differed from white girls' genitals was demonstrated by Paula's, Jane's, and Helen's direct sexual explorations (Example 31). A racially mixed group of three boys carried out a similar but defensively disguised exploration, through the common displacement downward from the genitals to the feet (Example 29). There is a strong suggestion of a confusion of sexual and color differences in Clark's experiencing of play in the doll corner as a sudden threat to his masculinity (Example 17). He had to assure himself of the like *sexual* identity of Donny, Andrew, and himself, each of whom had a different *skin color* identity. Then he had to rescue himself and his *boy* friends from the castration threat in the *girls'* doll corner.

In the midst of their penis envy many girls displace their conflicts about their genitals to their hair. Pigtails and ponytails readily serve as denials of—or disappointing substitutes for—the missing penis which they feel they are lacking. This displacement was very common among the Negro girls. In Paula, a child with a complicated and fully developed neurosis, this displacement to her hair was intense (Example 34). Abby, too, showed intense feelings of inferiority about her hair (Example 47).[7]

Nor was the displacement of the castration conflict to hair confined to the girls. Negro boys sometimes appeared ashamed of their fresh haircuts, sensing when their closely cropped heads reflected a parental wish to do away with an inferior, Negroid, part of their bodies. If sexual conflicts are displaced to the hair, it

---

[7] A visiting Negro physician told us an interesting example of the significance of hair differences for white and Negro girls in an African community she had visited. In a class of young children there was just one white child—a little girl living temporarily in Africa with her family. The physician observed a few of the African girls demonstrating boastfully to the lone white girl how they could make their hair stand up and the white girl could not.

is understandable that the parental wish to hide and get rid of his hair could be experienced as a frighteningly realistic castration threat by a Negro boy. Furthermore, he would sense in the castration impulses of his parents a judgment that his masculine sexuality—his phallic impulses and associated thoughts and feelings—is bad, uncontrollable, and deserving of destruction. The problems such a boy would have in achieving an identity as a Negro male are obvious. However, not only the parental castration threats were apparent; in the Negro boy's shame and effort to conceal his shaven head are contained his guilty masturbation conflicts. And for him, his punishment is to lose, symbolically, not only his masculinity, but also his skin-based identity, rooted in the unwelcome Negroid features. It is not just his hair, but his *Negroid* hair which is taken away from him. One Negro boy with a strong wish to grow long hair, rather than to have his head shaven, expressed much curiosity and confusion to a bald-headed white relative about what had happened to his hair. What he could not ask was why this Negro relative had white skin.

Many times children expressed interest in the problem of mixed marriages (Examples 2, 12). (See also Ruth and Bruce, reported in Chapter 3, and the teacher's management!) Frances brought the equation of her out-of-controlness (both her wetting and her oedipal excitement for her father) with dark skin, badness, and rejection in direct relation to the sexual conflicts of her oedipal development, through her revealing doll play (Example 30). (Frances is also discussed in Chapter 6.)

LATENCY, ADOLESCENCE, AND ADULTHOOD

The opportunity for clinical observation at the Hanna Perkins School comes to an end at about the beginning of latency. In order to do justice to the vicissitudes of racial conflicts within the personality from latency onward many more clinical data would be required. Ideally observational studies would need to be supplemented with data from psychoanalyses of latency children, adolescents, and adults. As was true in the preschool years, it is to be expected that racial problems could interweave with all aspects of personality development throughout all of life. Any study and discussion of racial attitudes in any particular developmental phase would have to draw upon almost everything that is known of the psychology of that phase. A study of latency, for example, would be especially helpful in tracing the relationships between skin color conflicts and ego and superego development and the developmental danger represented through the sense of guilt.

A few analysts already have anticipated, and in some instances demonstrated analytically, certain complications of race and personality development. Bernard (1953) anticipated that the analysis of Negro patients would draw upon and expand our knowledge of "the exception." Kennedy (1952) demonstrated analytically the complications in the ongoing development of the ego ideal which are introduced by racial conflicts. Gitelson anticipated in one of his aphorisms that analytic study of interracial marriage will draw upon and illuminate the psychology of love. Kramer (1967) quotes Gitelson: "An exogamous marriage is a reaction against an intense (negative or positive) oedipus complex" (p. 266). But these are only a few of the directions in which subsequent analytic studies could be expected to venture.

The work with the Hanna Perkins children can only stress the importance of establishing a basic foundation in the child that will enable him to accommodate himself realistically to racial differences as he meets them later in life. This is the best protection he can have against the later development of unrealistic, prejudiced attitudes.

Today we are passing through a necessary cultural instability en route from a stabilized environment that was predominantly prejudiced to the goal of a stabilized environment that will be predominantly free of racial prejudice. During this transitional period, whose length cannot be predicted, children, especially, need a healthy personality foundation that will enable them to withstand the instability and eventually to bring it to a desirable resolution. But for the present, most people have had to grow up without the benefit of actively working through skin color conflicts in the first few years of life. Either they never met the problem of racial differences in their early years, or they met it in disastrous circumstances and were forced to accept a distorted resolution of it. It is a testimony to the resilience and resourcefulness of the ego that many adults of all races are finding it possible to progress toward some psychological integration, without benefit of proper early-life preparation for this step. And what they cannot achieve for themselves, they are willing to allow the next generation to accomplish.

Our Hanna Perkins examples have extended from the third through the seventh year, with an additional borrowed example or two from the first year of life. It seems fitting to close this chapter with another borrowed example, from the tenth decade of life. It illustrates a healthy ego, of almost a hundred years, at work. When a Negro woman married a white man, his grandmother, in her nineties, in effect disowned him. But after a short time and probably much contemplation the aged woman came to the recognition that it was foolish to cut herself off from her favorite grandson in the closing years of her life. So she apologized to him and graciously met and accepted his Negro wife. In the few years before her death the two women succeeded in developing a respectful and affectionate relationship with each other.

6

SKIN COLOR ANXIETY
AND THE DEVELOPMENT OF
OBJECT RELATIONSHIPS

So basic a life task is the achievement of adult object relationships that Anna Freud (1965) has made use of it as a prototype
in illustrating her concept of developmental lines. She has named
this prototype line, "From Dependency to Emotional Self-Reliance and Adult Object Relationships," and has prefaced it, in
part, with the following comment. "This is the sequence which
leads from the newborn's utter dependence on maternal care to
the young adult's emotional and material self-reliance—a sequence for which the successive stages of libido development
(oral, anal, phallic) merely form the inner maturational base"
(pp. 64f.; my italics). In this statement Anna Freud shows us
drive development and the development of object relationships in
their proper perspective.

Chapters 4 and 5 dwelt upon skin color anxiety and its effects upon the inner maturational base of drive development. In
brief, successful resolutions of skin color anxiety promote drive
development; unsuccessful resolutions potentially support arrests and fixations of drive development. The present chapter
proceeds beyond this preoccupation with the maturational base
to the topic of object relationships built upon that base.

The culmination of the resolutions of skin color anxiety and
their effects upon the inner maturational base comes in the development of object relationships. Ultimately the success of these
resolutions must be measured along developmental lines concerning object relationships. It would indeed be a mistake to hold
forth a psychoanalytic view of our current racial conflicts merely
as oral or anal or phallic conflicts, or even skin color conflicts.

They are conflicts in object relationships. They are struggles between people, trying to protect and preserve their own identities, trying to appreciate and value others' different identities, and trying to build and maintain bonds between each other.

The attainment of emotional self-reliance and adult object relationships is a complex developmental achievement, in relation to persons of the same, let alone a different, race. In describing her concept of developmental lines, Anna Freud conveys the nature of the complexity. "Whatever level has been reached by any given child [along a developmental line] represents the results of interaction between drive and ego-superego development and their reaction to environmental influences, i.e., between maturation, adaptation, and structuralization" (p. 64). The achievement signifies a capacity to maintain one's own independent identity and at the same time to evaluate the identity of another person. At maturity the evaluation of another person will be largely according to the content of his character and will not be unduly influenced by some superficially different—and therefore often disturbing—physical, or psychological, trait. In mature interracial relationships skin color is just skin color—no more and no less. It is not the bearer of unresolved developmental conflicts with the inner drives. In a mature object relationship a person is secure in his evaluation of his own separate stabilized identity (his self representation, including his skin color as a part of his body image) and he is secure in his empathic evaluation of the character of the other person (the object representation, including a realistic recognition of the skin color of the object). That is, he recognizes the other person as an individual, who is both like himself and yet different, with a separate identity of his own, with his own physical and psychological characteristics.

There are two important developmental lines described by Anna Freud concerning object relationships, and progress along both of these lines is fundamental for attainment of healthy interracial relationships. In view of their importance her description of both of these lines is quoted here in full:

From Dependency to Emotional Self-Reliance and Adult Object Relationships

(1) The biological unity between the mother-infant couple, with the mother's narcissism extending to the child, and the child including the mother in his internal "narcissistic milieu" (Hoffer, 1952), the whole period being further subdivided (according to Margaret Mahler, 1952) into the autistic, symbiotic, and separation-individuation phases with significant danger points for developmental disturbances lodged in each individual phase;

(2) the part object (Melanie Klein), or need-fulfilling, anaclitic relationship, which is based on the urgency of the child's body needs and drive derivatives and is intermittent and fluctuating, since object cathexis is sent out under the impact of imperative desires, and withdrawn again when satisfaction has been reached;

(3) the stage of object constancy, which enables a positive inner image of the object to be maintained, irrespective of either satisfactions or dissatisfactions;

(4) the ambivalent relationship of the preoedipal, anal-sadistic stage, characterized by the ego attitudes of clinging, torturing, dominating, and controlling the love objects;

(5) the completely object-centered phallic-oedipal phase, characterized by possessiveness of the parent of the opposite sex (or vice versa), jealousy of and rivalry with the parent of the same sex, protectiveness, curiosity, bids for admiration, and exhibitionistic attitudes; in girls a phallic-oedipal (masculine) relationship to the mother preceding the oedipal relationship to the father;

(6) the latency period, i.e., the postoedipal lessening of drive urgency and the transfer of libido from the parental figures to contemporaries, community groups, teachers, leaders, impersonal ideals, and aim-inhibited, sublimated interests, with fantasy manifestations giving evidence of disillusionment with and denigration of the parents ("family romance," twin fantasies, etc.);

(7) the preadolescent prelude to the "adolescent revolt," i.e., a return to early attitudes and behavior, especially of the part-object, need-fulfilling, and ambivalent type;

(8) the adolescent struggle around denying, reversing, loosening, and shedding the tie to the infantile objects, defending against pregenitality, and finally establishing genital supremacy with libidinal cathexis transferred to objects of the opposite sex, outside the family [pp. 64f.].

From Egocentricity to Companionship

(1) a selfish, narcissistically orientated outlook on the object world, in

which other children either do not figure at all or are perceived only in their role as disturbers of the mother-child relationship and rivals for the parents' love;

(2) other children related to as lifeless objects, i.e., toys which can be handled, pushed around, sought out, and discarded as the mood demands, with no positive or negative response expected from them;

(3) other children related to as helpmates in carrying out a desired task such as playing, building, destroying, causing mischief of some kind, etc., the duration of the partnership being determined by the task, and secondary to it;

(4) other children as partners and objects in their own right, whom the child can admire, fear, or compete with, whom he loves or hates, with whose feelings he identifies, whose wishes he acknowledges and often respects, and with whom he can share possessions on a basis of equality.

In the first two phases, even if cherished and tolerated as the baby by older siblings, the toddler is by necessity asocial, whatever efforts to the contrary the mother may make; community life at this stage may be endured but will not be profitable. The third stage represents the minimum requirement for socialization in the form of acceptance into a home community of older siblings or entry into a nursery group of contemporaries. But it is only the fourth stage which equips the child for companionship, enmities and friendships of any type and duration [pp. 78f.].

These two lines have a coordinal importance as measurements of achievement in object relationships, especially when the additional complexity of a skin color difference is introduced. In the first of the two lines the emphasis is upon the step-by-step *separation from members of the family.* This progressive separation is a prerequisite for achieving adult status within the original family and for a releasing of energy for investment in new persons outside the original family. In the second of the two lines, the emphasis is upon the step-by-step discovery and *approach to strangers with the eventual awarding to these strangers their own rightful, realistic identities.*

There are people, both children and adults, who at first glance appear to have progressed well along both of these developmental lines, *provided that their impaired capacity to relate to someone of another skin color is overlooked.* But skin color anxiety may lead to exposure of otherwise ordinarily hidden weaknesses in development by highlighting arrests or precipitating regressions along either or both of these two important lines.

The skin color anxiety aroused by a differently colored person may stir some repressed drive conflict, which in turn carries the potential of reviving an old disturbance in a particular relationship to another family member. Various combinations of conflicts and solutions are possible, depending both upon the relative amounts of skin color and libidinal anxieties, and the structure of the defensive systems to cope with them. The skin color anxiety itself may be the greater and overwhelming pressure, and old incestuous conflicts may be revived more for defensive purposes, to ward off this underlying skin color anxiety. Then the old unresolved incestuous relationship is displaced onto the frightening stranger, to disguise him in a familiar protective coating. At once, the ability to award this stranger any recognition of his rightful identity is lost; his identity has been sacrificed to that of the conflictful incestuous object. A regression along the first of the above two developmental lines occurs, and the qualities of the new mixed-race relationship take on the characteristics of some immature level along this developmental scale. This level characterizes the weak spot in the old incestuous relation.

Of course, it is possible that skin color anxiety can be the lesser source of conflict, and that unresolved incestuous libidinal conflicts will contain the greater anxiety, and forever be threatening to overwhelm the ego. Then a displacement of incestuous conflicts onto a differently colored person would serve primarily to defend against their breaking out within the original family circle. From a descriptive, clinical point of view the end result would appear to be the same as in the first of these two possible combinations just described. A regression along the first of the two developmental lines would be evident, and the qualities of the new mixed-race relationship would take on the characteristics of some immature level along this developmental scale, characteristic of the original unresolved incestuous relationship. Only a psychoanalytic exploration could make clear the underlying metapsychological differences, by bringing to light the various psychodynamic and economic balances in each situation.

It needs to be stressed that in both of these situations the rightful identity of the person of different race is denied in the eyes of the beholder. To add insult to injury this person of different color is also *misused* as a person. On the one hand he is drawn within the sphere of old familiar incestuous conflicts, where he has no realistic significance, in order to try to tame him on familiar territory. On the other hand he is misappropriated as a pawn in an effort to solve overwhelming incestuous conflicts for which he has no realistic responsibility.

A point of disagreement here might be represented by the different view that it is only the pressure of the internalized unresolved incestuous conflicts which has any significance; if this pressure did not exist and spill over onto the new-colored person, the disturbed racial relationship would not arise. Without in any way minimizing the importance of such intense, unresolved, incestuous conflicts, I have represented the incestuous conflict as serving, *as well*, a defense against skin color anxiety. My view would be that to disregard the importance of the skin color component per se would be a denial of a reality—a denial of the existence of a basic skin color anxiety as a normal factor in human development. If skin color anxiety is denied, then its special conflicts, particularly those rooted in early separation and identity formation, can be denied.

A return to clinical examples may be clarifying. Frances, at five years, was at the height of her oedipal conflict (Example 30). During this period there was no evidence of any marked skin color anxiety, no evidence of difficulty with or having to avoid Negro friends in her class. But in her doll play she threw out the Negro girl dolls. On one level these girls represented herself in her oedipal defeat. The dolls got what she herself deserved for wanting to throw her mother away and have father for herself. On another, less obvious level the dolls probably represented her mother, reduced by Frances, in her oedipal victory, to a dark, dirty (recall her own wetting), castaway little Negro girl. Frances might have displaced this version of her oedipal conflicts onto the Negro girls in her class, and then had to fight with them and repeatedly reject them. (Here her solitary doll play served a valuable defensive purpose; she protected her friends from an aggressive treatment which she realized they did not deserve. Her disturbance in racial relations was confined to her dolls, and did not have to include her real Negro friends. This example demonstrates but one of the many values of having dolls of mixed race for children, of any color, to use in their play.)

Andrew was a child who often rejected his father, sometimes on realistic grounds but more often not. Whenever he found a way to belittle his father, in a comparison with white fathers, he took advantage of it. At times this belittling attitude was clearly that of a boy in an ordinary oedipal competition with his father. His father and mother would dress up and go out for a Saturday evening, leaving an openly jealous and distressed boy to remain at home with a babysitter. Sooner or later Andrew would strike a belittling blow at his father, subtly or openly criticizing him for being Negro. He cleverly knew how to succeed in his belittling so that father, mother and Andrew might *all* go through a stage of appearing to regard father as not very important, or grown up, or responsible. At these times Andrew found it all too easy to seize the throne his father had vacated next to his mother. Only when father recovered from the blow to his self-esteem would Andrew get dethroned, in a proper resolution of the oedipal rivalry. But at other times Andrew's belittling of his father's color appeared to contain very little of their oedipal competition. During times when Andrew was obviously in a stage of anxiety about his own color he blamed his father for having made him that color. In both of these states Andrew's mixed-race relationships became disturbed. He rejected Negro boys and men, as though they were his father, and he overvalued and demanded extra attention from white men (e.g., staff members and visitors to the school), trying to make them the idealized replacements for the father he had rejected and at the same time missed so much.

Should either of these children have remained fixed in these states of conflict they illustrate, it is possible that in later life these conflicts could appear as interferences in their racial relationships. Then they would become prejudiced people (see Chapter 7). Frances could reject Negro women, not so obviously for any skin color anxiety (which she had worked through in the formation of her friendships with Negroes) but as hated and degraded oedipal rivals. Andrew could idealize white men and reject Negro men in a defensive splitting apart of his oedipal conflicts onto separate good and bad fathers; or, he might do the same out of his unresolved skin color anxiety. Further, he might vacillate between these two different conflicts; at times using one as a defense against the other.

Another clinical example illustrates an earlier level of drive conflicts intertwined with skin color anxiety, and a corresponding difficulty in object relationships. A little Negro girl had many conflicts about her oral aggression. Since her aggressive impulses were often quickly pacified with sweets, reality tended to confirm her own estimate of the dangerousness of her biting and devouring impulses. The child also had many anxieties about her skin, which she cloaked in an oral disguise, in that she had many persnickety food fads, all based upon food colors. In her object relationships this little girl demonstrated marked characteristics of the oral phase of development. With some people she merged completely, needing to be not just with them but in every respect at one with and like them. With other people, she was totally rejecting, with the indiscriminate intolerance of an angry impatient infant toward anyone who is not the expected, demanded, gratifying mother.

Other clinical examples, illustrating progressive stages in the development toward mature object relationships with people of other races, are presented in the last section of Chapter 3. They require no further discussion here.

Skin color anxiety can lead to another kind of disturbance in object relationships, which can be measured along the second of the two developmental lines quoted above. In this disturbance a person who ordinarily appears able to make acceptable relationships reacts to his skin color anxiety by failing to make any meaningful relationship when confronted with a person of different skin color. He defensively withdraws into an egocentric state of caring only for himself and investing little or nothing in the threatening stranger. His withdrawal may be so complete that he avoids any confrontation at all, or even any awareness, of people with different skin colors. In effect, he notices and loves only himself; the threatening strangers do not exist. In this defensive shoring up of his narcissism with his self-love he is safeguarding his own identity, the integrity of his own personality. At the same time the strangely colored person ceases to be felt as a threat because he has little or no existence within the narcissistic limits of the world of self-love.

The clinical picture of such a disturbance (whether in a child or an adult) will be found to coincide with an immature level along the second of the two developmental lines described above. For the narcissistically withdrawn person, the other-colored person will not exist at all, or else he will bear the quality of an inanimate object, an obstruction, a toy to play with, a servant to be used, etc.

Once again, a point of disagreement might be raised by interpreting the defensive narcissistic withdrawal as a response to castration anxiety rather than a skin color anxiety. This interpretation says that the qualities "phallic" and "castrated" are displaced onto differing skin colors, and the castration anxiety then aroused by the sight of the different color is relieved by avoiding the "castrated" skin color and loving the "phallic" color. Such disturbances do exist and can be demonstrated clinically as an important etiology in some forms of disturbed racial relations. But once again, my view is that a displaced castration anxiety does not account for all narcissistic withdrawals from mixed-race relationships. Castration anxiety must not be used as a denial of skin color anxiety. And once again, only a psychoanalytic investigation of the clinical state can reveal what is castration anxiety, with its threat to sexual identity, and what is an underlying skin color anxiety, with its more basic threat to the earliest roots of identity as a separately existing individual.

A person who defensively retreats from a differently colored person into a state of heightened narcissism often needs some visible assurance of the intactness of his own skin color, and in turn his integrity of body and personality. He can get such assurance just by looking at himself, but he may also get it from his relationships with like-colored people. A person who must defensively cling to relationships with like-colored people may unconsciously be using them as reflections of his own image. He resembles the mythical Narcissus, who spent his time loving his own reflection in the pool, without recognizing that it was only himself he was gazing at so fondly. The racially prejudiced Narcissus of today relieves his skin color anxiety with the sight of his own reflection reassuringly shining back at him from his like-colored friends.[1]

In our nursery Jane was a child who avoided or withdrew from Negroes. She seemed especially frightened by the fact that some of the Negro girls so obviously made her their blond, white ego ideal, and either followed her about or reacted with open envy toward her. A puzzling observation about Jane came to light in assembling our cumulation of observations. Only then

[1] The myth of Narcissus is a story of castration anxiety and a narcissistic defense against it. While the anxiety is roused by the sight of castration, and not of differing skin color, the withdrawal to an egocentric self-love is the same defense mechanism as the one described above in relation to skin color anxiety. Narcissus rejected the Nymph, Echo, for whom he could feel no love. In her fated echoing of Narcissus' words, the story attempts to conceal Echo's fate as a *Nymph* that she could *not* "echo" his genitals. Narcissus' own sexual identity was too threatened by the sight of the "castrated" nymph to be able to love her. In a defensive effort to ward off the frightening sight, he gave his love instead to his own phallic reflection. The "echo" of his own reflection reassured him of the intactness of his own sexuality. An illustrator of the myth has demonstrated his understanding of Narcissus' conflict. He has drawn the naked Narcissus in profile, kneeling and gazing into the pool, but awkwardly positioned so that his genitals are protectively hidden by his buttocks, which dominate the picture. (See Thomas Bulfinch, *The Age of Fable*. New York: Heritage Press, 1942, pp. 101-104.)

did we discover that Jane was one of the very few children about whom we had made almost no observations. It was especially puzzling because we remember her as having been mentioned quite frequently during our work. But she had entered our observations primarily by means of the Negro children's views of her in working out their color conflicts. It seemed that we had tended to overlook evidence of Jane's own skin color anxiety and her efforts to resolve it. This oversight is a report not only about our own difficulty as observers but also about the nature of Jane's defense. Her defensive avoidance of and withdrawal from Negroes must often have proceeded quietly, without attracting any attention to herself. Jane all too easily got herself lost in the shuffle. Her skin color anxiety attracted attention only when she could not possibly avoid contact with Negroes.

Withdrawal to an egocentric position, especially if it is the sole reaction to a skin color anxiety, is a particularly dangerous mechanism because it leads away from object relationships. It cuts off not only new interracial relationships but also any helpful use of already existing relationships. So long as her teachers and family did not notice Jane's withdrawal they would not come to her aid. In contrast, a child actively struggling with his reactions to a child of a different race is striving toward formation of an interracial relationship. And in his struggles he is attracting attention and bidding for help. His efforts lead him to make good use of old relationships in order to expand his object world with new relationships.

The choice of mechanisms in response to skin color anxiety is a highly individual matter, not predictable and not yet fully understood, but determined by the individual's total biological and psychological development. It appears that primitive mechanisms are quite often aroused—introjections, projections, withdrawals, denials. All of these mechanisms carry the high price of forgoing any fair appraisal of and respect for the objective world of external reality. That is, a different-colored skin is no longer recognized for what it actually is, and its owner then cannot possibly be recognized for his own human and uniquely individual identity. It can be speculated that since skin color anxiety has its deepest root in the oral phase of development, through its threat to body image and the earliest foundations of identity, its arousal may favor a revival of primitive defensive mechanisms prevailing in the early phase of libidinal development.

It is possible to estimate a time at which a child ought to have acquired an ability to evaluate and relate to another person, of any color, as an individual in his own right. (There is no need to dwell further upon the fact that this time should be independent of the color of the skin and determined rather by the content of the character.) On the first of the two developmental lines quoted earlier in this chapter, a child must have attained Level Six; on the second line he must have attained Level Four (the final level). Not surprisingly, these levels correspond to the child's entry into latency. At that time the fundamental structural outlines of his own character are established. His early developmental conflicts have resolved and have undergone repression. His own identity has emerged and begun to stabilize as a result of the completion of the early developmental tasks, and he is capable of recognizing and allowing a similar, and yet different, identity development in others.

Perhaps, in our present state of social turmoil, it appears unrealistic to expect young latency children to achieve such an advanced level of interracial relationships. Nevertheless, it is reassuring that psychoanalytic formulations of intrapersonal development support our ultimate interpersonal goal of complete racial integration in our society. Psychoanalysts place a premium on the understanding of the content of the character as the final common pathway to improved relationships between people. They share with all unprejudiced people Martin Luther King's dream that the next generation will judge and relate to each other not by the color of their skin but by the content of their character.

7

A NOTE ABOUT PREJUDICE

The dictionary defines a prejudice as a judgment or opinion formed before the facts are known, and held in disregard of the facts that contradict it. Our clinical examples, with their ramifications throughout all developmental phases up to latency, abound with judgments and opinions formed before the facts are known, and held onto, at least for a while, in the face of contradictory facts. Yet there is not a single instance among them which would lead us to label it as an example of prejudice in any one of these children. Even before this declaration can be defended, most readers will sense at once the injustice of labeling as prejudice the mental processes at work in these developing minds. What the dictionary defines as prejudice must not fit the facts where these preschoolers are concerned. In spite of the dictionary their approaches to racial conflicts generally convey a healthy and unprejudiced quality, and we would like to be able to explain why this is so.

First, there is the matter of the *direction* in which each child's mental development is moving. These children are not controverting a reality they have already comprehended. Instead, in their "prejudiced" racial statements they are trying hard to discover more about a reality they have not yet had the opportunity to comprehend, in their young, undeveloped state. In so doing, they are moving in a healthy direction. A major developmental task facing them is the acquisition of an ability to appraise reality correctly, and they are trying to fulfill it. The intensity of their urge to comprehend the unknown reality compels our admiration, even when some of their conclusions about the world are obviously incorrect. Brown skin is not dirty skin. But we must allow a preschooler to draw this wrong conclusion, and even to contradict the facts presented to him for awhile, in order that he can come to discover his error and be stimulated to correct it. In fact, the more he can exercise this trial-and-error process, the better will be his eventual comprehension of reality, independent of whether it is pleasing or displeasing to him in relation to his inner fantasy world. The little girl who discovered for herself that the brown color of the Negro does not rub off was a true scientist (Example 10).

Second, there is the matter of *content* of the children's "prejudiced" statements. An examination of it (Chapters 5 and 6) soon leads us to an awareness of how familiar it all seems. The "prejudiced" statements are filled with nothing other than the old familiar developmental conflicts occupying the mind of any ordinary child in the years before latency. What gives these conflicts their prejudiced flavor is that they are being worked through in a place where, *eventually,* they will no longer belong —in the context of a mixed race relationship. But *at this point* their content is healthy and timely enough, when measured by normal drive and ego development, or particular events and traumas in an individual child's life. The fact that unrelated developmental conflicts intertwine with race conflicts does not at all suggest a prejudice formation in the prelatency child. On the contrary, this intertwining of skin color anxieties with other developmental conflicts is an aid to the resolution and segregation of both (Chapter 5). The temporary displacements of one upon the other are but a part of the healthy trial-and-error process toward conflict resolution and reality appraisal.

With the arrival of latency the dictionary definition of prejudice gradually becomes applicable. By the time a child reaches latency his early developmental conflicts are resolved and repressed and, under favorable circumstances, his skin color conflicts have also achieved some basic resolution. His reality appraisal is now quite well developed. He becomes capable of friendly, sustained relationships with another race, without danger of uncontrolled intrusions from unrelated, prelatency conflicts. And he does not feel the different-colored skin of a friend as a serious threat to his own identity formation. Internally his mind has become structuralized into organizations which allow him a growing regulation of his inner life. His sense of identity is gaining in stability, as are his appraisal and respect for conditions in the outer world.

If a child has not lived in an integrated community before latency, he has yet to experience the skin color anxiety produced in his first experiences with integration. But the combination of his ability to appraise reality and an overall healthy personality development leading into latency should provide him with the means to resolve his anxiety. During the resolution some old developmental conflicts may be reactivated, but their return should be transitory. With the arrival of latency a child should soon be able to come to a judgment or opinion about different-colored skin based upon fact. If instead he now fixes upon a judgment or opinion before the facts are appraised, and holds it in disregard of the facts that contradict it, then he may be on the way toward development of a prejudice.

The conclusion from the above is that racial prejudice is a condition which cannot appear before latency. At most, events before latency can lead to a suspicion that a young child may later on become prejudiced. Marked arrests and fixations in the face of ordinary developmental tasks and conflicts, when they become tenaciously attached to skin color differences, are ill omens.

The tendency to form prejudices is well recognized to be a universal human phenomenon. Generally the mechanisms and content of most ordinary prejudices can readily be detected as counterparts of the mechanisms and contents of ordinary developmental phases of early childhood. It is their misplacement from early childhood into later life which establishes them as prejudices. In this respect racial prejudices do not at all differ from other forms of prejudice, whether the rejected group is categorized by religion, residence, income, intelligence, etc.

"Prejudice" is only a descriptive, not a diagnostic (metapsychological) term. Like a fever, it can be symptomatic of a variety of conditions ranging in seriousness from an innocuous common cold to a fulminating pneumonia. In its mildest, most innocuous and transitory form a prejudice causes a remote enemy little harm and functions as a safety valve—although obviously not the most desirable form for a stabilizer—in the maintenance of an individual's psychic economy.[1] In its most malignant variant a prejudice can manifest itself in the form of malicious destruction of an enemy and/or collapse into serious mental disturbance, even psychosis.[2]

In the "ordinary" prejudice, although the content (racial, religious, etc.) varies, the basic mechanisms in its formation are quite uniform. A sector of reality—e.g., a differently colored person—rouses an unbearable anxiety. When this reality cannot be tolerated it may be avoided or denied. If it cannot be escaped by these methods, introjections and projections take over in order to rearrange reality, to cloak it in a disguise that will be bearable to the ego. This is not a psychotic process. The cathectic investments in reality are staunchly retained, and not relinquished as they would be in a psychotic process. Reality is only disguised, to suit the wishes and needs of the beholder. (In fact, from another viewpoint, these mechanisms leading to a disguising of reality can be seen as *protecting* the investment in reality, so that attachments to it can be maintained and psychosis warded off.) The mechanisms are infantile, not psychotic. But in the case of an infant they are healthy because he as yet has no way of appraising reality; he is busy trying to become better acquainted with it. Only in the older child and adult do the mechanisms take a turn away from health. The older child or adult has learned about and invested in reality, but out of anxiety about it he has given up his ability to appraise it correctly and respect it.

---

[1] See, in this connection, the summary of psychoanalytic contributions to the subject of prejudice, in Chapter 10, and in particular the reported discussion of a paper by Seitz (1960).

[2] See, in this connection, an account by Coles (1965) of the psychology of a paranoid member of a mob which was persecuting the first few Negro children to integrate a Southern school.

8

PSYCHOANALYSIS AND RACIAL INTEGRATION

At the present time psychoanalysis appears to have fallen into both public and professional disfavor, for reasons both sound and unsound. Among psychoanalysts themselves there is alarm for the future welfare of their profession. But healthy trends are unmistakably in evidence. Both public and profession are rejecting earlier unrealistically wishful expectations for psychoanalysis. Out of this shared disillusionment there seems to be growing a more realistic and discriminate use of psychoanalysis, both as a therapeutic and a research procedure. Furthermore, psychoanalysis is evidencing a growing appreciation for reality. This trend is reflected, for example, in the efforts of the American Psychoanalytic Association to find and use ways in which psychoanalysis can be in better touch with and contribute more effectively to the community. There is a recognition that sound community relationships are of mutual benefit and are necessary for the healthy survival of psychoanalysis.

In the earliest days of its existence the whole development of psychoanalysis for a time hinged upon Freud's recognizing that what his hysterical patients claimed as infantile realities were instead infantile fantasies. With this discovery there followed a general turning away from reality. Developmentally this *temporary* de-emphasis of external reality factors protected the penetrating investigations of inner psychological realities. (For example, in 1908, Little Hans's tonsillectomy was almost entirely overlooked during his analysis in the efforts to elucidate the internalized aspects of his phobic anxieties and developmental conflicts [Freud, 1909]. Nowadays, with the many advances psychoanalysis has made, Hans's tonsillectomy would have top

priority in his analysis.) But gradually, once inner world events
became better understood, verified, and accepted, psychoanalytic
attention could return again to outer world influences. The protective de-emphasis of reality had served its purpose, and to continue it further would only have delayed psychoanalytic development. As this de-emphasis of reality has been abandoned as an
anachronism, psychoanalysis has evinced a growing appreciation
for reality factors and the adaptational demands they make upon
the development of the mind.

The development of child analysis has helped greatly to redi-
rect psychoanalytic attention to the influences of the external
upon the internal world. Through his clinical work the child
analyst has reached a recognition of the power of the environment to distort a child's internal personality development, just as
the adult analyst before him had discovered the power of an adult
internalized disturbance to distort the external world. Anna
Freud (1965, pp. 51-52) comments:

> While the analysts of adults have to remind themselves of the frustrating,
> external, precipitating causes of the disorder of their patients, so as not to
> be blinded by the powers of the inner world, the child analysts have to
> remember that the detrimental external factors which crowd their view
> achieve their pathological significance by way of interaction with the in-
> nate disposition and acquired, internalized libidinal and ego attitudes.
>
> Together the two procedures, adult and child analysis, may help to
> maintain the balanced outlook demanded by Freud's etiological formula of
> a sliding scale of internal and external influences: that there are people
> whose "sexual constitution would not have led them into a neurosis if they
> had not had . . . [certain] experiences, and these experiences would not
> have had a traumatic effect on them if their libido had been otherwise dis-
> posed" (S. Freud, 1916-1917, p. 347).

In many of her writings Anna Freud has been especially concerned with "the translation of external events into internal experience" (see, for example, 1965, p. 56). In this process of internalization it is the developing personality within the child which
acts as the translator of the external event. *Internal* forces select
the special language of the child's translation. The process of
translation can at best be assisted, but not directed, by favorable

external influence such as an empathic adult can supply. (The adult can act as a buffer between the external and internal worlds of the child. Further, he can reinforce and supplement the child's tenuous secondary process—logical—thinking. In this way he can help to modify a child's tendency to misinterpret external events in terms of id-derived fantasies of abandonment, hostile attack, etc.)

In this country it is evident to all that at the core of our current social crisis is the problem of racial integration. This is an external reality which psychoanalysis cannot ignore. Much more important, it is a crisis to which psychoanalysis can make its own significant contribution.

In a variety of ways psychoanalytic findings support the need for external change. The most crucial finding is that racial integration is necessary for optimum development of the foundations of the personality in young children. But psychoanalysis also cautions that mere external change cannot determine the nature of the child's "translation into internal experience" of his racially integrated environment. If the cues of racial anxieties from the child's internal translators are not recognized, a personality foundation that is prone to later development of prejudice can still occur, even in the best racially integrated environment.

Psychoanalysis can make known the nature of the internal forces which operate within the child as he responds to an integrated environment. Psychoanalysis can explain the existence of a basic skin color anxiety as a normal and necessary internal response to confrontation with skin color differences. To know that such anxiety exists, and to know that it is a normal, expectable happening is fundamental to the healthy resolution of its accompanying conflicts. If this anxiety goes unrecognized, unnamed, then conflict resolution and in turn racial adaptation become immensely more difficult. Adults would deny evidence of racial anxiety in children, and children would be left on their own to find solutions to racial problems which they are not supposed to have or to notice. What psychoanalysis can do is to encourage the recognition of this normal skin color anxiety and to promote an understanding of the ways in which children can be helped to resolve it, particularly in the early stages of personality development.

Psychoanalysis can also make known the special gains in personality development that come from *early* racial integration. The racially integrated infant and preschooler gains a special advantage to his own identity formation. He gains a greater thoroughness of resolution of his ordinary developmental conflicts. He gains a greater ability to form and maintain object relationships, including those with members of other races.

This is vital information which psychoanalysis has at its disposition. It demonstrates that psychoanalysis is in full agreement with racial integration, not just on general moral and social principles, but upon unique *psychoanalytic* grounds. From a psychoanalytic point of view racial integration is not merely desirable but essential for sound personality development in a multiracial society. Neighborhoods and schools, including nursery schools, must bring racial integration into the lives of children.

PART III

THE LITERATURE

We conclude that in the field of public education the doctrine of 'separate but equal' has no place. Separate educational facilities are inherently unequal.

—Chief Justice Earl Warren
May 17, 1954

9

A HISTORICAL SURVEY

In 1929 Bruno Lasker published his book, *Race Attitudes in Children*. Although sometimes passed over as anecdotal and unscientific, it is in fact a forthright documentation of the evil effects of segregation upon children of all races, everywhere in the United States. It is the first of a series of publications whose combined pressures eventually helped move this country toward integration. After Lasker's book a decade went by—a decade of economic depression—before more publications began to appear.

In the 1940's and early 1950's the sociologists and anthropologists carried on Lasker's mission to expose the evils of segregation where they worked their worst effects—upon the development of children. Their styles and methods of investigation varied widely. Some stressed social scientific method as an end in itself and professed less concern with how the results of their studies might be used. Others concentrated less upon tests and statistical studies and more upon individual human examples, from which they tried to extract conclusions and recommendations. There can be no doubt, however, that all shared the same humane motivation to make a social scientific protest against segregation. A few writings by psychiatrists, psychologists, and educators appeared and confirmed the work of the social scientists. So did some sociological writings about prejudice, not confined to the age range of childhood (e.g., Allport's *The Nature of Prejudice*, 1954). Psychoanalytic publications of comparable quality, except for a few on anti-Semitic prejudice, do not exist from this period. Three psychoanalysts who did write about the Negro published their contributions in sociological references (McLean, 1946, 1949; Sterba, 1947; Spitz, 1951).

A review of this early literature makes it apparent that a consistent concern for the welfare of *children* living under segregation led the social scientists, more than any other professional group, to persist in their efforts. They were the ones who amassed the damning testimony of the effects of segregation throughout all of childhood and adolescence. The younger the child the graver seemed the evidence, and the facts they unearthed about the damage to three- and four-year-old children hit hard blows at segregation.

On May 17, 1954 came the Supreme Court's *Brown* decision, outlawing public school segregation. Chief Justice Earl Warren, delivering the unanimous opinion of the Court in one of the simplest and most moving documents in American history[1] wrote:

> We conclude that in the field of public education the doctrine of "separate but equal" has no place. Separate educational facilities are inherently unequal. Therefore, we hold that the plaintiffs and others similarly situated for whom the actions have been brought are, by reason of the segregation complained of, deprived of the equal protection of the laws guaranteed by the Fourteenth Amendment.

In a preceding paragraph Chief Justice Warren acknowledged the Court's reliance upon the work of social scientists:

> Whatever may have been the extent of psychological knowledge at the time of *Plessy v. Ferguson* [1896], this finding ["separate educational facilities are inherently unequal"] is amply supported by modern authority.[11] Any language in *Plessy v. Ferguson* contrary to this finding is rejected.

"Footnote 11," now famous, cites seven references. The first two are the work of Kenneth B. Clark, as summarized for the Midcentury White House Conference on Children and Youth (1950). These seven references are taken from an appendix to the appellant's brief, prepared by thirty-five leading social scientists, and presented to the Supreme Court. The appendix cites nearly sixty references.

---

[1] "Perhaps not since the Declaration of Independence has a public federal document stressed the importance of personal feelings as an item of political consideration. The Supreme Court decision was in part based on personal, psychological, and sociological data showing that segregation constitutes a psychological and personal handicap." (Group for the Advancement of Psychiatry Report #37, 1957, p. 13.)

On May 17, 1954 the United States committed itself to racial integration. Three years later our legal and moral commitment was broadened when Congress enacted a bill of civil rights.

It is of interest that prior to the *Brown* decision there does not seem to be much emphasis in the literature upon changing the laws as a means of undermining segregation. In their efforts to come up with recommendations based upon their findings, the social scientists confined themselves mostly to educational approaches, and particularly to approaches which would reach young children. For example, in *Race Awareness in Young Children*, Mary Ellen Goodman (1952, p. 217) wrote:

> The preceding chapters have surely demonstrated that there is no "it"—no prejudice unit-of-personality—in our children. . . . Still, prejudice is no simple unit-of-personality in adults either, and talking as though it were, only confuses the issue. . . .
>
> What we have to deal with is not a simple matter. It is a complex set of causes, lying behind a complex set of ideas, habits, and feelings. So, if grownups are to give children tools for building racial democracy, they must cope with complex causes and complex results. They must remove or alleviate the conditions which directly or indirectly promote the growth of antagonistic cross-racial orientations in children. They must also strengthen and support the conditions which directly or indirectly promote cross-racial friendliness or, better still, which promote a race-free view of society.
>
> Before we talk about ways and means of accomplishing these ends, we must acknowledge the fact that a great many earnest and informed people throughout the United States are working to accomplish them. *Our major point here, and the major practical implication to this study, is that too few of these people are working with young children.*

In the remainder of the chapter Goodman goes on to discuss how young children can be helped, through discussion with unprejudiced adults, to achieve democratic racial attitudes.

Why do sociological writings before the *Brown* decision reflect so little pressure to bring about integration through legal reform? Perhaps the Supreme Court's refusal to reverse the decision of the lower court in the case of Martha Lum, in 1928, was a major deterrent to any hopes for reforms through the Courts. In Martha Lum's case the Court was upholding the "separate but equal" doctrine proclaimed in its *Plessy v. Ferguson* decision in 1896 (a decision involving transportation, not education, of the races). Martha Lum was a nine-year-old Chinese child whose father protested her classification as nonwhite by the state of Mississippi, a classification which required Martha to attend a Negro school. For her, "separate but equal" meant attending a Negro school, where expenditure per child was $2.26, instead of a white school, where the expenditure per child was $43.33 (Lasker). Kurland, in his review of the legal background of the school segregation cases (in Kenneth B. Clark's, *Prejudice and Your Child*), calls the Court's action in the Lum case the "high-water mark of the separate but equal" doctrine.

In the years following the *Brown* decision there developed a widespread recognition that this legal reform had been an absolute prerequisite to achieving any social reform. The social scientists, now increasingly joined by the psychiatrists, discovered that only the necessity of obeying the law would bring the vast law-abiding citizenry to accept and practice some degree of racial integration. To have awaited a hoped-for voluntary change in mass racial attitudes, as a prerequisite to legal reform, would have been an endless wait. Such a change in psychological attitudes depended upon improved physical integration, and only a change in the law of the land could enforce this necessary physical integration. Only the reality of physical integration could force out of hiding and into open conscious conflict the many unconscious roots of racial prejudice which had so gripped the country.

In the 1960's, at Hanna Perkins School, we had to discover for ourselves what the pioneers of the 1950's had already learned. Psychological integration cannot proceed in a segregated environment. The everyday reality of physical integration is the absolute prerequisite of psychological integration.

In the era before the *Brown* decision, Lasker and his many successors had to demonstrate two important facts. Patiently and repeatedly they had to prove that there is no "prejudice unit-of-personality" (Goodman)—that prejudice does not arise from within as a manifestation of a bad seed. Consequently it was natural and necessary for them to *emphasize the cultural contributions* which induced prejudice and all of its bad effects in children. It was also natural and necessary to *underemphasize the child's own intrapsychic contributions*—his innate drives and his conflicts concerning them—to the formation of his prejudices. In the prevailing climate, it would have been almost impossible to give intrapsychic factors their due without at the same time being misunderstood as giving support to the erroneous bad-seed, "prejudice unit-of-personality" theory. With this underemphasis upon internal factors, the "intrapsychic" scientists could only stand by and wait. Meanwhile the social scientists steadily exposed the deformities in child development that were culturally induced by segregation and prejudice, and the realistic cultural guilt that belonged to them.

The second fact which the social scientists had to demonstrate was that the Negro is not an inferior being. They worked at exposing to the white majority the evidence that Negroes have thoughts and feelings which originate and function exactly like "white" thoughts and feelings. The white myth of the simple inferior Negro, happy in his childlike dependency, which had served so long as the favorite rationalization for white guilt, had to be dispelled. Powdermaker (1943), for example, exposed the enormity of human aggressive conflicts that arise within the Negro who is forced to live under the constraint of this white myth.

The *Brown* decision initiated slow but definite cultural changes. With nationwide attention focused upon the first Negro children to integrate Southern white schools, it was no longer possible for many whites to remain unaware of their prejudice and guilt.

As the country began to change, the social scientists began to draw in help from their colleagues. Desegregation brought conflicts about it to the surface within individuals caught up in this cultural change. In this way the process of desegregation brought about new conditions which invited the entry of the "intrapsychic" scientists into racial problems. Clinicians were needed to treat and to give advice about the newly evolving conflicts and anxieties. Significant psychiatric and psychological publications began to appear. Educators began looking for guides to understanding the psychological problems of segregation and desegregation, and themselves began to publish their own experiences. A significant publication in the 1950's was that of the Committee on Social Issues, of the Group for the Advancement of Psychiatry, *Psychiatric Aspects of School Desegregation* (1957). In the 1960's the writings of the psychiatrist, Robert Coles, are outstanding. Coles studied the psychological states of Negro children, their families, their teachers, and their white classmates and families in the process of desegregation.

Probably the most prominently observed intrapsychic condition in the race studies of the 1950's and 1960's has been that of self-esteem. The universal low self-esteem of Negro children, and the universal low esteem which white children had for them concerned everybody. While cultural factors lost none of their culpability, intrapsychic factors—such as the emotional significance of the color brown—began to draw some attention. Even so, the emphasis continued to be placed on the necessary altering of external factors as a correction for self-esteem conflicts. Indeed, there can be no letup in this emphasis until racial integration is achieved.

Now, in the late 1960's the first reports of improved self-esteem among Negro children are beginning to appear. They accompany the Negro's growing conscious awareness and constructive channeling outward of his aggression. In writing of Northern Negro children, in 1968, Coles says:

> In contrast to their counterparts in the South, these Northern Negro children evidence more explicit anger and bitterness toward white people. Their racially connected fears and resentments are more directly in their awareness, and have been expressed to this white observer far less hesitatingly than was the case in Georgia or Louisiana [p. 14].

In the same publication Coles quotes a Northern Negro mother at length. She stands in awe of her nine-year-old son's freely verbalized angry denunciations of the white people, and her five-year-old daughter's equally vehement words and feelings. She says that her children tell her:

> . . . we've got to keep pushing, and we can't let "the white" beat on us no more, and we should go across town [Boston] and tell them to give us what we should have been having three hundred years ago.

When this mother tried to silence her son he called her a "black coward."

> . . . he tells me we're to blame, because if we had gone and told the white man a long time ago that enough is enough, then they wouldn't be on top of us now.

Contrast her children's words with those of the same mother, describing her own Southern upbringing:

> My mother, she used to tell us kids we shouldn't even let *ourselves* know what we're thinking and wanting. And even in church, she'd say we should be careful what we pray for, because you never can tell, you can get in trouble for being "uppity," even if you *look* "uppity" when you comes out of church. The white man he'll see you and tell you, "Nigger, you look too smart!"

Coles comments:

> Since I first started my work, eight years ago, a sense of racial pride has become evident in many of these children—even as they continue to struggle with feelings of shame and worthlessness. Most of all, they seem hurt—not necessarily "damaged," but hurt—by what they sense to be an almost inescapable fate, which they yet struggle to overcome.
>
> . . . I find a certain angry cynicism in even the youngest of these children that I rarely encountered in the South from 1958 to 1965. I now find Southern children similarly cynical, but still less so than Northern ghetto children.
>
> . . . One is also impressed by the responsiveness these children show to contemporary events. Just as the Negro children of the South watched what happened in Little Rock or New Orleans as if they themselves were participants, Northern children are quick to speak the various slogans and claim as their own the various political or racial attitudes they hear voiced in the ghetto. I found these children—coming from diverse backgrounds—much more aware of the Negro's general problems in American society than I had expected. Again, perhaps Northern city life makes for such awareness, or such frankness. Or perhaps Negroes today have less hope—

or fewer illusions—than they did in 1960 or 1963 [pp. 7-11].[2]

There are as yet only a few psychoanalytic writings about skin color conflicts. Except for Spitz's brief report (1951), based upon his observations of institutionalized infants, there are no published studies by psychoanalysts regarding race and children. Only a few reports contain any clinical material about racial problems from psychoanalyses of adults—white or Negro. A few more contain generalized psychoanalytic formulations, loosely if at all tied to clinical evidence. The latter have a tendency to produce irritation in other professional people with extensive firsthand experience in the field of racial problems. In addition, when generalizations about unconscious processes are erroneously interpreted as universal facts about consciousness, there is a danger that they can distort the results of sound clinical studies.

As this chronological review has demonstrated, progress in racial problems has required an expansion of scientific activity

---

[2] In 1968 we extended our Hanna Perkins staff meetings for a time to include teachers from four other Day Nursery Association schools located throughout greater Cleveland. At semimonthly meetings there were both Negro and white teachers, representing schools of all degrees of integration and socioeconomic levels. Recently a Negro teacher in an all-Negro ghetto school asked each of her fourteen four-year-old nursery school children whether they knew what color they were. All but one knew they were "black" or "colored" or "Negro." ("Brown" has recently replaced "black" as the objectionable word.) Several combined their answers with current slogans or songs of black pride. Some even knew that they were "Afro-American." When the teacher later talked to the children's parents she learned that every parent had talked about race with his child and had told him what color he was! The teacher, who had had many reservations about undertaking this inquiry, even though it was her own idea, was astonished at what she learned. So was everyone at our staff meeting. Soon after, another Negro teacher, from an almost all-Negro school in a less deprived area carried out a similar inquiry in her own school. This time we were surprised at the contrasting results. Seven children knew their color correctly, two misidentified themselves as white, and four Negro children did not know what color they were. None of their parents had discussed race with their children or made it a point to identify their own color for them.

In the ghetto there is an active effort by the adults to reject whiteness and internalize blackness (see Chapter 4, footnote 2). This effort appears to promote a realistically colored body image as part of their identity formation in young children and in turn to promote a realistic self-esteem in them. In the less deprived Negro area, the persisting conflict between wishful white ideals and degraded brown self-images seems to be reflected in confused, ambivalent, and inhibited reactions of parents toward their children's racial conflicts. Development of a realistically colored body image and a realistic self-esteem in these children is then blocked.

from evironmental toward intrapsychic approaches. While this development is still in progress certain focal points of research in various fields are helping to unravel the complex issues of racial comparisons and contrasts. As already described, sociologists and others have endeavored to prove that racial prejudice is not inborn—in a sense, that the white race is not inferior through being born prejudiced. Psychological studies of Negro children have been conducted in an attempt to establish whether or not the Negro is inferior, especially in intellectual capacity. But test findings which seemingly demonstrate racial inferiorities require cautious interpretation; otherwise the interpretation itself might reflect only a prejudice of the interpreter.

Research into the effects of early deprivation, both physical and mental, is particularly significant. Factors which might be regarded as innate, constitutional, inherently inferior, are increasingly recognized as regularly associated with deprivations early in life, *regardless of race*. Longitudinal studies of the early effects of malnutrition suggest that intellectual capacity can be irreversibly stunted by malnutrition in the first two years of life (see Chapter 10). Psychoanalytic studies of infancy have demonstrated the devastatingly stunting effects of maternal deprivation upon the development of psychic structure.

These findings about the irreparable blocking of maturation through early deprivation of food and mothering have an important bearing upon any studies designed to demonstrate racial differences or inferiorities. As deprived infants age, but fail to mature adequately, they do indeed become inferior. Research findings on the effects of early deprivations prevent misinterpretation of findings of inferiority, later in life, as proofs of innate racial inferiority. Currently, the effect on the American Negro of early deprivations imposed by his poverty—a condition which has been denied as a part of the denial of racial conflicts—is just beginning to receive the nationwide concern that it needs. Adequate nutrition, adequate opportunity for early mothering (or substitute mothering, when an unmothered mother cannot be a mother), and early intellectual stimulation through specialized preschool programs are taking their proper places as basic issues upon which to base social reforms. Only when white and Negro children have an equal opportunity for comparable environments from the beginning of life will it be possible to obtain valid studies of innate racial differences.

Major omissions in this brief historical review of the modern literature of racial conflict are the fields of fiction and biography. Writers such as Lillian Smith, Richard Wright, and more recently others too numerous to name, have turned personal experience and talent into artistic expression of universal truths about personality development in racially conflicted America. They have much to tell us.

10

A REVIEW OF THE LITERATURE

The reviews which follow are arranged according to professional specialty. The references included do not represent an exhaustive review of the literature, particularly in the fields of sociology, social work, psychology, and education. Nor are the reviews of these references intended to be critical and complete. In each case the intent is to give a brief comprehensive review of the author's work, and then to select for special attention those sections which bear a close relationship to our own clinical and theoretical work.

SOCIOLOGY

Lasker's book, *Race Attitudes in Children* (1929) is a report of the work of a national organization, called "The Inquiry," composed of social, educational, and religious workers. They participated in discussion groups, collected reports, and reviewed results of an extended questionnaire mailed to 800 people throughout the United States who were known to be interested in race relations. Lasker acknowledges the unscientific method and the inevitable inaccuracies; nevertheless, the book contains much of interest. It also fulfills its goals of establishing evidence that race attitudes are present very early in life, and of calling attention to the need for further study of the effect of the prejudiced adult world upon young children. The book is arranged in four sections: I. Race attitudes of children; II. How they have been acquired; III. What intentional teaching has gone into their formation; and IV. How they may be modified. The book is excellent in its exposure of the many sources from which children learn prejudiced attitudes. The section on the biased presenta-

tions of history, civics, and geography in schools is no different
from the writings of today, which are finally leading to reform in
the content of these courses. The plea for removal of prejudiced
attitudes in that specialty of American literature, the comic strip,
is just now, forty years later, being recognized, as Negro children
begin to make their appearance in the daily comic strips and
Negro adults enter the white world of the *New Yorker* and other
magazine cartoons.

The book is especially good in the portrayal of children's
feelings, and consequently the case histories come alive as real
children who stick in the reader's memory. Lasker closes his
book with a forceful paragraph, which speaks better than any
description could do of the scope and character of the book's content (pp. 383f.):

> As we close the book, however, it is not so much of the technical tasks that
> we think, as of a procession of boys and girls we have met in these pages:
> Martha Lum, denied an education by decision of the Supreme Court of
> the United States, the little boy who was deprived of his white playmate,
> the bewildered southern boy in the northern school, the Jewish adolescent
> who grew too quickly into maturity to retain the friendship of his pals, the
> Chinese child "made much of" as a pet and subsequently neglected, the
> Mexican boy who fought himself into appreciative recognition by the Jew-
> ish and Italian gangs who could not come together on anything except to
> "beat up the niggers," the five-year-old in the Baltimore street-car, the
> innumerable children frightened with accounts of "black men" and pic-
> tures of bloodthirsty savages, children often crippled in mind and future
> experience by propagandist tools wielded for the benefit of selfish interest.[1]
> Generation after generation we see them pass by—children who are given
> the stones of fictitious stereotypes when they ask for the bread of knowl-
> edge, children of all races and all nationalities made the potential cannon-
> fodder of future wars because they are not permitted to develop in them-
> selves those qualities of mind that make for a sense of fair play, for mutual
> appreciation, for mental flexibility in response to changing situations. It is
> to these children, burdened with the material costs of past wars and with
> the inheritance of limiting social attitudes that society owes its greatest
> unacknowledged debt.
>
> [Lasker's footnote 1:] The *comprachicos*, according to Victor Hugo's
> novel, *The Laughing Man*, were a wandering gypsy tribe of the seven-
> teenth century, already well forgotten in the eighteenth, who plied a

ghastly and horrible business. The word, an abbreviation of the Spanish *comprapequenos*, means a buyer of children. These loathsome people never stole children, as certain gypsies are supposed to have done; they bought them, but for a terrible purpose. As our plastic surgeons seek today to eliminate physical defects and so to render the human face more beautiful, so these *comprachicos* studied how they might take the fair forms of children they had purchased and convert them into monstrosities and hunchbacks at whose antics the courtiers of Europe might be amused.

The day of the *comprachicos* is happily long since past. We would no longer tolerate the conversion of the young into hideous oddities. We insist on the right of all children to a normal and natural physical development. But there are still some who would force the spiritual and intellectual development of the child into cruel channels of dogma and curriculum, instead of allowing adequate opportunity for its individual nature to express itself.—*The World's Youth, April, 1926.*

In Chapter I Lasker includes many examples of racial attitudes in early childhood, illustrating fear, cruelty, combativeness, and ridicule in children's reactions. Many of his examples duplicate our own, and those of others to be reported below. He quotes the example of a one-year-old white baby taken by the parents to visit a grandmother living in a Mexican colony. The infant was very frightened of the dark Mexicans, but not of the strange white grandmother. Lasker points out that it is, of course, necessary to know more of the circumstances before the child's anxiety could be realistically attributed to the dark color of the Mexicans. (An unavoidable difficulty throughout the book lies in the unknown capacities and limitations of the countless observers.) However, he goes on to mention the lack of fear of Mexicans in an eight-month-old white baby, raised from birth in a Mexican community, "where colored or other people of a very distinct race form part of the accepted daily environment, children are not afraid of them, normally." (See our Example 4.)

There are many examples of racial reactions in young children believed to have been raised in both prejudiced and unprejudiced homes. One example, of a child said to be from an unprejudiced home, I have not come across elsewhere in the literature or in our own work. Lasker describes a five-year-old white boy's growing apprehension as a Negro classmate approached him. When the Negro came too close to bear, the white child said, "Look out, little black child, don't breave your black bref on me!" (See Chapter 4, footnote 3, regarding Freud's case of the Wolf Man.)

Lasker notes the importance of the different look of another race to a child. Concerning the nature and origin of a child's fear, he says the following:

> The existing confusion on the nature of first exhibitions of fear in children in the presence of certain phenomena is simply due to faulty observation; and the controversy as to whether certain fears are instinctive or acquired might quickly yield to agreement if there were a sufficient body of accurate and complete data. . . .
>
> All observations made carefully and over a sufficient length of time suggest that it is unprofitable to study race attitudes apart from other aspects of child psychology. If most of the noticeable reactions of small children to race are fear reactions, as seems to be the fact, we shall do well to acquaint ourselves more thoroughly with the nature and causes of fear in childhood. [pp. 8, 10].

In these words Lasker has expressed the aims of our work at Hanna Perkins.

Concerning the question of instinct, Lasker—in 1929— briefly mentions Freud's work, and notes that instinct theory is "at the present time one of the most controversial topics in the whole field of psychology." It is evident that he is eager to disprove the concept of an inherent "instinctive" race attitude and to expose it as a rationalization for cultural guilt. Like so many others, he appears to confuse an inherent "instinctive" capacity for anxiety with the concept of an inherent "instinctive" prejudice.

In 1940 Allison Davis and John Dollard published their book, *Children of Bondage: The Personality Development of Negro Youth in the Urban South.* It is a worthwhile sociological study of the effects of deprivation and segregation on the Southern Negro child. Their emphasis is upon portrayal of individuals through extensive interviewing. They give recognition to the fact that personality development arises from "reactive tendencies" in the child which meet family and cultural pressures. In the Southern Negro the end result of personality formation is an individual whose main concern is with his own survival and his efforts to maintain sufficient self-esteem to value survival. In another publication Davis (1939) reports the appalling statistics of broken families in the Negro population of various states throughout the country. He demonstrates how ineffective such homes are for raising children who must live in American society. In 1946 Davis and Havighurst studied "Social Class and Color Differences in Child Rearing" by means of interviews with 200 mothers, equally divided among four groups—middle-class whites and Negroes, and lower-class whites and Negroes, in Chicago. Their findings about feeding, weaning, toilet training, and encouragement of ego functions in these social groups are of great interest. Among their conclusions, they state:

> There are considerable social class differences in child-rearing practices, and these differences are greater than the differences between Negroes and whites of the same social class. . . . The same type of difference exists between middle- and lower-class Negroes as between middle- and lower-class whites. . . . Thus there are *cultural differences* in the personality formation of middle-class, compared with lower-class people, *regardless of color*, due to their early training [pp. 707, 710].

The work of Davis and his colleagues goes a long way toward dispelling the notion that Negroes are inherently inferior people.

Powdermaker (1943) studied the vicissitudes of aggression in the Negro, in the course of her field work in the rural South. She asks the question whether the Negro really did accept his position as a slave, or whether it aroused aggression. She says it was a "myth" that during slavery there were no criminal Negroes. Some risked horrible punishments—among them, castration—in committing every conceivable crime. Thousands ran away. Powdermaker is more concerned, however, with the Negro who appears on the surface to be unaggressive. She borrows from psychoanalysis to explain the repression of aggression in the course of the Negro's development. Following the freeing of the slaves the Negro remained dependent upon the white man. Then he defensively displaced his aggression from the white man to other Negroes, and at the same time he identified with his white employer to achieve a gain in self-esteem. He developed a masochistic defense (T. Reik), which relieved his guilt and permitted him to gain power by enduring suffering for a later reward in heaven. Powdermaker stated that in the Negro this character was not neurotic, but adaptive to the culture and to his survival in it. She said that this type of character, with its walling off of direct expression of aggression, describes many Negroes she met in the course of her work in the South. Like Davis's work, Powdermaker's observations and conclusions do a great service in elevating the Negro to the rank of a human being with ordinary human drives, feelings, and conflicts. Powdermaker does not stop there. She draws the very important conclusion—in 1943—that the Negro's goals will have to be obtained by the release of aggression in the service of an aggressive struggle with American segregated culture. The struggle must be carried out in *this* world, not later in heaven. Now, twenty-five years later, her predictions are coming true.

The Mark of Oppression, by Kardiner and Ovesey (1951), although often quoted as authoritative, contains little to recommend it. The authors used Negroes as subjects to demonstrate "the application of psychodynamics to a specific problem [the problem of race] in the social sciences." The authors dispensed with previous sociological studies of the American Negro and in effect claimed to be the first to demonstrate the influences of cultural pressure on the Negro "for our data derive from the examination of new source material, namely the Negro individual himself." Their method is that of "psychodynamic biography." Twenty-five Negroes were studied by "psychoanalytic interview technique" consisting of once, twice, or three times weekly sessions, for a minimum of 20 to a maximum of 100 visits. One author studied or treated the cases, the other drew the psychodynamic conclusions from the protocols, and Goldfarb, a psychologist, interpreted Rorschach tests administered to all the subjects by another psychologist. His scoring was "blind" in that he was given no other information about the subjects. The subjects for the study were obtained from "the lure of therapeutic gain" (12 cases), "the incentive of scientific cooperation" (2 cases), and the lure of monetary remuneration (11 subjects).

This study in no sense establishes conditions necessary for valid psychoanalytic investigation, and therefore the conclusions about unconscious dynamics and personality structure cannot be regarded as valid. Cultural and intrapsychic factors are confused. The conclusions even suggest a discrimination and prejudice. For example, the authors state, "The affectivity potential is apparently higher [in middle and upper class Negroes] than in lower class Negroes and they have more capacity for relatedness." Although claiming themselves to be psychoanalytic, the authors do not understand defenses against feelings. In claiming that any Negroes have less capacity to feel, they dehumanize and depreciate them. In so doing, they counteract the efforts of other sociologists, e.g., Powdermaker, to demonstrate the human and equal worth of the Negro precisely because of his equal capacity to feel, as well as to defend from consciousness his unbearable feelings. More broadly, the authors state, "Is there such a thing as a basic personality for the Negro? This work proves decidedly that there is . . . a caricature of the corresponding white personality." But in their wish to discover universal personality characteristics in Negroes, through original scientific investigation, they produce only another version of a racial stereotype of Negroes. They do not make clear any difference between constitutional difference and weakness, and developmental distortions of personality.

A remarkable feature of the Rorschach reports is that 88 percent of the group tested showed color shock to the test cards, and 100 percent showed shading shock. Interpretations of these findings were made in relation to anxiety and hostility, but no comment was made about their meaning in relation to skin color and shading.

In 1952 Goodman's book on *Race Awareness in Young Children* was published. In his Introduction, Kenneth Clark calls this book "a model of systematic and objective research." He further states, "The work . . . may be viewed as an important bridge between those studies which were primarily seeking an understanding of the development of racial attitudes in children [Lasker, Eugene and Ruth Horowitz] and those which were concerned with the personality concomitance of racial awareness and identification [Kenneth and Mamie Clark]. On the levels of both theory and method, her work is eclectic. Her principal focus, however, is that of the cultural anthropologist. . . . Through a series of intensive case studies, Dr. Goodman investigates the complex processes underlying intergenerational persistence of the culturally predominant pattern of 'white over brown' " (p. 11). In her own introduction, Goodman says, "There are offered here some inventories of the thoughts and feelings of young children, brown and white, and some evidence concerning the background hows and whys. These inventories focus upon a rather little-known part of the young child's thought and feeling systems—upon his awareness of race differences and his feelings about those differences" (p. 13). In the years 1943 to 1948, Goodman and her co-workers studied 103 four-year-old children, 57 Negro and 46 white, attending three different nursery schools in a "transitional" zone of a large Northeastern seaboard city. It is a sensitive study, respectful in the dignity of its four-year-old subjects, their parents, and their teachers. The investigators spent enough time in the schools, before undertaking any formal studies, so that children and teachers became acquainted with them. On the strength of their relationships they then undertook a series of interviews and tests with the children. They asked them questions, gave them puzzle tests, showed them pictures, and gave them dolls to play with. The tests, pictures, and dolls were representative of both Negro and white children, and the overall approach was aimed at encouraging the children to reveal to a friendly and known observer as much as possible of their racial awareness. Sometimes it was necessary to explore painful thoughts and feelings which the children presented, and Goodman notes how painful this was for the examiners to do. But through their efforts the children readily told them a wealth of information about their extensive racial awareness.

When their parents and teachers learned of the results of the investigation they were amazed at what their children knew. In their own unawareness there was concealed a massive denial of their children's reactions to racial difference.

Goodman quotes many individual examples from these four-year-olds. They differ hardly at all from our examples of Hanna Perkins children, twenty years later, from a large Northern city on the coast of the Great Lakes. Skin color was the main focus of concern; hair quality, though important, was secondary. The Negro children sometimes denied their color, sometimes called it dirty and wanted to scrub it off, and uniformly presented a low self-esteem and an envy of white skin. White children shared the same judgmental attitude about the superiority of white skin. Goodman says, "Not all our children feel so strongly, or perhaps they are not so much given to putting their feelings into words. But a fourth of them said enough to make it clear that, among four-year-olds, their systems of race-related values are strongly entrenched" (p. 47).

As part of her study Goodman related racial awareness and feelings to other aspects of personality development. She was concerned mainly with ego growth, and did not consider the inner drives or developmental conflicts involving these drives. Through her juxtaposition of comments about racial attitudes and the "purity" illusions of grownups about childhood, or the comparison of racial and sexual guilt, she strongly implies that race and drives do intertwine. But further investigation of these internal relationships lies beyond the scope of her study. For example, she gives a detailed discussion about the words, "clean" and "dirty" in connection with skin color, and quotes a four-year-old white boy's reaction to viewing a picture of a brown boy. "He's black! He's a stinky little boy.—He's a stinker—he sh---! Take it away! I want another little boy' " (p. 71). But she does not link the confusion of anal drive and racial conflicts in this child. Other comments in the book are as follows:

> Even parents and teachers are inclined to overlook the significance of the few [racial] clues they do get. They may be too busy to

notice. They may also be ignoring or selectively forgetting matters which are distasteful because Americans like to believe in the "purity" of childhood. Precocious sexuality shocks them and so does precocious raciality [p. 44] .

It is natural enough to avoid a topic about which one has guilty feelings, especially when it is so easy to convince oneself that no good can come of discussing it anyway. For example [in avoiding the topic of race with their children parents say] , "Things (race relations) have been this way for generations and they're not going to be much different," or "There's nothing I (we) can do about it anyhow." [Another example from a parent] : "When it comes to the question of color I never say anything. They just have to meet problems and take care of themselves. We don't tell them anything about it, but still, *they know.*" [Goodman concludes,] There is a prevalent feeling among our parents that race, like sex, is a rather hazardous topic and one best left alone, at least so far as the children are concerned. They feel so partly because both topics rouse their own emotions [pp. 136f.] .

Goodman is a strong advocate of honestly and openly discussing racial awareness and racial conflicts with young children. However, she is handicapped in her approach through the unrecognized isolation of racial and drive conflicts. For example, in encouraging a frank discussion about color with children she recommends acknowledging to a child the obvious fact that Negroes are of different shades, even within the same family. But in omitting any explanation of the origin of skin color, like life itself, from the sexual union of the parents, she goes astray. She suggests the facts be "embellished with a little fantasy." "Wouldn't it be funny if the trees were shades of brown and pink and we were shades of green!" (p. 220f.). Saying that all living things come in different shades is like trying to explain human sexuality by defensive retreat to the birds and the bees.

Another problem introduced by the limitation in understanding of intrapsychic life comes in the failure to recognize unconscious defenses. Children are categorized into low, medium, and high awareness with regard to noticing racial differences. Generally, these ratings paralleled observations of development of ego skills. However, it is apparent that in some cases defensive activity aimed at not noticing a painful racial difference interfered as well with other ego activity dependent upon "noticing." Goodman's example of William illustrates such a disturbance. William is described as a boy of "low awareness;" he is not clear about or interested in the matter of color. He calls white paper blue and is apt to call brown clay white one moment and brown the next. Medium dark William tells the examiner he looks like the white, not the brown doll. He thought that when he was a baby he looked like the medium brown and light brown babies. "He was positive about only one thing—he didn't look like the dark brown baby. 'I wasn't no colored baby like that (dark brown)! I was a red baby like this (light brown).' (He is quite right.) It is the only strong statement he ever made to us" (p. 52). Under William's denial ("low awareness") lie clear perception and intensely felt conflicts about his own color.

As a part of this work eight children were studied in greater detail and their family backgrounds were more extensively investigated. The conclusions from this part of the study have less value than the actual observations of the children, since the concentration is too exclusively on what is transmitted of the culture, through the parents. Once again, the omission of the contribution of the child's own personality limits realistic conclusions.

Goodman's epilog, like Lasker's, is a forceful protest against segregation:

> It is shocking to find that four-year-olds, particularly white ones, show unmistakable signs of the onset of racial bigotry.
>
> So here is a grim, hard fact to be added to the growing collection of grim, hard facts about race relations in America. It is all too clear that the race prejudice which flourishes among us . . . sends its taproots deep, and even into early childhood.
>
> As an equally grim corollary we have another fact. It is all too clear that Negro children not yet five can sense that they are marked, and grow uneasy. They can like enormously what they see across the color line, and find it hard to like what they see on their side. In this there is scant comfort or security, and in it are the dynamics for rendering personality asunder. . . .
>
> The thoughts and feelings of our four-year-olds, white or brown, do not come out of the blue. Neither do they come simply and directly from parent to child. They rather *grow* in each child, a unique result of a unique combination of conditions. Each child grows his own set of

thoughts and feelings about race, and he achieves them out of the materials at hand. The materials can be sorted into types and labeled, personal, social, and cultural [pp. 245f.].

In an excellent chapter appended to the second edition (1964) of her book Goodman presents "an overview of research" and includes an extensive bibliography. She also makes many wise recommendations for further investigations, including further investigation of the individual personality development of children in relation to the problems of race.

There is a moving refrain, quoted throughout her book. Joan, a four-year-old Negro child, offered this "acute commentary on American society" to one of Goodman's colleagues (p. 45):

The people that are white, they can go up.
The people that are brown, they have to go down.

Gordon Allport published his extensive and authoritative book, *The Nature of Prejudice*, in 1954. He takes exception to the anthropologists, influenced by Freud, who look for a "basic personality structure" to account for ethnic group differences. (Unfortunately, it is especially the work of Kardiner and Ovesey which is misunderstood as representative of Freud.) In contrast, Allport places greater emphasis upon the culture and early child-rearing practices, and sees prejudice primarily as a cultural problem imposed upon the individual from without. While he agrees with Freud that the characteristic way in which an individual handles his aggressive impulses is an important feature of his character structure, he says, "Unlike Freud, however, we are assuming that aggression is a capacity rather than an instinct. It is primarily a reactive matter."

In writing of the origins of prejudice, Allport stated, "If there is any instinctive foundation for group prejudice it lies in this hesitant response that human beings have to strangeness. We note the startled reaction infants often display to strangers. . . . In a sense the reaction is never outgrown" (p. 130). Here Allport comes close to a recognition of what I have described as skin color anxiety.

Chapter 18 of Allport's book is entitled "The Young Child." Here he is especially concerned with styles of child rearing—permissive, rejective, neglectful, overindulgent, inconsistent—and their relationship to prejudice. He puts the "dawn of racial awareness" at about two and a half years, and gives an example which is almost an exact duplicate of the first Hanna Perkins example (Chapter 3). A two-and-half-year-old white child, sitting by a Negro child, said, "Dirty face." Allport comments, "an unemotional remark, prompted only by his observing a wholly dark-skinned visage—for the first time in his life."

Following the dawn of racial awareness there come successive stages in the development toward prejudiced attitudes. He quotes a six-year-old child, asking his mother, "Mother, what is the name of the children I am supposed to hate?" Allport states that from six to ten years prejudice is first learned and then taken over as a "total rejection" of the object against whom it is aimed. This overlaps with a phase lasting until about fourteen years, when prejudices become modified with "escape clauses" —rationalizations which conceal the full extent and nature of the underlying prejudice. Allport is especially interested in the development of verbal statements as indicators of changes in the underlying growth toward prejudice. He concludes, "The paradox, then, is that younger children may talk undemocratically, but behave democratically, whereas children in puberty may talk (at least in school) democratically but behave with true prejudice."

Allport describes an interesting example of initial fear in three- and five-year-old white siblings when a new Negro maid came into their home. After a few days the children accepted her, and in the next five or six years they grew to love her, as did all the family. Several years later, when the children were young adults, the family was reminiscing about the happy period of this maid's service in their household. Both of the grown-up children were "utterly astonished" to learn, during the conversation, that the maid was colored. They insisted that they had never known this fact or had completely forgotten it if they ever knew it. Allport says, "Situations of this type are not uncommon. Their oc-

currence makes us doubt that instinctive fear of the strange has
any necessary bearing upon the organization of permanent attitudes." A psychoanalyst would have to disagree, and would interpret the "forgetting" as a defense prompted by anxiety and
conflict involving the different-colored skin. The knowledge, as
a result of the defense, has been banned to the unconscious. And
the resulting denial to the beloved maid of an important part of
her rightful identity—her own color—is, in an adult, a manifestation of unconscious prejudice. Allport says, "The theory of
'home atmosphere' is certainly more convincing than the theory
of 'instinctive roots.'"

The work of Kenneth Clark, often assisted by his wife,
Mamie, is generally regarded as outstanding in the field of social
investigation of racial problems. His many publications are
summarized in his book, *Prejudice and Your Child*, first published in 1955. In a pocket edition, enlarged and published in
1963, there are many additional bonuses. There is a chapter, by
Philip Kurland, on the legal background of the school segregation cases. There is the complete text of the Supreme Court
Opinions of May 17, 1954. There is the appendix to the appellant's brief, prepared for the Court by Clark and other social scientists. There is Clark's reply to criticisms of the social scientist's
role in the desegregation cases, and finally his presidential ad-
dress to the Society for Psychological Study of Social Issues
(Chicago, 1960) in which he considers further the role of the social sciences in desegregation. The middle section of the book, "A
Program for Action," is a series of chapters about what schools,
social agencies, churches, and parents can do regarding prejudice
and segregation.

Part One is entitled, "The Problem of Prejudice." At once
Clark asks the questions, "Are children born with racial
feelings? Or do they have to learn, first, what color they are and,
second, what color is 'best'?" He elaborates that modern social
scientists have refuted theories held a half century earlier that
racial and religious prejudices are inborn. "Social scientists are
now convinced that children learn social, racial, and religious

prejudices in the course of observing, and being influenced by, the existence of patterns in the culture in which they live." Clark's own approach to the problem is revealed in the questions he poses:

(1) How and when do children learn to identify themselves with some people and to differentiate themselves from others?

(2) How and when do children acquire racial attitudes and begin to express these attitudes in their behavior?

(3) What conditions in the environment foster the development of these racial attitudes and behavior?

(4) What can be done to prevent the development and expression of destructive racial prejudices in children? [p. 17].

Through tests of young children, with dolls, the Clarks established that among three-year-old Negro children in both North and South, more than 75 percent knew the difference between "white" and "colored:" 37 percent of Negro children, three years of age, identified themselves correctly with the Negro doll; 87 percent of seven-year-olds made the correct identification. Some children as young as three years indicated a preference to be white. Clark sees this as a reflection of "their knowledge that society prefers white people." White children were generally found to prefer white skin. Clark discusses the conscious and unconscious ways in which family and society communicate to young children the idea that white is superior and Negro is inferior. He discusses the influence of movies, radio, television, schools, churches. Like Goodman, he makes a comparison of the reticence (in this case, of the schools) to talk about race to the reticence that prevails in talking about sex to children.

The following extended quotation from *Prejudice and Your Child* describes the "coloring test" administered to young children by the Clarks, and some of their conclusions about their findings:

The investigator gave each child a sheet of paper with drawings of a leaf, an apple, an orange, a mouse, a boy, and a girl, plus a box of twenty-four colored crayons which included brown, black, white, yellow, pink, and tan. Each child was tested alone and asked to color the leaf, apple, orange, and mouse. If the child responded correctly, it was assumed that he knew what color things really are. If the child was a boy, the investigator then said: "See this little boy? Let's make believe he is you. Color this little boy the color that you are." After the child responded, he was told: "Now this is a little girl. Color her the color you like little girls to be." (If the child being tested was a girl, the questions were altered accordingly.) Of the responses to the "coloring test," only those of the children between five and seven seemed consistent enough to be analyzed. There were 160 children in this age group.

These children generally made spontaneous comments as they colored the little boy or the little girl or as they reacted to the questions asked during the "dolls test." (In view of the discovery that children are sensitive to many racial nuances and may have their responses influenced by the skin color of the observer, it may be important to point out that the person who conducted these experiments was of medium-brown skin color.)

In the "coloring test," all of the Negro children with very light skin color colored the figure representing themselves with the white or yellow crayon; these children were reacting in terms of the color they could see that their skin was. These responses were interpreted as accurate. But 15 per cent of the children with medium-brown skin color and 14 per cent of the dark-brown children also colored their "own" figure with either a white or a yellow crayon or with some bizarre color like red or green. Yet these same children were quite accurate in their ability to color the leaf, the apple, the orange, and the mouse. Their refusal to choose an appropriate color for themselves was an indication of emotional anxiety and conflict in terms of their own skin color. Because they wanted to be white, they pretended to be.

When these children were asked to color the child of the opposite sex the color they preferred, 48 percent of them chose brown, 37 per cent white, and 15 per cent a bizarre or irrelevant color. It is significant that 52 per cent of these children refused to color their preference either brown or black. This finding supports the conclusions of the "dolls test," in which 60 per cent of these children preferred the white doll or rejected the brown doll.

The discrepancy in the percentage of Negro children who rejected the brown doll compared to the percentage who refused to color their preference brown may be due to the fact that the "coloring test" required a greater effort from the child. It subjected him to a greater strain in indicating his preference. In the "dolls test," he could solve the conflict merely by pointing to a certain doll. In the "coloring test," he not only had to choose a crayon of a certain color, but also had to use this crayon long enough to color the drawing. Many of these children spent a long time in looking at all of the different colors before making a deliberate choice. Some of them picked out one crayon, looked at it, put it back, and chose another one—

usually of a lighter color. Their behavior revealed how deeply embedded in their personality is the conflict about what color they are and what color they want to be. Some of these children, who colored the leaf and the fruit and the mouse rather carefully and correctly, revealed their inner turmoil by coloring the picture representing themselves with a scribbling vigor. Others, even when making an obviously wishful, evasive, or inappropriate response, colored the picture with great tenderness and care.

How do northern Negro children differ from southern Negro children in this respect? Nearly 80 per cent of the southern children colored their preferences brown, whereas only 36 per cent of the northern children did. Furthermore, over 20 per cent of the northern children colored their preferences in a bizarre color, while only 5 per cent of the southern children did. A record of the spontaneous remarks of the children showed that 82 per cent of the southern children spoke as they worked, but only 20 per cent of the northern children did so. Most of the remarks of the northern children were concerned with the desirability of one or another skin color. While the same was true of the southern children, a substantially higher proportion of them supported their color preferences by remarks relating to the ugliness or prettiness of one or another color. The only two children who made spontaneous remarks indicating a derisive rejection of the brown color were southern children. On the other hand a substantially higher proportion of the northern children made evasive remarks.

Some of the children reacted with such intense emotion to the "dolls test" or to the "coloring test" that they were unable to continue. One little girl who had shown a clear preference for the white doll and who described the brown doll as "ugly" and "dirty" broke into a torrent of tears when she was asked to identify herself with one of the dolls. When confronted with this personal conflict, some children looked at the investigator with terror or hostility. Many of these children had to be coaxed to finish the tests.

The only children who reacted with such open demonstrations of intense emotions were northern children. The southern children when confronted with this personal dilemma were much more matter-of-fact in their ability to identify themselves with the brown doll which they had previously rejected. Some of them were able to laugh or giggle self-consciously as they did so. Others merely stated flatly: "This one. It's a nigger. I'm a nigger."

On the surface, these findings might suggest that northern Negro children suffer more personality damage from racial prejudice and discrimination than southern Negro children. However, this interpretation would seem to be not only superficial but incorrect. The apparent emotional stability of the southern Negro child may be indicative only of the fact that through rigid racial segregation and isolation he has accepted as normal the fact of his inferior social status. Such an acceptance is not symptomatic of a healthy personality. The emotional turmoil revealed by some of the northern children may be interpreted as an attempt on their part to assert some positive aspect of the self [pp. 42-46].

Clark also reports studies involving older children, and work involving white as well as Negro children. He describes very effectively some of the adverse effects of prejudice in the personalities of white children. Here he follows the work of Adorno, Frenkel-Brunswik, and others at the University of California, concerning the "authoritarian personality."

Chapter VI, "The Effects of Prejudice and Discrimination," in Witmer and Kotinsky's book on the Midcentury White House Conference on Children and Youth was prepared by Clark. He stresses the damages of segregation, quoting Goodman (1952) and Horowitz (1939) for evidence of *early* damage. He deals with the stresses of being taught democracy but having to live under enforced segregation, of the frustrations produced by segregation, of the sense of inferiority that arises. The low self-esteem of the Negro child is, throughout his work, a special concern of Clark's. He considers the submissiveness, martyrdom, feelings of persecution, withdrawal tendencies, self-ambivalence, and aggression that are likely to develop, as well as the distortions of the sense of reality, in the victims of segregation. This report, as already indicated, was one of the seven cited in Footnote 11 of the Supreme Court Opinion.

In another publication, undated, Clark considers "How to Protect Children Against Prejudice." He advises minority group parents of their extra responsibility to their children. Wisely he recommends that they, as parents, try to counteract negative social forces that tend to rob their children of their self-esteem. He stresses loving, understanding, and making the child feel wanted. He cautions about realistic aspirations for children. He advises realistic discussions of children's questions and conflicts. Prejudice must be recognized as a reality of life, but taught to be wrong, unfair. Minority status must not be used as an excuse for undesirable personal characteristics. Aggressive, antisocial, delinquent behavior cannot be condoned as solutions. Children must be helped to develop tolerance. Clark's advice is not merely excellent; it is inspirational. It is evident how concerned he is with correcting the distorted, damaged, demeaned self-image so widespread in the Negro race, and with introducing high, but realistic ideals to replace the infantile unattainable ideal of becoming white.

Nobody can question the great value of Clark's work. *Prejudice and Your Child* is a "must" book for anyone—parent, professional, or lay—at all interested in this field. Yet, it is just because of Clark's longstanding stature as a leader in the field of racial problems that his tendency to discount the importance of individual intrapsychic studies is a disappointment.

PSYCHOLOGY

Through various forms of psychological testing psychologists have demonstrated many of the adverse effects of prejudice and segregation, on both white and Negro children. An early publication is that of Ruth Horowitz (1939). This particular report, a part of a larger study, deals with the "beginnings of race consciousness conceived as a function of ego development." Twenty-four nursery school children, two to five years of age, were tested with projective techniques. Horowitz interprets the test results as demonstrating the first stage of self-identification as a discovery of one's own body, and the second stage as one of discovery of similarities and differences with others. Her test results demonstrate that a state of conflict about his color adversely influences the development of a young child's realistic self-identification.

In 1946, as a part of his doctoral dissertation, Parrish demonstrated, by means of questionnaire studies, the judgmental linking of character traits with shades of skin color in the Negro race. The darker the skin the worse the misassociated character trait and the worse the connotation of the particular slang expression describing the skin color shading. His tests included adults and junior high school students.

As a part of her work with T. W. Adorno on the "authoritarian personality," Frenkel-Brunswik (1948) carried out a research project on ethnic prejudice in children and adults. From a group of 1,500 boys and girls, eleven to sixteen years of age, she studied 120 who were found on testing to score either very high or very low with regard to prejudicial attitudes. She then studied the reactions of these 120 children to fifty slogans reflecting racial prejudice or tolerance. She interpreted the findings as indicating that prejudicial attitudes are already well set in adolescence, and attempted to derive a typical personality structure characterizing the prejudiced child. The prejudiced child was more oriented toward power, and the unprejudiced child toward love. She regarded the most important problem the child's attitude toward authority and stressed that forced submission to authority is to be avoided. There should be a "deliberately planned" democratic school and family life. A weakness in the study is that the relationship of prejudice or lack of it to adolescent development is not sufficiently considered.

In 1952 Boyd noted the large number of studies which psychologists had done in recent years to compare intelligence levels of Negro and white children. His own study was of levels of aspiration in 25 white and 25 Negro children, of similar and normal IQ range, attending a nonsegregated school in Portland, Oregon. He found that the Negro group had a higher level of aspiration —as evidenced by goals for travel, occupation, income, and car size. Boyd interpreted that the higher aspirations stemmed from desires to improve social conditions of Negroes and from feelings of insecurity. However, the administration and interpretation of the tests are both open to question. The children were deceived in that they were told the examiner. was making a comparison of boys and girls; the Negro-white comparison was concealed from them. As for the "higher" aspirations of Negro children, they appear rather to represent an ego ideal still infused with infantile wishes rather than realistic goals. If this is indeed the case, then prejudice and segregation have contributed to the stunting of a mature ego ideal development in Negro children. An infantile, unattainable, ego ideal defeats rather than stimulates a child in his efforts to improve his lot in life.

Landreth and Johnson (1953) tested 228 three- and five-year-old children, white and Negro, upper and lower socioeconomic status. The results of the study, which used picture completion tests, demonstrate that children as young as three years of age know that skin color is important, and are capable of regarding white as desirable and dark as undesirable.

Hammer (1953) tested 400 "normal" white and Negro children, attending grades one through eight in Virginia. He used the H-T-P test—a free-hand drawing of a House, a Tree, and a Person. The results of the rather intricate scoring placed the mean of the white children's scores between "mildly neurotic" and "neurotic." The mean for the Negro children was placed at a rating of "severely neurotic." Hammer cautions against too quick an interpretation of neurosis from such tests, when cultural factors are so important.

Graham (1955) studied the doll play of 30 Negro and 30 white children, ages six to eight and a half years, attending two different integrated schools. From three different ten-minute sessions, each involving different combinations of Negro and white dolls, he attempted to categorize the fantasies which the play seemed to demonstrate. As with so many reports of brief tests administered to large groups of young children, the significance of the child's understanding of the test and his relationship to the examiner is overlooked in the interpretation of the test results.

Vosk (1966) tested 50 first grade Negro children in Harlem, who were singled out because of their learning and behavior disorders. In addition to the WISC and Leiter tests, which she administered with modifications—mainly special measures to give the child added assurance and encouragement during the test— she observed the children in class and acquainted herself with their family backgrounds. She describes her test results as not "objectively creditable," although qualitatively very revealing. Many of the nonlearners lived in a state of *real* fear of events they could neither predict nor control. For example, one child lived in dread that his father would return, because he had witnessed his father's attempt to kill his mother. As part of her conclusions, Vosk places emphasis upon the need for extra love and encour-

agement from teachers. She tends to view the educational problem in these children as one of conscious, or unconscious, rejection by the teacher, frustrated in her efforts to teach the non-
learner. In this teacher-nonlearning-pupil contest, she emphasizes the teacher's responsibility to teach, but not the child's to
learn. This interpretation appears to pass over the child's internalized conflicts and at the same time expects teachers to be able
to surmount these conflicts within the child through love and
encouragement. A teacher cannot help a child to learn if his unconscious defense is not to learn in order not to be informed
about some unbearable reality facing him elsewhere in his life.
But a teacher's understanding of this defense can lessen her own
narcissistic hurt as a teacher and consequently her need to reject
the child. If learning is regarded as a shared responsibility of
both teacher and child, and if it is the child who is incapable of
meeting this responsibility because of his personality crippling,
then the realistic teacher can accept her limitations as an educa-
tor, who cannot be expected, through love, to straighten crippled
personalities.

SOCIAL WORK

Although the profession of social work has been in the fore-
front both in integrating its own ranks and in working with
clients of all races, caseworkers have not published much about
their experiences. They contributed to two Round Table discussions at annual meetings of The American Orthopsychiatric
Association (to be reviewed in the section on Psychiatry). A recent article by Gochros (1966) mentions the "long and curious
dearth" in the social work literature concerning racial problems.
Gochros wrote about the effect of race upon the worker-client
relationship. She noted the unwillingness on the part of social
workers to plunge into exploring racial attitudes with clients,
and recognized the possible merits in such reticence. Premature
pointing out and interpreting of racial conflicts may fit the client
(and the worker) into patterns of presumed racial attitudes, and
block the caseworker-client relationship. But too long a delay

can be wrong too, because it also can lead to a relationship block. Gochros discussed the entry into and working through of racial problems "when appropriate" with the individual client, and in so doing stressed the value of the individual identities of both client and worker. She also cautioned about the importance of the white worker's being able to recognize his own prejudice and guilt, as a white person living in the United States. For the Negro worker, she believed, the problem may be one of being viewed by the client as a collaborator of the white enemy. She also considered problems of intrastaff mixed race relationships.

In an earlier publication Smith (1946) discussed racial casework problems and placed the same stress on the preservation and valuation of individual identity. He noted that sociological studies are informative, but not sufficient for the individual caseworker attempting to work with an individual Negro client.

Tyler (1946) wrote about experiences at a Harlem agency, with racially mixed staff and Negro clients. She was especially concerned with the problem of passive resistance in the Negro and the frustration this resistance could cause a caseworker in trying to help Negro parents regarding plans for the care of their children. She took strong issue with another social work publication, from the South, suggesting that tremendous shifts are necessary in a (white) worker's attitudes, opinions, and philosophy of practice in dealing with Negro clients. Tyler forthrightly elaborated the obvious fact that "Negro resistance" is no different from forms of resistance which white clients can call up, and it does not require a special approach. Nor does it require a special color of worker. "No caseworker can hope to do an objective casework job when she is approaching people, not in terms of understanding them as individuals, but in terms of reflecting the attitude of the dominant group in the community by thinking of them as different from others because of their racial identity. . . . The race of the worker need not be an important factor. The significant factor is the security and skill with which each caseworker is able to accept and understand people and their needs." Tyler, too, lamented the dearth of social work literature, and made a plea for social work schools to give students more help in understanding racial problems which they will meet in their future work.

Houwink (1948) also wrote of the problem of racial difference between client and worker, but illustrated it with an interview in which the white guilt of the giving worker to the Negro client appears to be largely unrecognized.

The field of social work has not yet contributed much direct information to advance our knowledge about racial anxiety in children. So far, its efforts have had to be directed more toward reaching and working with adults—with parents of children. An exception, however, comes from a residential treatment center for children. In 1967 several members of the staff of Bellefaire, a children's residential treatment center in Cleveland, published their experiences with the first Negro children admitted to Bellefaire, a Jewish institution (see Chethik et al.). They described in the Negro children an initial period of "hyper-race consciousness," followed by a period of "color blindness" and then a period of "loyalty conflict." They regarded this third period as a manifestation of an identity crisis. The new "good white" environment had become symbolic of health, while the old "bad black" culture stood for pathology. It was as if the child were saying, "Each time I improve I get a little whiter." Change then implied desertion of race. The Bellefaire staff expressed concern with the offering of opportunities for positive identification for Negro children—e.g., "with positive images emanating from the Negro figures in the present civil rights struggle." The circumstances defining their field of work (age of child, degree of disturbance) do not permit any extensions of their conclusions about identity crisis into the realm of identity formation in the first few years of life.

EDUCATION

In the field of education, particularly nursery education, the theme of race has been the subject of institutes, special addresses, and research review articles. In an Institute, "The Roots of Prejudice," held by the Child Study Association (1944), Eisenbud, a psychoanalyst, discussed prejudices against Negroes, Jews, and other minorities. For the prejudiced person the Negro, Jew, etc., represented a fantasied threat to his liberty, life, and possessions. Eisenbud placed the root of such a prejudice in overly harsh, aggressive parental restrictions in the early years of a child's life, when the parents indeed appeared to threaten the child's life, liberty, and possessions. The early parental handling became an ever-present source of emotional energy, available for prejudice formation in later life.

Ausubel (1958) spoke of the importance of school integration for healthy ego development in Negro children. Under integration the Negro children entered healthy competition with real white children. The opportunity for competition, comparison, and contrast promoted realistic self-concepts and self-esteem. Under segregation the Negro children lacked any real competition. In their competition, comparison, and contrast with fantasied idealized white children, their own identity and self-esteem suffered greatly.

In 1955 *Child Study* published a group of articles by various professional people, under the general heading, "The Many Faces of Prejudice." In one of these articles, "How Prejudice Begins," M. M. Lawrence presents examples of how a child's color attitudes can become confused with developmental conflicts, and how they can be understood and sorted out with a child. Lawrence also says that "it is an easy step to substitute expressions of dislike for dark-colored people for expressions of the primary and more emotionally important fear." She writes of her work with weekly parent-teacher discussion groups and urges that more such groups be formed as an aid to integration. At Hanna Perkins we came to share Lawrence's view of the importance of the ongoing efforts necessary to support and promote true psychological integration. Lawrence quotes Lillian Smith (from "Now is the Time"): "Integration is a creative job —a process that will take effort, imagination, and faith."

In 1959 Arter published an excellent "inventory of research"

on the effects of prejudice on children. Arter also pointed to the
future with thoughtful questions about "whither current research." In 1967 Stevenson published a somewhat similar research review article, "Studies of Racial Awareness in Young
Children." He pointed to the need for research "to determine
what kinds of environments and what kinds of experiences will
prevent racial awareness and early discriminations from developing into firm prejudice." A still more recent article (1968) in
the same vein is Munat's "Four, Poor, Nonwhite and Out-of-
Sight."

A special educational project concerned with developing
democratic attitudes in young children, the "Philadelphia Early
Childhood Project," is detailed in a book by Trager and Yarrow
(1952). Goals included a large-scale study of racial attitudes of
children, parents, and teachers, and a study of the influences of
teacher attitudes and values upon children. Teachers, pupils,
parents, and school administrators from kindergarten, first and
second grades in each of six different Philadelphia schools all
were involved in the project. The first year was one of work with
groups of teachers. The second year was one of estimating social
attitudes through tests and interviews with children and their
parents. As with every study of young children's racial attitudes,
the Philadelphia group soon learned that young children not
only are racially aware, but also know the meaning of social
classes and their consequences. In the third year an "experiment" was conducted, in which an attempt was made to change
social perceptions and attitudes of first and second grade children. For a period of seven weeks, by means of special "club"
meetings, teachers attempted to teach either democratic or prejudiced attitudes to separate groups of children. The teachers consciously, deliberately assumed roles and attitudes which they
then presented to the children as genuine reflections of the teachers' personalities and beliefs. (Oddly, only one teacher vigorously
rebelled at this scheme, and she was regarded as emotionally disturbed.) At the end of the seven-week period, the children were
specially tested, and the conclusion was: "The changes achieved

in the experiment demonstrate that democratic attitudes and prejudiced attitudes can be taught to young children." While much in this three-year project appears to have been a worthwhile effort to accomplish both physical and psychological integration, through bringing together racially mixed groups of teachers, parents, and children, the final "experiment" was carried out at the intolerable expense of an honest and trusting relationship between teachers and children, and therefore goes a long way to cast doubt on the validity of the entire project.

PSYCHIATRY

In 1939 Bender published one of the first modern psychiatric reports about Negro children, based on a study of 1,100 Negro children under sixteen years of age, admitted over a fifteen-year period to the children's ward of the Psychiatric Division of Bellevue Hospital. Physical studies, though often revealing evidence of neglect and deprivation, tended to disprove actual racial differences or primitivity of the Negro race as accounting for differences between the white and Negro races in mental and nervous diseases. Bender noted the underlying emotional conflicts of Negro children, and commented, "So far, we have seen that the problems of Negro children are not necessarily different from those that any child may be subjected to, but the Negro child may react with a different type of response such as sleepiness, mutism, catalepsy, blocking, dancing motility or vivid hallucinatory experiences. These are adaptive mechanisms which express the child's needs. It is possible that they represent somewhat different brain functions in the Negro child." Bender suggests that these symptoms may be evidence of psychological defenses at work upon internalized conflicts, but that they also might have an underlying organic basis.

Recent longitudinal studies of the effects of malnutrition in early life tend to confirm the possibility of stunted brain development, along with poor intellectual and emotional development, as a result of early malnutrition. Stoch and Smythe (1963) studied the height, weight, head circumference and IQ at periodic intervals of two groups of twenty-one Cape Coloured children in South Africa. The two groups, matched in age (ten months to three years) and sex, differed markedly in nutritional level. The control group was well nourished and its physical growth and IQ measurements did not suggest any racial inferiority. The poverty-stricken, grossly malnourished group of children had a significantly smaller head circumference (a fair estimate of brain size early in life) and lower IQ, measured for periods of up to seven years while the study was in progress. (See also Cravioto and Robles, 1963; and National Academy of Science-National Research Council, 1966.) Thus Bender's suggestion in 1939 that the Negro child has "somewhat different brain functions" should not be regarded as a prejudiced remark implying that Negroes are inferior. It can be understood simply as a plausible speculation about an unexplained finding in her extensive study of 1,100 Negro children admitted to a psychiatric hospital.

In 1946 Gardner and Aaron studied the histories of childhood and adolescent adjustment of Negro sailors who were psychiatric casualties during World War II. They concluded that the same antecedent constitutional, familial, developmental, social, and economic factors existed in the backgrounds of Negroes with a psychiatric illness, as in white people with psychiatric illnesses.

In a most unusual psychiatric report about the effect of race upon children, Glasser (1958) has reported a child guidance clinic evaluation of a Negro child reared as white. The case is a bizarre tragedy of physical illness, mismanagement by legal and social professions, and consequent severe rejection of a child. The physical and environmental pathology obscures the structure of the child's internal psychopathology. But the importance of race in relation to child adoption procedures is, sadly, illustrated all too well.

In 1963 and 1964 Brody published his studies on color and identity conflict in young boys from five to ten years of age. His aim was to identify the significance of color status for white and Negro boys (selected from children attending a psychiatric clinic), the relation of their perceptions in this regard to their mothers' attitudes, and the relevance of such perceptions for the children's sense of their own identity. He studied the children in two individual sessions of puppet play with Negro and white hand puppets, and he interviewed the mothers of each boy on two occasions. All sessions were tape-recorded and observed through a one-way screen. He found that almost all children displayed evidence of racial conflict, and that some expressed it directly. "I feel sad about being dark-skinned. I felt that way since I was a baby," one boy told him (1961). Prominent themes in the children's play indicated the Negro as a bad, sad, weak, lonely, and inferior figure. A corollary theme was the suggestion of guilt in the dominant white puppet and of fear in the white when the Negro showed flashes of hostility. In the Negro boys there were conflict-laden wishes to assume the more powerful white and to abandon the less rewarding Negro identity. The resulting confusion in identity was related to a need to identify with the white aggressor.

The white boys did not reveal any clear wishes to be Negro, but tended to project onto the Negro unacceptable feelings of inferiority, aggression, anxiety, and guilt within themselves. Among the mothers there was extensive denial of the children's racial conflicts. The transmission of messages, both conscious and unconscious, from mother to son was found to be significant. Brody (1964) observes, "The interesting possibility here is that mixed or conflictful feelings, rather than purely hostile or deprecatory ones, may be evoked in a boy through interaction with a prejudiced mother who consciously feels that she should instill attitudes in him which are not congruent with her own basic point of view." The mother's conscious message may be, "People are all the same inside. . . . We are all human. . . . People are what they are and the skin color is unimportant." But her unconscious message, "mediated through affective and behavioral clues," can be translated, "While I tell you that people are the same inside, I expect you to behave as though this is not true, and, in fact, I don't believe it myself" (1963). (It is interesting to consider these latency observations in relation to Allport's observations on the development of prejudice.)

In 1955 and again in 1957 there were Round Table discussions on problems of segregation and desegregation at the annual meetings of the American Orthopsychiatric Association. The importance of both of these meetings lay not in their contribution of new findings, but in their bringing together a wide variety of experts in various fields, with equally varying personal backgrounds. Negroes and whites, Northerners and Southerners, and even a South African representative participated. They focused professional attention, on a national scale, to all aspects of racial problems. Bingham Dai, in discussing research implications, encouraged intensive case studies of selected normal Negro school children—studies which Robert Coles began a few years later. Not much attention was given to the importance of the preschool years in childhood development. Dai, for instance, referred to the years from six to sixteen as "the crucial years for personality development." Whitney Young, in speaking of the community organizer's role, urged that we not forget the capacity of all people to change. While he recognized the necessity of compromise methods in setting time schedules for school desegregation, he distinguished the importance of not compromising on principles and goals. Viola Bernard spoke of the fact that the social psychologist and not the clinicians had borne the brunt of the work so far in connection with school desegregation. They helped in changing the law, preparing communities, and educational planning. With desegregation moving into actual daily living, "the time and opportunity for clinical activity seems at hand." She anticipated the need for psychiatrists as personal problems arose in connection with desegregation. She foresaw them working with school staffs, with parents, and with children as the new experiences of desegregation roused internal anxieties. (Two years later the G.A.P. report [see below] was issued by a group of psychiatrists expressly for educators, counselors, social workers, psychologists, and school administrators—the people immediately responsible for putting into effect the Supreme Court's desegregation decision.)

Several psychiatric publications in the 1950's reaffirmed the importance of cultural aspects of prejudice and segregation as adverse influences upon children's personality development. Usually the authors did not consider the significance of intrapsychic development, except as it appeared in reaction to the cultural (or familial) influences. Some authors even cautioned against an overemphasis upon Freudian instinctual theory, implying that such emphasis might negate the obviously important cultural factors. It is evident that, although clinicians have increasingly entered the scene, their attention for the time being remained almost too exclusively with the cultural aspects of racial conflict (Bernard, 1958; Chess, Clark, and Thomas, 1953; Lief and Stevenson, 1958; Milner, 1953).

A number of psychiatric publications dealt with the problems in adult psychotherapy when the patient—or the therapist —is Negro (Adams, 1950; Rosen and Frank, 1962; Grier, 1967). They emphasized the following concepts: the white therapist must be realistically informed about the cultural conflicts of Negroes; he must recognize and not deny racial reactions in Negro patients, as well as prejudices and signs of white guilt within himself; racial reactions within the doctor-patient relationship must come to light and be worked through.

Adams (1950) cautioned against ascribing all problems of Negro patients to cultural and racial conflict and pointed out that the Negro patient "uses race as an unconscious defense to conceal more basic conflicts." Adams recognized, in psychotherapeutic work with adults, the same difficulties that we observed in children who had to sort out their racial and developmental conflicts. However, Adams appeared to deny the significance of racial conflicts in *early* childhood, and consequently he viewed their adult form only as defensive against basic (early childhood) conflicts rather than an evolution of the racial conflicts of early childhood. He stated, "It is generally agreed that the basic personality traits and patterns of reaction are formed by the age of six, a period when children have little reflective understanding of the true and import of racial social symbols." This conclusion is at variance with the evidence presented by Goodman, Clark, and many others.

Grier (1967) examined the transference development of a white patient with himself, a Negro therapist. "The therapist's race presents a stimulus from the outset which evokes a response in the unconscious of the white patient." Here Grier comes close to a recognition of skin color anxiety. However, he appears to view the unconscious response as being due to essentially nonracial—e.g., oedipal—conflicts rather than to any basic unconscious reaction to skin color difference. In three clear and engaging case reports he traces his sensitive handling of racial aspects of the transference conflicts as the treatment progressed in each case. He copes with external reality, with drive derivatives, with race used as a defense, with the "Negro stereotypes," all within the transference development and its used to investigate and relieve the patient's conflicts.

Like Adams and Grier, Rosen and Frank (1962) wrote sensitively of racial problems in psychotherapy. They stressed the importance of feelings being brought into the open in treatment, rather than subjected to an intellectual review which avoids racial conflicts. They also valued individual identity. "The personal problems of each patient are unique regardless of the color of his skin, and each must be treated as an individual."

In 1948 Myers and Yochelson reported their experiences at St. Elizabeth's Hospital (Washington, D.C.) on a service of almost 1,000 psychotic Negro male patients. They noted the frequency of concern with color in Negro psychotics and recognized that psychotic symptoms in a Negro often included elements which reflect a need to solve the problems of skin color and the difficulties of being Negro. They recognized the Negro as being chronically anxious and attributed it to his being the victim of prejudice. Brody (1961) has reported similar impressions of psychoses in Negroes.

Racial conflicts between Negroes and whites seem so much an American problem that it comes as a surprise to discover an article by a European psychiatrist about it. The article, by Sclare (1953), comes from his experiences in the United States, while a Commonwealth Fund Fellow in the Department of Psychiatry at Cincinnati. From Glasgow, Sclare wrote (in the *British Journal of Medical Psychology*) an informative article for European readers. It is a description of racial conditions in the United States, a consideration of defensive-adaptive personality features among Negroes, and an account of experiences in psychotherapeutic treatment of Negro patients.

An excellent and lengthy report, "Psychiatric Aspects of School Desegregation" was issued by the Committee on Social Issues, of the Group for the Advancement of Psychiatry (1957). It includes a useful bibliography. Prepared primarily for educators and school personnel, it emphasizes "relevant psychiatric principles rather than . . . their practical application." The function of racial myths and prejudices as defenses against anxiety is well explained. The myths "have deep roots in individual childhood experience and are sustained by ongoing social and economic forces." The psychodynamics of prejudice is lucidly reviewed, and the psychodynamics of changing attitudes, during the process of desegregation, is well discussed. The same can be said for the psychological responses of children, parents, and educators regarding their individual reactions to desegregation.

It is unnecessary to review this lengthy reference in further detail here, since its concern, though largely about children, is not with their personality development so much as with their immediate reactions to a cultural crisis. However, the following remarks about skin color are pertinent.

> Through lifelong association of specific meanings to certain colors, there is an automatic tendency to impute to those presenting a particular color, psychological qualities which they may or may not possess. . . .
>
> Skin contacts form an essential part of the important relationships from infancy through childhood, and a variety of emotional attitudes come to be associated with particular colors, forms, and textures of the skin. . . .
>
> In this culture, yellow, brown, or black tend to be associated with ideas

of dirtiness or destructiveness or unpleasant smell, while light colors, especially white and pink, tend to be associated with ideas of cleanliness, purity, innocence, and chastity. Since the skin and its extensions—the hair and nails—cloak the entire body, it becomes that part of a person most quickly accessible to superficial perception and evaluation. Consequently, the association of particular meanings to certain colors and textures of skin often determines the manner in which one person relates to another. It would seem that negative associations to their skin color combine with the other reasons we have considered so far in accounting for the disesteem of Negroes in this country. That it cannot be the sole factor is shown, for instance, by the high social value placed on sun tan by many white people [pp. 22f.].

This is one of the clearest statements about the skin in relation to personality development and racial conflict that I have come across in my review of the literature. In fact, specific statements about the importance of skin color are seldom spelled out; rather, as a rule, the topic is taken for granted. In the above statement the displacements of drive conflicts, particularly those of the anal stage, onto the skin are clearly implied. (The report also contains a detailed discussion of both sexuality and aggression, as portrayed in the Negro stereotypes.) While the importance of the skin in the earliest relationships in life is recognized, it is not discussed more specifically in relation to skin color anxiety and identity formation.

The report stresses as the humanitarian goal that it is "a fundamental right of human beings to be judged as individuals and not as members of this or that ethnic group," but also recognizes that the current adult generation, raised under segregation, cannot radically restructure their entire personalities. The realistic goal for the present has to be that both white and Negro parents accept the fact that their children will be exposed to a fundamentally different experience, so that their earliest steps in identity formation will occur within an integrated society.

In the past few years the work of Robert Coles stands apart as a monumental contribution to the understanding of racial conflicts. For his scientific and lay publications he has merited both psychiatric and literary awards. His work is the product of years of zealous personal dedication, by a man who combines scientific training with the spirit of the creative artist. Much of it is reported in his book, *Children of Crisis: A study in Courage and Fear* (1964). Later publications report the expansion of his studies from Southern to Northern locales. (See also Chapter 9 for a report of his recent Northern studies.)

Children of Crisis tells of Coles's observations made in the midst of the first and most violent attempts to desegregate Southern schools, in New Orleans and Atlanta. Most of his observations come from frequent and regular interviews with white and Negro children, their parents, their teachers, and even the wide range of onlookers and agitators who participated in the early school desegregations. In New Orleans the pioneers were first, second, and third grade children; in Atlanta they were high school students. One of the most remarkable features of his study Coles, too modestly, never explains. It is a mystery how he, a Northern white man, ever managed to be permitted by any, let alone all, of the participants to carry out his work. Another remarkable feature is Coles's method of study. He relied primarily on establishing a personal relationship with all of the subjects of his study, ranging from the frightened little six-year-old Negro girl and her family to the angriest, most paranoid, white agitator at the demonstrations outside of the schools being integrated. His objectivity and his respect for the identity of *all* of these people stands out in his reporting. Furthermore, Coles has maintained his personal interest in them—particularly the children—ever since he first began his work. Now, years later, he is still making visits to these children. In his studies Coles, like many others, relied heavily upon observations of children's play and their drawings, for which he had a special fondness. In that he obtained the drawings through his relationship with the children, his interpretations of them can be trusted far more than drawings obtained for the sake of a test, in the absence of personal acquaintance with or adequate explanation to a child.

It is not possible to summarize here the many facets of Coles's work. Many of his findings confirm those of earlier investigators, especially with reference to the self-esteem and distorted body image of Negro children. But he more than confirms past findings, obtained mostly under stabilized, often segregated, conditions. He conveys as well the effect of the new social disruption, brought about by desegregation, upon personality development of school age children. A description of the reciprocal relationship between the problems of a little Negro girl facing a mob and one of the members of the mob tormenting her is especially insightful (1965; also 1964, Chapter IV). It brings to mind Loewenstein's "cultural pair" of Gentile and Jew (see below).

Although Coles did not work directly with pre-school children, he observed some of them in his family visits. Some of this part of his work is singled out here because of its relevance to the Hanna Perkins experiences. The quotations are from *Children of Crisis* (pp. 336f., 61-64, 71):

> My clinical impression—slowly consolidated over these past years of working with Negro children—is that most of the "usual" problems and struggles of growing up find an additional dimension in the racial context. In a very real sense being Negro serves to organize and render coherent many of the experiences, warnings, punishments and prohibitions that Negro children face. The feelings of inferiority or worthlessness they acquire, the longing to be white they harbor and conceal, the anger at what they find to be their relatively confined and moneyless condition, these do not fully account for the range of emotions in many Negro children as they come to terms with the "meaning" of their skin color. . . . [A child's grandmother said,] "It takes a lot of preparing before you can let a child loose in a white world. If you're black in Louisiana it's like cloudy weather; you just don't see the sun much."
>
> The "preparation" for such a climate of living begins in the first year of life. At birth the shade of the child's skin may be very important to his parents—so important that it determines in large measure how he is accepted, particularly in the many Negro marriages which bring together a range of genes which, when combined, offer the possibility of almost *any* color. What is often said about color-consciousness in Negroes (their legendary pursuit of skin bleaches and hair-straightening lotions) must be seen in its relentless effect upon the life of the mind, upon babies and upon child-rearing. A Negro sociologist [has said] "when a Negro child is shown to his mother and father, the first thing they look at is his color, and then they check for fingers and toes." . . . I made a point of asking many

parents what they thought of it—and found them unashamedly in agreement.

As infants become children, they begin to form some idea of how they look, and how their appearance compares with that of others. The issue of what skin color means is already confronting the child by three, let alone school age. In my interviews with grown-up Negroes and whites their memories hark back to one event or another that marks a first awareness of skin color and its implications. . . . Some of the children I have come to know were three when I first started talking with them—they were the nursery school brothers, sisters, and cousins of the older children I was visiting.

One three-year-old girl obviously avoided using those two colors [brown and black] in the pictures she made; instead she used her fingers as if *they* were crayons. After watching her use green and orange, then rub her hand alongside them, I asked her what she was doing. She said, "Nothing, just trying to make a picture." Her mother . . . explained . . . "She has been telling me on and off for weeks that she knows she can rub some of her brown skin off and use it for coloring. My two boys talked like that for a while when they were two and three and then they got over it. So I guess she will, too."

Before he is born the Negro child's color is likely to matter a great deal to his parents. By the third year of life the child is asking the kinds of questions that ultimately will include one about his skin color. A mother of five children in Jackson, Mississippi, described it to me rather explicitly: "When they asks all the questions, they ask about their color, too. They more than not will see a white boy or girl, and it makes them stop and think. They gets to wondering, and then first thing you know, they want to know this and that about it, and I never have known what to say, except that the Lord likes everyone because He makes everyone, and nothing is so good it can satisfy Him completely, so He made many kinds of people, and they're all equal before Him. Well, that doesn't always satisfy them; not completely it doesn't. So I have to go on. I tell them that no matter what it's like around us, it may make us feel bad, but it's not the whole picture, because we don't make ourselves. It's up to God, and He can have an idea that will fool us all. He can be trying to test us. It's the favorite child sometimes who you make sure you don't spoil."

I asked her when she found such conversation necessary. "I'd say about two or two and a half." she answered rather quickly. A bit deferentially she turned to me and asked: "Do you think that's too early for children to know?" I said no, I didn't. I said that what she told me confirmed some of my own observations. She smiled, a little proud but still a little nervous. She wanted to pursue the matter further: "I know I'm right on the age; I've gone through it with too many to forget when it happens. But to tell the truth I never have been certain what to say. That's why I try to talk about God. No one knows what color He is. . . . I read to them from the Bible, and remind them that the Lord is a mighty big man, and what He thinks is not the same as what white folks do, or even black folks. He's bigger than all of us. I tell them, and I hope that makes them feel satisfied, so they don't dislike themselves. That's bad, not liking your own self."

As one little Negro girl in Mississippi said after she had drawn a picture of herself: "That's me, and the Lord made me. When I grow up my momma says I may not like how He made me, but I must always remember that He did it, and it's His idea. So when I draw the Lord He'll be a real big man. He has to be to explain about the way things are."

In Chapter XI, "The Meaning of Prejudice," Coles refers briefly to psychoanalytic conceptions of the influence of early developmental conflicts upon later prejudices. It is beyond the scope of his work, a psychiatric study primarily of latency and adolescence, to delve more deeply into the earliest nature of skin color and developmental conflicts.

PSYCHOANALYSIS

Prejudice

Prejudice has been the subject of a number of psychoanalytic publications. In 1939 Freud published *Moses and Monotheism*, in which he discussed various determinants of anti-Semitism. Several post-World War II publications were about anti-Semitism. Zilboorg (1947), in a wide-ranging article, stressed the unconscious basis of prejudice. Ackerman and Jahoda (1948) attempted to encompass a prejudice syndrome, based on data from 25 psychoanalytic cases, collected from as many different analysts. Like most other psychoanalytic writers, they stated that prejudice is not a single clinical entity. They described the prejudiced person's defenses and their effects upon his identity. "The central dynamisms around which defense patterns cluster are the renunciation of parts of the patient's personal identity, the elimination of these unwanted parts through projection, and parallel with this the partial substitution of a borrowed identity through introjection." For the prejudiced person the Jew may represent unconscious aspects of either the conscience or the primitive uncontrollable drives. Anti-Semitism becomes a defense against self-hate; the prejudiced person blames the outside world rather than himself, and does not develop a true depression with turning of the aggression upon the self. In the genesis of prejudice Ackerman and Jahoda found that unfavorable preoedipal experiences fixated a basic passivity to stern, controlling, parents, with corresponding repression of aggression. This situation strongly hindered oedipal development. The oedipal conflict was intense, invested with much confusion and anxiety, never adequately resolved, and consequently the process of identification with the parent was seriously distorted.

Other analysts have elaborated upon various aspects of Ackerman and Jahoda's early paper. Waelder (1949) noted the variety of mechanisms which can underlie prejudice, ranging from those derived from normal psychology to those resulting from a psychotic illness. Kris (1949) stressed the importance of the mechanism of projection. He stated that prejudice functions as a channel for aggressive impulses, and stressed the importance of the fate of the aggressive drive in early childhood. Intensely ambivalent attitude, with polarization of values, accompanies prejudice. Loewenstein (1951), in his book *Christians and Jews*, analyzed the "cultural pair" formed by Gentile and Jew. (Much of what Loewenstein has to say of the tie between the perpetrator of prejudice and his victim might apply to an American "cultural pair" of white and Negro.)

In a more recent account of the nature of prejudice, Wangh (1964) not only lays stress upon the preoedipal stages, but particularly draws attention to the separation-individuation phase of development:

> Prejudice is a composite defense against instinctual strivings to which, paradoxically, it also offers an avenue of discharge. Regression to oral, anal, and phallic discharge-levels of primarily, but not exclusively, aggressive impulses, is combined in prejudice with projection, introjection, object and affect displacement and splitting, generalization and identification. . . . .
>
> The genetic, infantile model for the use of projection and displacement is to be found in the primordial beginnings of individuation. Psycho-anal-

ysis has long postulated that in the process of differentiation of self from non-self, irritant stimuli are first ascribed to the periphery of the mother-child unit, then to the differentiating maternal object. In later phases of development this displacing process establishes a new periphery—the stranger. A defective individuation experience, and a consequently disturbed object-relationship, will manifest itself early by just such displacement of aggressive cathexes on to the stranger. With the further completion of self-differentiation this displacement becomes projection. This projection on to the stranger will result in fear of him, which in turn will strengthen the need to seek refuge with the prime object. Ethnocentrism and xenophobia, the polar points of prejudice, have their basic roots in these infantile patterns. When individuation is impeded, the sense of identity remains unstable. Prejudices, by declaring 'This is not I', can help to reinforce the delineation of ego-limits. Projection and the concomitant intensified clinging to the prime-object are undertaken to aid impulse control, to preserve the love-object, and to preserve the integrity of the self. However, these defensive maneuvers may have an adverse effect. The more projections take place, the more debilitated become both the sense of reality and the sense of identity. An ever-widening repudiation of that which belongs to the self brings about an ever-increasing need to define the limits of the self in terms of that which is not self through a detailed delineation of the characteristics of the out-group. In consequence, the ego knows less and less of its own feelings and desires, and supposedly, more and more of those of the alien group. In this connection, attention may be drawn to the vast bulk of Nazi publications dealing with the character of the Jews [pp. 386f.].

In an earlier paper Bird (1957) stressed the oedipal origins of prejudice, noting that the cause of a prejudice may lie in an unsuspected rivalrous relationship toward a third, favored, person. He based his conclusion in part upon the analysis of a case in which an acute attack of prejudice arose during analysis as a defense against erotic oedipal impulses reawakened in the transference. The triangularly complex oedipal relationship is, of course, a far more advanced developmental stage than is the separation-individuation phase, involving only two people whose boundaries sometimes merge into one. Bird considered in some detail the mechanisms of introjection and projection in prejudice formation and maintenance—and in so doing also suggested the importance of earlier, preoedipal phases of development, in which these mechanisms predominate.

Seitz (1960) described a "projective exploitation" of a child by a parent. The child, through adaptive identification with the parent's ego defense mechanism of projecting inner feelings of "badness" to smaller and weaker persons, then developed his own prejudice. Some of the discussants of this paper noted "constructive aspects of prejudice," in the service of ego integration and maintenance of primitive forms of object relationship. Similar views of prejudice have been expressed in the literature by other analysts. Seitz took exception to the "constructive aspect of prejudice." He regarded this view as arising from the failure to distinguish between prejudice and the defense mechanism of projection. (Any symptom formation, physical or psychological, serves in part a defensive, homeostatic purpose. But this "constructive" function—to prevent further advancement of a destructive process—must not be mistaken for absence of pathology.) Heinz Kohut, discussing Seitz's paper, made the intriguing suggestion that prejudices might be classified according to intactness of object relations in the depths of the unconscious.

In their studies of anti-Semitism, Loewenstein (1951) and others have noted the importance of the skin shading and color, in the prejudice of predominantly blond people against dark-haired, olive-skinned Oriental or Latin types of people.

The Negro and Racial Conflict

The Negro has received less attention than the subject of prejudice, especially anti-Semitism, in the psychoanalytic literature. A book published in 1923 bears the remarkable title, *Duality: A Study in the Psycho-Analysis of Race*. As Flugel says in his review, "The use of the word 'psycho-analysis' in the sub-title is to be regretted, since very little use is made of psycho-analytic conceptions in the strict sense." Bradley, the book's author, divides the human race into two racial types—long heads from Africa and short heads from Asia. In the personalities of the former, feminine and unconscious features predominate; in the latter masculine and conscious features predominate—according to Bradley.

In 1942 and 1943 a series totaling nine papers, was published at intervals, mostly in the *Psychoanalytic Review*, under the general heading, "Psychoanalytic Studies in Race Psychology." They were arranged and edited by Ben Karpman. In general they are of uneven quality, and tend toward psychoanalytic generalizations not tied to clinical findings or to distinctions between conscious and unconscious mental properties. Charles has given a psychoanalytic interpretation of Bigger Thomas, from Richard Wright's *Native Son*. Other articles in the series have to do with mixed marriages (Little), Negro athletes (Hollomon), color conflicts (Bovell), and psychophysical aspects of race (Maddox).

In 1953 Viola Bernard, writing in the first volume of the *Journal of the American Psychoanalytic Association*, alerted the psychoanalytic profession to the Negro. With the wider public acceptance of analysis and the improved availability of analysis for minority groups, psychoanalysis, Bernard felt, should extend itself to more treatment as well as investigation of minority groups. Bernard noted especially the challenge and importance of systematic investigation of the transference-countertransference situation, as affected by racial differences. She discussed the necessity of the white analyst's being informed of the cultural problems, of not succumbing either to the patient's color denial or his exaggeration of the significance of his "Negro-ness." She also considered the problem of being among the "first" Negroes in analysis and therefore qualifying as "exceptions." In view of so much hate, fear, mistrust, guilt, envy, and ambivalence between white and Negro races in this country, Bernard regarded it as "something of a major feat in human relations when the degree of mutual trust required by the analytic situation can be achieved between them." Bernard did not consider how "Negro-ness" affects the basic formation of the personality, but stated that as an analysis of a Negro progresses the superficial recognition of the color difference progresses to the more comprehensive view of the basic formative ingredients of the personality, of which being a Negro is a part.

Reiser (1961), in a frankly speculative article, examined the origins of hatred toward Negroes, relating darkness to various drive-associated meanings in the oral, anal, and phallic stages of development. He saw taboo feelings then becoming externalized onto Negroes. Kubie (1965) also speculated on the "Ontology of Racial Prejudice." His hypothesis is that prejudice has at least three nearly universal roots in early human development: (1) a child's oscillation between secret guilty pride and hidden feelings of profound aversion toward his own body; (2) a child's inability to conceive of himself as ever becoming an adult; (3) a child's inability to accept on all psychological levels the anatomic differences between the sexes. While some of his interpretations are no doubt correct, his basic premises appear not to take into consideration a conception of *progressive* drive and ego development and interplay between them in the child. These developments lead to profound evolutions in a child's attitude toward his body, and toward acceptance of sexual differences. As for conceiving of himself as an adult, experience with children readily reveals how much of their fantasy and play activity aims toward growing up and fulfilling just such predictive self-conceptions. Hamilton (1966), in his consideration of factors underlying anti-Negro prejudice, regarded the most important dynamic mechanism to be the anal sadism of the white person.

McLean (1946, 1949), reviewed many aspects of psychodynamic factors in race relations. Like Powdermaker and others, she humanized the Negro by exposing the vicissitudes of his aggression. She described especially the frustration and chronic rage of the Negro man. If he has a passive subservient façade, his masculine pride and feelings of prestige are outraged; if he is self-assertive, he is considered rebellious. "Only a few gifted individuals have the ability to express their rage in sociological, scientific, or aesthetic form" (1946). McLean did not report specific analytic case material, but made the following comments based upon her experience as a psychoanalyst of Negro men and women. "I have yet to see a Negro who did not unconsciously have a deep fear of and hostility toward white people. This conscious and unconscious fear and hostile guilt produces in the Negro self loathing and self hate. He hates the pigmented skin which makes him feel like a depreciated human being and he hates in part others who suffer a like fate. Repeatedly in the dreams of Negro patients is expressed this self loathing and the wish to be white" (1948). Thus McLean bared dynamic aspects of Negro racial reactions, especially in relation to the prevailing culture. It would be of interest to know whether her clinical findings might also reveal more of the genesis of the skin color conflict and its relation to other early developmental conflicts.

Kennedy (1952) studied problems in the analysis of Negro patients and contributed to the literature two welcome analytic case reports. She observed that the Negro patient presents himself for treatment with fear, suspicion, and distrust of white *and* Negro therapist. She noted the difficulty which the Negro has in establishing an individual identity. "There is more room for the individual elaboration and perception of experience in the white population. The Negro patient reflects in a unique way the fate he shares with every member of his ingroup. Hence his specific life experiences are only secondarily elaborated, and *the development of the individualized ego is blurred by the phenomenon of color.*" Of her analyses of two Negro women, Kennedy wrote, "The cause of the neuroses of these two patients appeared to be the conflicts arising from a *hostile white ego ideal.* The self-hatred, generated by the fact of not being white, started with earliest infancy." During the psychoanalytic treatment this ideal must be altered, not lowered. "The therapist must reduce the fact of color to its proper size in the patient's self-esteem system." She noted that a Negro child reared in a Negro neighborhood develops an *abstract,* unrealistic, unattainable ego ideal. But a Negro child reared in a white community suffers the *concrete* development of a hostile white ego ideal. (See also a similar report by Ausubel, quoted above.) Kennedy stated that further research is necessary and made the interesting suggestion that a psychoanalytic team, made up of both Negro and white therapists—one to act as analyst, the other as a supervisor—might be beneficial in conducting a psychoanalysis of a Negro patient.

From his analyses of white patients' dreams, Sterba (1947) discerned two types of unconscious motivations which can underlie the conscious irrational antagonism of the white person toward the Negro. The first he described as a "general negative reaction," a "constant and general antagonism" against all members of the Negro race, regardless of sex. The white person so afflicted harbors a repressed hostility to a younger sibling. This hostility gets displaced onto the Negro, and thereby gains a substitute outlet. Such a white person does not want a Negro to advance, just as he did not want a younger sibling to advance and "dethrone" him. His horror of mixed marriage is especially great since this would represent "complete acceptance into the family" of the hated and feared younger rival. The second type of unconscious motivation for antagonism to the Negro, has its roots in repressed hostility of the son for the father. Here it is especially the Negro man who becomes the target for the displaced aggression. Sterba found that the race riots in Detroit in 1943 stimulated dreams revealing the son's wish to kill the father, in certain patients who unconsciously harbored such hostility to the father. In the dreams the father appeared thinly disguised as the Negro, whom the patient wanted to kill. Sterba suggested that the attraction which some white men feel to the aggressive excitement rampant in a race riot is that of the sons herded together in the hunt to kill the father.

As a part of his widely known studies on infants reared in institutions during the first year of life, Spitz (1951) made some meaningful observations about "Environment versus Race." In his comparisons of white and Negro infants he demonstrated that racial difference was not a significant factor in the course of their development, as measured at monthly intervals by the Hetzer-Wolf test—a well-standardized test providing data on perception, body mastery, social behavior, learning, manipulation of objects, and intelligence. Spitz's observations were of infants cared for in an institution by their own mothers during their first six months, and then cared for by their own and another mother, sharing responsibility, during the second six months. Sometimes the second mother would be of a different skin color. His findings are well known—that the babies in this institution, who had maternal care, fared far better than infants in another institution where maternal care was lacking. Spitz noted that the introduction of the second mother, in the second six months, made for a change in emotional climate for the infant. He did not report any specifically observed reactions of infants in the second six months to the sight and touch of a woman whose skin differed in color from the infant's own mother. Spitz comments:

> For the clinician the importance of racial factors dwindles into insignificance compared to the overwhelming impact of the emotional climate and its consequences. Racial traits, during the first year of life, at least, could be completely neglected in our investigation, were it not for the fact that racial prejudice is apt to create variations in emotional climate. These variations, as we have shown, can have the most far-reaching consequences for which then race is blamed.
>
> The therapeutic problem therefore becomes that of an adequate environment in infancy and childhood. One of the prerequisites of this is elimination of racial prejudice. That is a responsibility of society which the psychiatrist can share; but he cannot carry it alone. He can and should, however, share with the pediatrician the responsibility of creating a favorable emotional climate for the development of the infant [pp. 40f.].

Since Spitz's work there has been a growing interest among psychoanalytic investigators in the effects of early maternal deprivation upon the child's subsequent psychic development. The serious and permanent intrapsychic defects caused by such deprivation have been well documented and this research is having its influence upon social programs aimed at improving the lot of the poverty-stricken victims of racial prejudice. Negro children, raised in a distorted family setting and deprived of adequate mothering have been forced, through early environmental influence, to develop into inferior adults. The psychoanalytic findings help to establish that this adult inferiority is not due to inherent racial defect but to environmental circumstances imposed by racial prejudice.

SUMMARY

The literature contains countless confirmations, from many socioeconomic settings, of the childhood observations we have made about race at Hanna Perkins School. It also extends racial observations to include older children and adults, and in a few instances younger children and infants. A review of this literature places our contribution in both a historical and professional perspective. The special circumstances of our work with preschool children and their parents and our psychoanalytic frame of reference have led to interpretations of our observations which go beyond—or sometimes conflict with—the reports reviewed in this chapter.

As yet there are not sufficient psychoanalytic studies of infants and young children or of adults to confirm or refute the basic skin color anxiety postulated in Part II. Many others have touched upon important elements of this postulate. The skin as a libidinized organ, the separation-individuation phase of development, and the problem of identity at the root of many racial conflicts, the underlying anxiety in racial difference conflicts—all have received at least passing reference from various professional specialties.

Displacements and distortions linking racial and drive conflicts are well documented in the literature, especially in clinical work with adults. Some authors seem to see the defensive use of one set of conflicts to conceal and distort the other as a sort of culturally induced defense. The implication is that drive conflicts and their resolution must come first in the course of development, and racial conflicts can only be imposed later on. Our work confirms the existence of such distortions and displacements. It also demonstrates that in favorable (integrated) circumstances racial and drive conflicts coexist, probably even before the end of the first year of life. Our work further demonstrates that the separation and working through of these two sets of conflicts can be well under way before a child reaches latency. When this is so, the child's own personality development benefits and, in addition, he gains a protection against a later development of prejudice.

In the extensive literature on prejudices the various dynamic constellations are more clearly delineated and agreed upon than are the origins. The psychoanalytic literature traces the roots of prejudice into all of the prelatency stages of drive development. Our work offers clinical demonstrations of all of these suspected roots, but leads to a formulation that prejudice as such cannot be diagnosed until a child has established himself in the latency phase of his development.

Spitz has spoken of the "adequate environment in infancy and childhood"—the environment which sustains a "favorable emotional climate." Perhaps the most valuable conclusion to come from this review of the literature is a sociological one. It is that there is nothing in the literature to refute and much to support the claim that an "adequate environment in infancy and childhood" in our society must be an integrated environment.

BIBLIOGRAPHY

Ackerman, N. W. & Jahoda, M. (1948), The Dynamic Basis of Anti-Semitic Attitudes. *Psychoanal. Quart.*, 17:240-260.

Adams, W. A. (1950), The Negro Patient in Psychiatric Treatment. *Amer. J. Orthopsychiat.*, 20:305-310.

Allport, G. W. (1954), *The Nature of Prejudice.* Cambridge: Addison-Wesley.

American Orthopsychiatric Association (1956), Round Table. Desegregation: Its Implications for Orthopsychiatry. Chairman, K. B. Clark. *Amer. J. Orthopsychiat.*, 26:445-470.

—— (1958), Round Table. Segregation-Integration: Some Psychological Realities. Chairman, S. J. Beck. *Amer. J. Orthopsychiat.*, 28:12-35.

Arter, R. M. (1959), The Effects of Prejudice on Children. *Children*, 6:185-189.

Ausubel, D. P. (1958), Ego Development among Segregated Negro Children. *Ment. Hyg.*, 42:362-369.

Barnes, M. (1964), Reactions to the Death of a Mother. *The Psychoanalytic Study of the Child*, 19:334-357. New York: International Universities Press.

Bender, L. (1939), Behavior Problems in Negro Children. *Psychiatry*, 2:213-228.

Bernard, V. W. (1953), Psychoanalysis and Members of Minority Groups. *J. Amer. Psychoanal. Assn.*, 1:256-267.

—— (1958), School Desegregation: Some Psychiatric Implications. *Psychiatry*, 21:149-158.

Bird, B. (1957), A Consideration of the Etiology of Prejudice. *J. Amer. Psychoanal. Assn.*, 5:490-513.

Bovell, G. B. (1943), Psychological Considerations of Color Conflicts among Negroes. *Psychoanal. Rev.*, 30:447-459. (See also Karpman, B.)

Boyd, G. F. (1952), The Levels of Aspiration of White and Negro Children in a Non-Segregated Elementary School. *J. Soc. Psychol.*, 36:191-196.

Bradley, R. N. (1923), *Duality: A Study in the Psychoanalysis of Race.* London: Routledge.

Brody, E. B. (1961), Social Conflict and Schizophrenic Behavior in Young Adult Negro Males. *Psychiatry*, 24:337-346.

—— (1963), Color and Identity Conflict in Young Boys: I. Observations of Negro Mothers and Sons in Urban Baltimore. *Psychiatry*, 26:188-201.

—— (1964), Color and Identity Conflict in Young Boys: II. Observations of White Mothers and Sons in Urban Baltimore. *Arch. Gen. Psychiat.*, 10:354-360.

Bulfinch, T. (1855), *The Age of Fable.* New York: Heritage Press, 1942, pp. 101-104.

Charles, C. V. (1942), Optimism and Frustration in the American Negro. *Psychoanal. Rev.*, 29:270-299. (See also Karpman, B.)

Chess, S., Clark, K. B., & Thomas, A. (1953), The Importance of Cultural Evaluation in Psychiatric Diagnosis and Treatment. *Psychiat. Quart.*, 27: 102-113.

Chethik, M., Fleming, E., Mayer, M. F., & McCoy, J. N. (1967), A Quest for Identity: Treatment of Disturbed Negro Children in a Predominantly White Treatment Center. *Amer. J. Orthopsychiat.*, 37:71-77.

Clark, K. B. (1955), *Prejudice and Your Child*. Boston: Beacon Press (2nd edition, 1963).

——— (undated paper), How to Protect Children Against Prejudice. New York. Child Study Assn. of America.

Coles, R. (1963), Southern Children under Desegregation. *Amer. J. Psychiat.*, 120:332-344.

——— (1964), *Children of Crisis:* Boston: Little, Brown.

——— (1965), Racial Conflict and a Child's Question. *J. Nerv. Ment. Dis.*, 140:162-170.

——— (1968), Northern Children under Desegregation. *Psychiatry*, 31:1-15.

Cravioto, J. & Robles, B. (1963), The Influence of Protein-Calorie Malnutrition on Psychological Test Behavior. In: *Mild-Moderate Forms of Protein-Calorie Malnutrition,* ed. G. Blix. Stockholm: Almqvist & Wiksells, pp. 115-126.

Davis, A. (1939), The Socialization of the American Negro Child and Adolescent. *J. Negro Educ.*, 8:264-274.

——— & Dollard, J. (1940), *Children of Bondage: The Personality Development of Negro Youth in the Urban South.* American Council on Education. Republished: New York: Harper & Row, 1964.

——— & Havighurst, R. J. (1946), Social Class and Color Differences in Child Rearing. *Amer. Sociol. Rev.,* 11:698-710.

Eisenbud, J. (1944), The Roots of Prejudice: Hostilities Begin in the Nursery. *Child Study*, 6:74-75.

Ellison, L. (1968), Cities Aflame. . . . Young Imaginations on Fire. *Young Children*, 23:261-264.

Flugel, J. C. (1924), Book Review of Bradley, R. N., *Duality: A Study in the Psychoanalysis of Race. Int. J. Psycho-Anal.,* 5:105-108.

Frenkel-Brunswik, E. (1948), A Study of Prejudice in Children. *Human Relations,* 1:295-306. Reprinted in: *Readings in Personal and Social Adjustment,* ed. E. Kubie & C. F. J. Lehner. New York: Prentice-Hall.

Freud, A. (1965), *Normality and Pathology in Childhood.* New York: International Universities Press.

Freud, S. (1909), Analysis of a Phobia in a Five-Year-Old Boy. *Standard Edition*, 10: 3-149. London: Hogarth Press, 1955.

—— (1916-1917), Introductory Lectures on Psycho-Analysis. *Standard Edition*, 15 & 16. London: Hogarth Press, 1963.

—— (1918), From the History of an Infantile Neurosis. *Standard Edition*, 17:87-88. London: Hogarth Press, 1955.

—— *(1939)*, Moses and Monotheism: Three Essays. *Standard Edition*, 23: 3-137. London Hogarth Press, 1964.

Furman, R. A. (1964a), Death and the Young Child: Some Preliminary Considerations. *The Psychoanalytic Study of the Child*, 19:321-333. New York: International Universities Press.

—— (1964b), Death of a Six-Year-Old's Mother during His Analysis. *The Psychoanalytic Study of the Child*, 19:377-397. New York: International Universities Press.

—— & Katan, A., Eds (1969), *The Therapeutic Nursery School*. New York: International Universities Press.

Gardner, G. & Aaron, S. (1946), The Childhood and Adolescent Adjustment of Negro Psychiatric Casualties. *Amer. J. Orthopsychiat.*, 16:481-495.

Glasser, A. J. (1958), A Negro Child Reared as White. In: *Clinical Studies in Culture Conflict*, ed. G. Seward. New York: Ronald Press, pp. 41-61.

Gochros, J. S. (1966), Recognition and Use of Anger in Negro Clients. *Soc. Work*, 11:28-34.

Goodman, M. E. (1952), *Race Awareness in Young Children*. Cambridge: Addison-Wesley Press. New, revised edition: New York: Collier Books, 1964.

Graham, T. F. (1955), Doll Play Phantasies of Negro and White Primary School Children. *J. Clin. Psychol.*, 11:29-33.

Greenacre, P. (1958), Early Physical Determinants in the Development of the Sense of Identity. *J. Amer. Psychoanal. Assn.*, 6:612-627.

Grier, W. H. (1967), When the Therapist Is Negro. *Amer. J. Psychiat.*, 123: 1587-1592.

Group for the Advancement of Psychiatry, Committee on Social Issues (1957), *Psychiatric Aspects of School Desegregation*. Report No. 37. G. A. P. Publications Office, 1790 Broadway, New York.

Hamilton, J. W. (1966), Some Dynamics of Anti-Negro Prejudice. *Psychoanal. Rev.*, 53:5-15.

Hammer, E. F. (1953), Negro and White Children's Personality Adjustment as Revealed by a Comparison of Their Drawings (H. T. P.). *J. Clin. Psychol.*, 9:7-10.

Holloman, L. L. (1943), On the Supremacy of the Negro Athlete in White Athletic Competition. *Psychoanal. Rev.*, 30:157-162. (See also Karpman, B.)

Horowitz, R. E. (1939), Racial Aspects of Self-Identification in Nursery School Children. *J. Psychol.*, 7:91-99.

Houwink, E. (1948), Color Is an Additional Problem. *Ment. Hyg.*, 32:596-604.

Jacobson, E. (1964), *The Self and the Object World.* New York: International Universities Press.

Kardiner, A. & Ovesey, L. (1951), *The Mark of Oppression: A Psychosocial Study of the American Negro.* New York: W. W. Norton.

Karpman, B. (1942-1943), *Psychoanalytic Studies in Race Psychology,* ed. B. Karpman. (For individual references, see Bovell, G. B.; Charles, C. V.; Holloman, L. L.; Little, G. & Maddox, A.)

Kennedy, J. A. (1952), Problems Posed in the Analysis of Negro Patients. *Psychiatry,* 15:313-327.

Kramer, C. H., Ed. (1967), Maxwell Gitelson: Analytic Aphorisms. *Psychoanal. Quart.,* 36:260-270.

Kris, E. (1949), Roots of Hostility and Prejudice. In: *The Family in a Democratic Society* [Anniversary Papers of the Community Service Society of New York]. New York: Columbia University Press, pp. 141-155.

Kubie, L. S. (1965), The Ontology of Prejudice. *J. Nerv. Ment. Dis.,* 141:265-273.

Landreth, C. & Johnson, B. C. (1953), Young Children's Responses to a Picture and Inset Test Designed to Reveal Reactions to Persons of Different Skin Color. *Child Develpm.* 24:63-80.

Larick, N. (1965), The All-White World of Children's Books. *Saturday Review,* September 11, pp. 63-65, 84-85.

Lasker, B. (1929), *Race Attitudes in Children.* New York: Henry Holt & Co.

Lawrence, M. M. (1955), How Prejudice Begins. *Child Study,* 33:2-26.

Lief, H. I. & Stevenson, I. P. (1958), Psychological Aspects of Prejudice with Special Reference to Desegregation. *Amer. J. Psychiat.,* 114:816-823.

Little, G. (1942), Analytic Reflections on Mixed Marriages. *Psychoanal. Rev.,* 29:20-25. (See also Karpman, B.)

Loewenstein, R. M. (1951), *Christians and Jews.* New York: International Universities Press.

Maddox, A. (1943), Some Psychological Aspects of the Race Problem. *Psychonal. Rev.,* 30:325-329.(See also Karpman, B.)

McDonald, M. (1963), Helping Children to Understand Death: An Experience with Death in a Nursery School. *J. Nursery Educ.,* 19:19-25.

―――― (1964), A Study of the Reactions of Nursery School Children to the Death of a Child's Mother. *The Psychoanalytic Study of the Child,* 19: 358-376. New York: International Universities Press.

McLean, H. V. (1946), Psychodynamic Factors in Racial Relations. *Annals Amer. Acad. Pol. & Soc. Sci.,* 244:159-166.

―――― (1949), The Emotional Health of Negroes. *J. Negro Educ.,* 18:283-290.

Milner, E. (1953), Some Hypotheses Concerning the Influence of Segregation on Negro Personality Development. *Psychiatry,* 16:291-297.

Munat, C. E. (1968), Four, Poor, Nonwhite, and Out-of-Sight. *Young Children,* 24:4-14.

Myers, H. J. & Yochelson, L. (1948), Color Denial in the Negro. *Psychiatry,* 11:39-46.

Myrdal, G. (1944), *An American Dilemma.* I. The Negro Problem and Modern Democracy. New York: Harper.

Parrish, C. H. (1946), Color Names and Color Notions. *J. Negro Educ.,* 15: 13-20.

Powdermaker, H. (1943), The Channeling of Negro Aggression by the Cultural Process. *Amer. J. Sociol.,* 48:750-758.

Pre-School Malnutrition. Publ. 1282. Washington, D. C.: National Academy of Science-National Research Council, 1966.

Reiser, M. (1961), On Origins of Hatred toward Negroes. *Amer. Imago,* 18: 167-172.

Rewald, J. (1961), *The History of Impressionism.* New York: Museum of Modern Art, pp. 431-433.

Rosen, H. & Frank, J. D. (1962), Negroes in Psychotherapy. *Amer. J. Psychiat.,* 119:456-460.

Sclare, A. B. (1953), Cultural Determinants in the Neurotic Negro. *Brit. J. Med. Psychol.,* 26:278-288.

Seitz, P. F. D. (1960), Parental Behavior, Projection, and Prejudice. (Abstract by the author.) *Bull. Philadelphia Assn. Psychoanal.,* 10:156-157.

Seitz, W. C. (1960), *Monet.* New York: Harry N. Abrams, p. 29.

Smith, J. C. Jr. (1946), Understanding the Negro Client. *The Family,* 27:87-95.

Smith, L. (1949), *Killers of the Dream.* New York: W. W. Norton, p. 78.

—— (1955), *Now Is the Time.* New York: Viking Press, p. 91.

Spitz, R. A. (1951), Environment Versus Race. In: *Psychoanalysis and Culture,* ed. G. Wilbur & W. Munsterberger. New York: International Universities Press, pp. 32-41.

—— (1965), *The First Year of Life.* New York: International Universities Press.

Staples, R. (1933), The Response of Infants to Color. *J. Exp. Psychol.,* 15:119-141.

Sterba, R. (1947), Some Psychological Factors in Negro Race Hatred and in Anti-Negro Riots. *Psychoanalysis and the Social Sciences,* 1:411-427. New York: International Universities Press.

Stevenson, H. W. (1967), Studies of Racial Awareness in Young Children. *The Young Child* (Reviews of Research), ed. W. P. Hartup & N. Smothergill. Washington: National Association for the Education of Young Children, pp. 206-213.

228   BIBLIOGRAPHY

Stoch, M. B. & Smythe, P. M. (1963), Does Undernutrition During Infancy
    Inhibit Brain Growth and Subsequent Intellectual Development? *Arch.
    Dis. Child.*, 38:546-552.
Trager, H. & Yarrow, M. R. (1952), *They Learn What They Live: Prejudice
    in Young Children.* New York: Harper.
Tyler, E. B. (1946), Casework with Negro People. *The Family,* 27:265-273.
Vosk, J. S. (1966), Study of Negro Children with Learning Difficulties at the
    Outset of the School Careers. *Amer. J. Orthopsychiat.*, 36:32-40.
Waelder, R. (1949), Notes on Prejudice. *Vassar Alumni Magazine,* 34. Re-
    printed in: *Bull. Philadelphia Assn. Psychoanal.,* 4:71-81, 1955.
Wangh, M. (1964), National Socialism and the Genocide of the Jews. *Int. J.
    Psycho-Anal.,* 45:386-395.
Witmer, H. L. & Kotinsky, R. (1952), *Personality in the Making: The Fact-
    Finding Report of the Midcentury White House Conference on Children
    and Youth.* Chapter 6: The Effects of Prejudice and Discrimination. New
    York: Harper.
Young, W. M. (1968), Why We Should Suspend the Studies of Negroes. *The
    National Observer,* April 1.
Zilboorg, G. (1947), Psychopathology of Social Prejudice. *Psychoanal. Quart.,*
    16:303-324.

INDEX OF CHILDREN

(I = Indian; N = Negro; O = Oriental; W = White)

NAME INDEX

Aaron, S., 202, 225
Ackerman, N. W., 212-213, 223
Adams, W. A., 205-206, 223
Adorno, C., 192-194
Allport, G. W., 165, 186-188, 204, 223
American Orthopsychiatric Association, 196, 204-205, 223
Archer, L., viii
Arter, R. M., 199-200, 223
Ausubel, D. P., 199, 218, 223

Barnes, M. J., viii, 65 n., 223
Beck, S. J., 223
Beeke, C., viii
Bender, L., 201-202, 223
Bernard, V. W., 141, 204-205, 216, 223
Bigger Thomas, 216
Bird, B., 214, 223
Bovell, G. B., 216, 223, 226
Boyd, G. F., 194, 223
Bradley, R. N., 215, 223, 224
Brody, E. B., 202-204, 206, 223
Brown decision, 3, 163, 166-169
Bulfinch, T., 152, 223

Charles, C. V., 216, 224, 226
Chess, S., 205, 224
Chethik, M., 198, 224
Clark, K. B., 31 n., 166, 168, 182, 188-193, 205-206, 223, 224
Clark, M., 182, 188-192
Coles, R., 109, 128, 158 n., 170-171, 204, 208-212, 224
Cordes, N., viii, 74
Cravioto, J., 202, 224

Dai, B., 204
Daunton, E., viii, x
Davis, A., 178-180, 224
Dollard, J., 178-179, 224

Eisenbud, J., 199, 224
Ellison, L., 65 n., 224

Fairman, D., viii
Fetter, L., viii
Fiedler, E., viii
Fleming, E., 198, 224
Flugel, J. C., 215, 224
Frank, J. D., 205-206, 227
Frenkel-Brunswik, E., 192-194, 224
Freud, A., ix, 89, 93, 95, 143-146, 160, 224
Freud, S., 109, 159-160, 178, 186, 212, 224-225
Furman, E., viii
Furman, R. A., viii, 11, 65 n., 225

Gardner, G., 202, 225
Gitelson, M., 141, 226
Glasser, A. J., 202, 225
Gochros, J. S., 196-197, 225
Goodman, M. E., 167-168, 181-186, 189, 192, 206, 225
Graham, T. F., 195, 225
Greenacre, P., ix, 105, 225
Grier, W. H., 205-206, 225
Group for the Advancement of Psychiatry, 166 n., 170, 204-205, 207-208, 225

Hamilton, J. W., 217, 225
Hammer, E. F., 195, 225
Hamre, M., viii
Havighurst, R. J., 179, 224
Hoffer, W., 145
Holloman, L. L., 216, 225, 226
Horowitz, E., 182
Horowitz, R. E., 182, 192, 193, 225
Hosley, E., viii
Houwink, E., 198, 226
Hugo, V., 176

Jacobson, E., viii, 125, 226
Jahoda, M., 212-213, 223

SUBJECT INDEX

238

SUBJECT INDEX

of strangers, 146-148
threatened by: death, 118-119;
illness, 37-38, 57, 117-118;
skin color anxiety, 116-119;
suntan, 39, 56, 96-97, 118, 208
Infants
institutionalized (Spitz), 172,
219-220
observations of different skin col-
or, 33, 102, 117, 177
Inferiority-superiority, see Narcissism
Institutions
infants in (Spitz), 172, 219-220
Bellefaire, treatment of Negro
children in, 198
Bellevue, study of Negro children
in, 201-202
Integration, racial
importance for realistic self-esteem and ego ideal, 89, 199,
218
necessary for personality development, 115, 129, 156-157, 161-
162, 222
physical and psychological, 4-10,
168, 199
psychoanalysis and, 159-162
see also School integration
Intelligence, 194-196, 201-202
Interpretation of children's defenses, 35-37
Interracial marriage, 79-80, 90,
140, 141, 219
children's attitudes and fantasies,
35, 40-41, 70-71
effect on children, 104
Interracial transference, see Transference
Introjection, 119-125, 153-154

Latency, 140-142, 154, 222
prejudice becomes possible, 156-
157
Libidinal development, stages of,
and skin color anxiety, 115-142
Loyalty conflict

between mother and teacher, 21,
86, 91
between parents of different race,
90
effect on racial identity in Negro
children, 198

Malnutrition, 173
effect on intelligence, 201-202
Masai tribe, 110
Masochistic defense (Reik), 180
Maternal deprivation, 51, 173, 220
Maturity in racial relations, see
Development
Minority groups and psychoanaly-
sis, 216; see also Negro
Money, linked to race, 34, 128
Moses and Monotheism, 212
Murder
Chicago nurses, 60-61
Martin Luther King, 18, 65-74,
135

Narcissism
and skin color, 89-90, 98-99,
106-107, 109
in anal phase, 126, 130-134
in phallic phase, 138-140
narcissistic reflection of person of
same race, 152
narcissistic withdrawal as defense
against different race, 151-154
Negro
aggression in, 217-218; see also
Aggression
as human being, 143-144, 179-
181
as not inferior, 169, 173-174
in psychoanalytic literature, 212-
222
masculinity conflicts, 217
Northern, 170-171, 191-192
Southern, 170-171, 178-180,
191-192
white ego ideal in, 4, 130, 218

Object relations